DAVID EDGAR

Plays: 3

Our Own People
Teendreams
Maydays
That Summer

with an introduction by the author

D0112702

Methuen Drama

METHUEN CONTEMPORARY DRAMATISTS

This collection first published in Great Britain 1991 by Methuen Drama
Reissued in this series in 1997 by Methuen Drama
an imprint of Reed International Books Ltd
Michelin House, 81 Fulham Road, London SW3 6RB
and Auckland, Melbourne, Singapore and Toronto
and distributed in the United States of America
by Heinemann, a division of Reed Elsevier Inc.
361 Hanover Street, Portsmouth, New Hampshire NH 03801 3959

Our Own People first published by Methuen London Ltd., in 1987. Copyright
© 1987 by David Edgar
Teendreams first published by Eyre Methuen Ltd., in 1979, revised 1987.
Copyright © 1979, 1987 by David Edgar and Susan Todd
Maydays first published by Methuen London Ltd., in 1983, revised 1984.
Copyright © 1983, 1984 by David Edgar
That Summer first published by Methuen London Ltd., in 1987. Copyright ©
1987 by David Edgar

This collection copyright © 1991 by David Edgar
Introduction copyright © 1991 by David Edgar

The author has asserted his moral rights

A CIP catalogue record for this book is available from the British Library

ISBN 0 413 64850 8

Printed and bound in Great Britain by Cox & Wyman Ltd., Reading, Berkshire

CAUTION
These plays are fully protected by copyright. Any enquiries concerning
rights for professional or amateur stage production should be addressed
to Michael Imison Playwrights Ltd., 28 Almeida Street, London N1.

This paperback is sold subject to the condition that it shall not, by way of trade
or otherwise, be lent, resold, hired out, or otherwise circulated without the
publisher's prior consent in any form of binding or cover other than that
in which it is published and without a similar condition including this condition
being imposed on the subsequent purchaser.

David Edgar

Plays: 3

Our Own People, Teendreams, Maydays, That Summer

Our Own People: 'A courageous and intelligent discussion of race and industrial relations which is important, relevant and should be seen.' *City Limits*
'A firm, skilfully paced, ruefully funny play.' *Guardian*

Teendreams, written with Susan Todd: 'A painfully accurate portrait.' *Guardian*

Maydays: 'One of Edgar's many achievements is to give us a rich sense of the ironies of history . . . A big public play on a big public theme. Its territory is nothing less than the map of post-war politics. But its achievement is that it unites the epic and the individual. Edgar gives us a sense of the patterns of history, but he still manages to focus on the individual conscience . . . A play of staggering richness.' *Guardian*
'Stimulating, revelling in the breadth of its theme, firing off ideas in profusion.' *The Times*

That Summer is an 'elegantly tangential treatment of the 1984 miners' strike' (*Plays & Players*): 'Edgar never lets his drama simplify into ideological diagram . . . This elegant, humane play keeps its emphasis on the modest but fruitful results that can ensue when diverse lives briefly brush against each other.' *Independent*

David Edgar was born in 1948 in Birmingham. His stage work includes *Excuses Excuses* (1972); *Dick Deterred* (1974); *Saigon Rose* (1976); *Wreckers* (1977); *Mary Barnes* (1978); *Teendreams* (with Susan Todd, 1979); *That Summer* (1987) and *Entertaining Strangers*, a community play first commissioned by Ann Jellicoe and the Colway Theatre Trust and adapted for performance at the National Theatre, London in 1987–8. He has written five plays for the Royal Shakespeare Company: *Destiny* (1976); *The Jail Diary of Albie Sachs* (1978); *Nicholas Nickleby* (1980); *Maydays* (1983); and *Pentecost* (1994). Plays for the National Theatre include *Entertaining Strangers* (revised version 1987) and *The Shape of the Table*. He received the John Whiting award for *Destiny*, the Society of West End Theatres Best Play award for *Nicholas Nickleby* (which also won him a Tony award in New York), the *Plays and Players* Best Play award for *Maydays* and the *Evening Standard* Play of the Year award for *Pentecost*. His television work includes adaptations of *Destiny*, *Jail Diary* and *Nicholas Nickleby*, *Buying a Landslide* (1992) and a three-part play *Vote for Them* (BBC, 1989). His radio work includes *Ecclesiastes* (1977), *A Movie Starring Me* (1991) and *Talking to Mars* (1996). His first film, *Lady Jane*, was released in 1986. He is Professor of Playwriting Studies at the University of Birmingham.

by the same author

DAVID EDGAR PLAYS: 1*
The Jail Diary of Albie Sachs, Mary Barnes,
Saigon Rose, O Fair Jerusalem, Destiny

DAVID EDGAR PLAYS: 2*
Ecclesiastes, Nicholas Nickleby Parts I & II,
Entertaining Strangers (the National Theatre Version)

THE SHAPE OF THE TABLE
THE STRANGE CASE OF DR JEKYLL AND MR HYDE
PENTECOST

EDGAR: SHORTS
Ball Boys, The National Theatre, Bloodsports,
The Midas Connection, Baby Love

THE SECOND TIME AS FARCE
A book of essays

also available
by Susan Painter

EDGAR THE PLAYWRIGHT*

* published by Methuen Drama

Contents

To Sarah and her family

A Chronology of Plays and Screenplays

Two Kinds of Angel (Bradford University, July 1970; Basement
    Theatre, London, February 1971) Published by Burnham House,
    London, 1975
The National Interest (General Will Theatre Group, July 1971)
Tedderella (Pool Theatre, Edinburgh, December 1971; Bush Theatre,
    London, January 1973)
Excuses Excuses (Belgrade Theatre Studio, Coventry, May 1972;
    Open Space, London, July 1973)
Death Story (Birmingham Repertory Theatre Studio, November
    1972; New End Theatre, London, November 1975)
Baby Love (Soho Poly Theatre, London, May 1973; BBC TV Play
    for Today, November 1974)
The Eagle Has Landed (Granada Television, April 1973)
Operation Iskra (Paradise Foundry Theatre Group, September 1973)
Dick Deterred (Bush Theatre, February 1974) Published by Monthly
    Review Press, New York, 1974
I Know What I Meant (Granada Television, July 1974)
O Fair Jerusalem (Birmingham Repertory Theatre Studio, May
    1975) Published by Methuen, London, 1987
Blood Sports/Ball Boys (Birmingham Arts Lab, July 1975; Bush
    Theatre, June 1976) *Ball Boys* published by Pluto Press, London, 1978
The National Theatre (Open Space, London, October 1975)
Saigon Rose (Traverse Theatre, Edinburgh, July 1976; BBC Radio Three,
    April 1979)) Published by Methuen, London, 1987
Destiny (Royal Shakespeare Company at the Other Place and
    subsequently the Aldwych Theatre, September 1976, May 1977;
    BBC TV Play for Today, January 1978; BBC Radio Four, January
    1979) Published by Methuen, London, 1976/78
Wreckers (7:84 Theatre Company, February 1977) Published by
    Methuen, London, 1977
Ecclesiastes (BBC Radio Four, April 1977)
Our Own People (Pirate Jenny Theatre Company, November 1977)
    Published by Methuen, London, 1988
The Jail Diary of Albie Sachs (Adaptation) (Royal Shakespeare
    Company at the Warehouse, June 1978; Manhattan Theatre Club,
    New York, October 1979; productions in Los Angeles, San Francisco
    and Seattle; BBC Television, 1981) Published by Rex Collings, 1978
    and Methuen, London, 1988
Mary Barnes (Based on the book by Mary Barnes and Joe Berke)
    (Birmingham Repertory Studio, 1978; Royal Court, January 1979;
    productions in New Haven, New York, Los Angeles and San Francisco)
    Published by Methuen, London, 1979
Teendreams (with Susan Todd) (Monstrous Regiment, January 1979)
    Published by Methuen, London, 1979

Nicholas Nickleby (Adaptation from Dickens) (Royal Shakespeare Company, Aldwych Theatre, July 1980; Plymouth Theatre, Broadway, New York, October 1981; Channel Four, November 1982) Published by Dramatists Play Service, New York, 1982 and Methuen Drama, London, 1990

Maydays (Royal Shakespeare Company, Barbican Theatre, October 1983) Published by Methuen, London, 1983, 1984

Entertaining Strangers (Colway Theatre Trust, Dorchester, 1985; National Theatre, October 1987) Published by Methuen, London, 1986

Lady Jane (Paramount picture, 1986)

Entertaining Strangers (new version) (National Theatre, Cottesloe Theatre, London, 1987) Published by Methuen, London, 1988, 1990

That Summer (Hampstead Theatre, London, July 1987; BBC World Service, August 1993) Published by Methuen, London, 1987

Vote for Them (with Neil Grant) (BBC Television, June 1989) Published by BBC, 1989

Heartlanders (with Stephen Bill and Anne Devlin) (Birmingham Repertory Theatre, October 1989) Published by Nick Hern Books, 1989

The Shape of the Table (National Theatre, Cottesloe Theatre, London, November 1990; BBC Radio Four, June 1993) Published by Nick Hern Books, 1990

The Strange Case of Dr Jekyll and Mr Hyde (Royal Shakespeare Company, Barbican Theatre, London, November 1991) Published by Nick Hern Books, 1992

A Movie Starring Me (BBC Radio Four, November 1991)

Buying a Landslide (BBC Television, September 1992)

Citizen Locke (Channel 4 Television, April 1994)

Pentecost (Royal Shakespeare Company, The Other Place, Stratford upon Avon, October 1994) Published by Nick Hern Books, 1995

Talking to Mars (BBC Radio Three, October 1996)

Introduction

There has been much talk of late of the decline of new writing in the theatre. Statistically, we are faced with the prospect of wall to wall *Twelfth Nights* (or musicals, or adaptations of Jane Eyre); culturally, we note elaborate, post–structuralist arguments for the move away from theatre into novels and films. Certainly, as the eighties turned into the nineties, many critics pointed to the paucity of major new playwriterly talents, particularly in the sphere of political theatre. Whatever party might have existed in the seventies, by the mid–eighties, we were told, it was over.

Well things are not so bleak. It is I suppose possible to claim that few new political playwrights have come on the scene, but only (frankly) if it is compulsory for them to be called Howard, David or John. Deem it conceivable for them to be called Clare, Sarah or Charlotte and the picture changes considerably. The rise of the women playwrights in the eighties has been one obvious and dramatic phenomenon; another has been the resilience of the playwrights of the seventies. Despite reports to the contrary, David Hare has remained a major figure on the scene, and so has Howard Brenton. Howard Barker and Caryl Churchill have achieved cult status. And the plays they wrote have continued to address the times. (Indeed, arguably, *Pravda* and *Serious Money* touched the mid–eighties with a sharper needle than any equivalent play of the seventies).

What has gone, perhaps, is the sense that behind many if not all the plays of the time is a story (the literary theorists would call it a grand narrative) on which everyone agrees, and into bits of which almost all works can be seen to slot. Put together, this narrative would begin with the Second World War, and the fact that (for all the wrong reasons no doubt) Britain ended up on the right side of it; that as a result the country was in a unique position afterwards to correct the inequities of the thirties and bring about an egalitarian and classless society; that this chance was squandered through the inadequacies of the post–war Labour government and the consumerism of the post–imperial 'long boom' of the fifties and sixties; that in the seventies we awoke from that party with a severe economic hangover, to find the institutions and principles of the forties corrupt and decayed; and that out of that understanding would come the realisation that the revolution of the forties had indeed been half-hearted and now was the time for 'real socialism' to emerge.

The fact that something very different emerged from the crumbling of welfare socialism was the first indication that there was something wrong with the thesis. The conclusive collapse of 'actually existing' socialism ten years later confirmed that the plotting was fundamentally flawed.

What took the place of the grand narrative play, first of all, was the snapshot play, the piece that demanded of its audience: hey, look at this bit of the scene – the City, Fleet St, advertising, Benidorm, strippagrams, whatever it is – *this* is the way to see the eighties, this the defining metaphor of the time. But then there began to emerge plays suggesting that in the wake of the single grand narrative there might be some other narratives, possibly even more than one, which might take its place (or even, had already). One of the defining things about the seventies political play was that it hopped about in time (and often space); what's striking is how much of the new women's drama, supposedly so humdrum and domestic, does exactly the same. Charlotte Keatley's *My Mother Said I Never Should* (for instance) covers over 50 years, and poses the uncomfortable suggestion that while the big male story has been bouncing merrily along, there has been another, invisible story tiptoeing quietly along beside it. And overlapping with the women's story (and its sub- or super-plot, the crisis-of-masculinity story) is the crisis-of-modernity story, which suggests that one of the problems of the grand-progress-towards-inevitable-socialism plot (and *its* counter-plot, the inevitable process-towards-the-end-of-history) is that progress itself is a delusion, and that if we're to survive as a species we have to get rid of it and its consequences fast.

I think the question that artists are going to have to worry between now and the millennium is whether the ecological epic and the Woman's Tale (not to mention the north-south saga, as yet in mere prologue) are indeed grand narratives in the manner of the Great Proletarian Adventure Story. The fashionable view of course is that they aren't, and that we are going to have to get used to living without unitary models and single explanations (with the exception, naturally, of the market and Islam). I am not sure what I think about that; but I am sure that the extraordinary resilience and tenacity of various forms of social idealism has something to tell us about the importance to the species of the notion of human collective emancipation, even if we know that our reach in this matter will always exceed our grasp.

All of these plays were written in the prospect – if not always the consciousness – of the collapse of state socialism. *Our Own People* and *Teendreams* were written in the late seventies (in the latter case with Susan Todd), and concern the emergence of two movements – feminism and anti-racism – that were to pose a considerable threat to the unitary model. In both plays, people originally committed to the idea that the only division that matters is class are forced to come to terms with the notion that there are other divisions between people as deep and perhaps even more painful.

Maydays is about as grand a narrative play as it's possible to be this side of *Tamburlaine the Great*. It covers the period from 1945 to now, and it crosses half the world. Its starting point was the insight that the unique thing about the conservative revival of the late seventies was that it was led largely by defectors from the left; which accounted (among other things) for the particular iconographic importance of east European dissidents, people who behaved like (and often looked and spoke like) lefties but were in fact confronting left-wing regimes. Most of the defecting intellectuals had been communists or socialists before the Second World War, during it or shortly after; in order to write the play convincingly, however, I had to draw on my own experience in the left of the 1960s, and speculate as to how my generation would move to the right if it was to do so. (The fact that it has moved neither as fast nor as far as the Alfred Shermans, Irving Kristols, Bernard Levins or Kingsley Amises is I think an indication of the flexibility and pluralism of the post-68 left, though I appreciate that those gentlemen would regard it as yet more evidence of the infinite powers of human self-delusion.)

Maydays finishes at a kind of Greenham Common, and thus at the starkest point of confrontation between feminism and the traditional left. To say that that's where *That Summer* begins is on the surface perverse. But, although in a domestic setting, this play too stretches its characters across a yawning class, gender, age and indeed political divide. It was a matter of alarm to some that I'd chosen to place a play about the miners' strike in a single set peopled with under ten characters on a welsh hilltop. But the extraordinary thing about that strike was how important one-to-one human relationships were, both within the communities and between those communities and the networks of supporters that sprung up around the country. Or perhaps, in fact, it wasn't that extraordinary, and merely served to confirm that the only narratives that will work now are ones that place such matters in the foreground of our attention and concern.

David Edgar, 1991

Our Own People

Our Own Trophe

Our Own People was first presented by Pirate Jenny at the Half Moon Theatre and on tour, in November 1977, with the following cast:

BARONESS COCKBURN, Inquiry Chair	Victoria Plum
JILL WATTS, Barrister	Sue Glanville
MANSUR HUSSEIN, Committee Chair	Tariq Yunus
MUHAMMAD LATEEF, Interpreter	Regee Ranjha
SAVITRI BHANDARI, Committee Member	Indira Joshi
HAMEED FARUQI, Shop Steward	Tariq Yunus
RANJIT SINGH SANDHU, Committee Member	Reggee Ranjha
GEORGE JOWETT, General Secretary	John Gillett
FRANK KITCHEN, Senior Steward	Malcolm Raeburn
JOAN DAWSON, Shop Steward	Chrissie Cotterill
NICHOLAS CLIFFORD, Barrister	Malcolm Raeburn
ERIC HARPER, Managing Director	John Gillett
ASHUYA RIDLEY, Conciliation Officer	Indira Joshi
A VISITOR	Victoria Plum
A YOUNG PAKISTANI	Reggee Ranjha
AN OFFICIAL	Malcolm Raeburn

Directed by Walter Donahue
Designed by Di Seymour
Lighting designed by Eddie Heron
Stage Managed by Sue Lovett

Our Own People is based around a fictional industrial dispute in Yorkshire in the 1970s. A chronology of the events of this dispute is included as an appendix to the text of the play.

ACT ONE

Scene One

The Court.
  Enter CHAIR, WATTS, CLIFFORD, JOWETT, HUSSEIN, LATEEF, BHANDARI *and* DAWSON.

DAWSON. In the late spring and early summer of 1975, there was a strike at a weaving mill in Beckley, a small textile town near Bradford in Yorkshire.

BHANDARI. It wasn't a very big dispute. The firm employed under 200 people, less than half of whom came out on strike.

HUSSEIN. What made this strike special, however, was that all the strikers were Asians, and nearly all the people who stayed at work were white.

  HUSSEIN *sits*.

LATEEF. The strike began as a dispute over pay, but it soon escalated into a bitter conflict over the treatment of Asian workers by the company, the union, and their fellow employees. Pickets were mounted, and several ugly incidents took place.

  LATEEF *sits*.

CLIFFORD. In the seventh week of the strike, the Department of Employment set up a Court Of Inquiry to investigate the affair. At the Inquiry, the company, Darley Park Mills Ltd, was represented by Nicholas Clifford, Barrister-at-Law. Mr Clifford had made his name defending companies before the Monopolies' Commission.

  CLIFFORD *sits*.

JOWETT. The National Union of Weavers was represented by George Jowett, its General Secretary. Mr Jowett was noted in Trade Union circles for his vigorous advocacy of selective import controls.

JOWETT *sits.*

WATTS. The strikers's case was put by Jill Watts, another Barrister. Mrs Watts, who had been involved in a variety of radical causes, agreed to accept the brief for a nominal fee.

WATTS *sits.*

CHAIR. The Court Of Inquiry was chaired by the Baroness Cockburn, a former junior Minister who was elevated to the peerage after Labour's defeat in 1970. Baroness Cockburn, a director of the BBC and a prospective member of the Equal Opportunities Commission, was also presently chairing the Royal Commission on River Pollution in England and Wales.

CHAIR *sits.*

BHANDARI. The Inquiry was held in the Mechanics Institute, Beckley.

DAWSON. It took place on the third and fourth of July, 1975.

Exit DAWSON *and* BHANDARI. *The* CHAIR *introduces the Inquiry.*

CHAIR. Good morning, ladies and gentlemen. This is the opening of the Inquiry. My name is Ruth Cockburn and I am an independent person appointed by the Secretary of State for Employment with the following terms of reference: 'To inquire into the causes and circumstances of the present dispute between employees of the Darley Park Mills Company Ltd, and their employer, and to report.'
The Secretary of State has not laid down any specific rules of procedure and I can therefore decide the ground-rules we shall adopt. I don't intend to permit cross-examination, but questions can be asked through the chair at my discretion. The Inquiry will be in public, but we can go into camera if I feel it's necessary. There will be no evidence on oath and I want proceedings to be as informal as possible.

That's all I wish to say by way of introduction. I shall now ask Mrs Watts to open proceedings for the Strike Committee.

WATTS. Madam Chairman, the Strike Committee welcomes the chance to put its case to you, a case which is, I believe, one for simple justice. The strikers feel that they have been discriminated against by the company in terms of pay, conditions of work, and promotion. They have tried to resolve their grievances peacefully, and only as a last resort have they gone on strike. I intend to ask the strikers, as far as possible, to present their own case to you. But I feel it would be helpful to give a brief summary of the dispute, which my witnesses will as it were flesh out in their evidence. I shall be making a number of general points about arrangements at the Mill, and if I make any errors of fact I trust that the other parties will intervene.

CHAIR. I'm sure you will make no mistakes, Mrs Watts, and I am equally sure that if you do so, they will be corrected.

WATTS. Darley Park Mills employs nearly 200 workers. Just over half of them are employed as yarn-preparers, cloth-menders, and in general labouring and clerical capacities. The 90 or so actual weavers are concerned with overseeing the weaving machines.

There are, however, two major dividing lines between the weavers, which lie at the heart of this dispute. The first concerns the job itself. On any one shift, there are two types of weaver; ordinary weavers, who look after a certain number of looms, and a smaller number of time-weavers, who are in general more experienced and who assist weavers when they cannot solve a particular problem. The time-weavers are so-called because they are paid on a fixed-rate basis, which works out at between £5 and £10 more than the ordinary weavers' piecework earnings.

CHAIR. Can you give us rough proportions?

WATTS. Well, on an average shift of say 20 ordinary weavers, there'd be four time-weavers.

CHAIR. About one in five. Thank you.

WATTS. The other major division between the weavers is the

machines they work. Since the early 1970s, the company has been scrapping its old Dobcross looms and replacing them with new Sultzer weaving machines. This process has now been half-completed. The weavers on the new machines work a rotating three-shift system, and are therefore all men –

CHAIR. Forgive me, this is because of legal restrictions on women working nights?

WATTS. That's right, whereas the Dobcross operation is still two-shift, and does employ women on days. There is, therefore, a permanent nightshift on the old looms.

CHAIR. Again, can we have the rough proportions?

WATTS. Yes, indeed. On the Dobcross dayshift, there are about 25 women, including eleven Asian women. The Dobcross nightshift is, of course, all men, of whom the vast majority are Asian. There are about 40 Sultzer weavers, including about half a dozen Asians. That is the general position now.

CHAIR. Perhaps before you go on, Mrs Watts, we had better just double-check that everyone is in agreement thus far, and then we can take it as read. I'm sure there can be no basic –

CLIFFORD. Well, there is one point, Madam Chairman –

CHAIR. I spoke too soon. Mr Clifford.

CLIFFORD. It's really whether we want to discuss the transfer of machinery at this point. Obviously this is going to come up again later, but we could clear it up now.

CHAIR. I think it might be better to leave it until it comes up of its own accord.

CLIFFORD. Very well.

CHAIR. Mrs Watts.

WATTS. Thank you. The dispute began, in fact, with a complaint about bonus payments among the Dobcross nightshift weavers. However, this grievance as it were exposed a number of other grievances, about the treatment of Asian women on the dayshift, and, more importantly, the whole question of whites and Asians having equal opportunities for promotion to time-weaving posts. Through the union, the Asians presented all these grievances to management, and having failed to get any satisfaction, the Asian workers came out on strike on the 16th of May. Because all the strikers were Asian, the company invited a conciliation officer from the Manchester Community Relations Council, Anshuya Ridley, to mediate. An agreement was reached, and the first strike ended on the 28th.

CHAIR. For everyone's information, Mrs Ridley will be available to give evidence tomorrow.

WATTS. When the strikers returned, however, they found that two time-weaving vacancies had been filled by white workers while they had been out. The Asians viewed this as a breach of the spirit of the agreement and came out on strike again. Since then, the strikers have been sacked, and the dispute has been made official.
The only other major event, Madam Chairman, was the acceptance by the nonstriking workers of a redundancy and productivity scheme presented by the management three weeks ago. Because this meant that the company could not guarantee to take back all the striking workers, a solution of the dispute had been impossible to reach, and the present stalemate solution has continued to the present time.
I should now like to call the chairman of the strike Committee. I should mention that Mansur Hussein intends to give his evidence in English, but we have an interpreter to assist him should that prove necessary.

CHAIR. I'm happy with that.

WATTS. Mr Hussein, how long have you worked with the company, and in what capacity?

HUSSEIN. I have been employed since 1970, on the nightshift, in old looms.

WATTS. Could you explain the overtime position?

HUSSEIN. Well, there was a basic shift, but often we were told to work up to 12 hours.

Asian women on the dayshift, and, more importantly, the

WATTS. This was compulsory? You were told to do it and you did it?

HUSSEIN. Yes.

WATTS. Were you happy with this situation, initially?

HUSSEIN *looks at* LATEEF.

LATEEF (*in Urdu*). Initially.

HUSSEIN. Oh, yes. It was work. And with overtime, better money.

WATTS. What made you become less happy?

HUSSEIN. Well, for various reasons, I didn't wish to work nights all the time, and not to know when overtime would be.

WATTS. Can you say what the various reasons were?

HUSSEIN. Mostly, I got married.

CHAIR. I think that is as near as we are likely to get to the perfect answer.

WATTS. Indeed. Wasn't it also true that the pay became less attractive?

HUSSEIN. Yes. When I began, there was a differential bonus on permanent nights of about 15 per cent. By now it is – (*He speaks to* LATEEF *in Urdu*.) Reduced to?

LATEEF. Eroded.

HUSSEIN. Is eroded to about only five or six per cent.

WATTS. And that was your first basic demand, to have that differential restored, put back?

HUSSEIN. That is so.

WATTS. Thank you. I want to deal with promotion now. Almost all the nightshift workers are Asian. Has there ever been an Asian time-weaver on the shift?

HUSSEIN. Well, only one. The rest have been white. The one was appointed two years ago.

WATTS. Can you tell me how that appointment was made?

HUSSEIN. Yes. There was a vacancy, and the company appointed a white, who had worked on Sultzers. We indicated that we thought it should be an Asian from the shift.

WATTS. When you say 'indicated'?

HUSSEIN. We stopped working.

WATTS. Yes. And then?

HUSSEIN. Well, they caved in, and we started working again. They made an Asian a time-weaver.

CHAIR. Sorry, this was in addition to the other new one?

HUSSEIN. Yes.

WATTS. Now, Mr Hussein, I'd like to come to the build-up to the strike itself. How did you pursue your grievances?

HUSSEIN. Well, for a long time we have been trying to talk to Mr Kitchen.

WATTS. Mr Kitchen is the senior shop steward?

HUSSEIN. Yes, and we had some meetings with him, but very little seemed to be happening. We became quite frustrated, in fact. And so we wrote to Mr Jowett.

WATTS. What happened then?

HUSSEIN. Well, we had a meeting with Mr Kitchen, and Mr Jowett. And they wrote to management with our demands.

WATTS. And what was management's response?

HUSSEIN. Well, there was a meeting, and they turned down our demands. Two days later, we asked Mr Jowett to give strike notice and they wrote to management. A week later, we saw Mr Kitchen and asked him what had happened and he said nothing. We said we would come out on strike, but he said we must wait till we see Mr Jowett, who we met on Friday the 16th. He told us not to strike.

WATTS. He had given strike notice but he advised you not to strike?

HUSSEIN. That's right.

WATTS. So what did you do?

HUSSEIN. We set up our own committee and came out.

WATTS. Lastly, Mr Hussein, I'd like to deal with the agreement the strikers reached for a return to work, 12 days later, the deal reached with Mrs Ridley's assistance. In broad terms, could you describe it?

HUSSEIN. Well, the most important point was that there should be equality in promotion, between Asians and whites, to time-weaving jobs.

WATTS. Yes. And was there an agreement on the nightshift bonus?

HUSSEIN. Yes, there was a – um – (*To* LATEEF, *in Urdu.*) Interim?

LATEEF. Interim.

HUSSEIN. Oh, yes, interim bonus for nights.

WATTS. Why only interim?

HUSSEIN. Well, because the idea was that the firm should finish phasing out the Dobcrosses quickly, and transfer everyone to Sultzers, so there would be no more permanent nights problem.

WATTS. And on the basis of that agreement, you returned to work on Wednesday 28th May.

HUSSEIN. Yes. And then we found –

WATTS. Forgive me, Mr Hussein. I'll be dealing with what you found, with the next witness. That's all I have at this stage.

CHAIR. I have only one question. You said 'We came out' on the 16th. Who was 'we' at this stage? I mean, who was on strike?

HUSSEIN. Well, all the nightshift, almost, some of the dayshift, and some of the Sultzer people. Also a few labourers and menders and so on.

CHAIR. I have to ask if all the strikers were Asian.

HUSSEIN. Yes.

CHAIR. And a large number of them, I mean, the Sultzer people and the non-weavers, had nothing to do with the dispute?

HUSSEIN. Not directly, no.

CHAIR. So can I ask you why they joined the strike?

Pause.

HUSSEIN. They joined the strike because it is normal that when there is a dispute in a factory everyone is involved. That is normal even when people are not directly affected. Or that is what we thought.

Lights change.

Scene Two

CHAIR, WATTS, JOWETT, CLIFFORD.

WATTS. Madam Chairman, before my next witness, as the issue of the phasing out and the Sultzer transfer has come into the story, perhaps we could deal with it now.

CHAIR. Thank you, Mrs Watts. Mr Clifford, perhaps you could explain all this.

CLIFFORD. Yes, Madam Chairman. As Mrs Watts correctly pointed out, Darley Park Mills is about half-way through a process of transferring from old Dobcross looms to new Sultzer weaving machines.

CHAIR. This is a general technological development that has been going on throughout the industry?

CLIFFORD. It is indeed. The Sultzer machines are much more competitive in many ways. It requires less pre-preparation of materials, it's faster, and requires less staff. In general, one weaver minds four Dobcrosses, but the same weaver can cope with eight Sultzers.
There are, however, fairly obvious redundancy implications.

Any firm would want union agreement, but in this case it was imperative, because there is a Government grant-aid scheme for firms undertaking the transfer, and written union agreement is a condition of assistance.

CHAIR. When did this scheme begin?

CLIFFORD. In 1971. In effect, the company reached agreement with the union at that stage, but the union withdrew from the arrangement in 1973.

CHAIR. Perhaps Mr Jowett could explain why.

JOWETT. Well, basically Madam Chairman, the initial agreement was mainly concerned with female redundancies. We agreed on a programme of early retirement, natural wastage and other forms of voluntary de-manning –

CHAIR. I'm not sure 'de-manning' is quite the right expression under the circumstances.

JOWETT. Well, de-womaning or de-personing or whatever. There were some blokes involved as well. In any event, in 1973, the company came back and said that all this hadn't reduced the labour force by a sufficient amount, and that they'd have to sack a few. We refused this, and the company said it couldn't afford to continue the transfer under those circumstances.

CHAIR. Would the company accept this?

CLIFFORD. Well, more or less. In fact, the union took a generally much more belligerent line in 1973.

CHAIR. By 'belligerent' you mean that the union drove a hard bargain in 1973, whereas management had done rather well in 1971?

CLIFFORD. Well, yes. In fact, on the first agreement, there were really no strings attached at all.

CHAIR. A splendid deal.

CLIFFORD. It sometimes happens, Madam Chairman.

CHAIR. I really ought to let Mr Jowett comment on this. His reputation is at stake.

JOWETT. Well, you win some and you lose some. In '71 the industry was in recession, and I suppose we accepted things we wouldn't take in a boom year like '73. There's a bit of a fatalistic feeling in this industry, you know, that each downturn'll be the last. It's not, of course, or else we'd not be here.

CHAIR. So we can say that the transfer was as it were frozen in the 1973 position?

CLIFFORD. Yes. The situation remained the same until this year, when the company was forced to reopen the question.

CHAIR. Why 'forced'?

CLIFFORD. Well, frankly, because the government's grant-aid scheme stops next year.

CHAIR. That, as they say, figures.

CLIFFORD. The company re-opened negotiations in April. They were in progress when the present trouble broke out.

CHAIR. I'm sorry, I'm confused. I thought Mrs Ridley had recommended that the transfer question should be reopened at the end of the first strike, as part of the deal for a return to work. Were negotiations already in progress at that time?

CLIFFORD. They were. I think Mrs Ridley's point was that they should be pursued with vigour.

CHAIR. I see. I have only two more questions: first, can you give approximate figures on the weaving workforce in 1971, and when the transfer is complete?

CLIFFORD. Yes, I think so . . . Yes. There were 121 weavers in 1971. The projected figure is just over 60.

CHAIR. And finally, Mr Clifford, following that, the company did present a new scheme to the workforce during the second strike? A new scheme that was similar to the one they'd rejected in 1973?

CLIFFORD. Yes, the company did so. This new scheme was, I must confess somewhat to the company's surprise, overwhelmingly accepted by the non-striking workers on the 18th of June.

CHAIR. Thank you.

Lights change.

Scene Three

The Court.
CHAIR, WATTS, BHANDARI, LATEEF, CLIFFORD, JOWETT.

WATTS. My next witness is Savitri Bhandari. Mrs Bhandari, when did you start working at the mill?

BHANDARI. In 1973.

WATTS. You had in fact come to England from Uganda in 1972?

BHANDARI. Yes.

WATTS. Where did you work in the mill?

BHANDARI. I was on the Dobcross dayshift.

WATTS. Now, I want mainly to deal with the reasons for the second strike, but before I do that I'd like to ask you about various other grievances among the Asian women. Particularly, I'm thinking about the overlookers.

CHAIR. Mrs Watts, what are overlookers?

WATTS. Overlookers are in charge of shifts. They perform some skilled maintenance work and act in a general foremanly capacity.

CHAIR. I see. I'm sorry, Mrs Bhandari. You were about to tell us about your grievances.

BHANDARI. Well, there were a number of things. Attitudes. The Asian women felt, for example, that the overlookers tended to come to their machines last when they broke down, that sort of thing. And there was rudeness about lengths of tea-breaks. Small things.

WATTS. Wasn't there also something to do with toiletry arrangements?

BHANDARI. There were some problems, yes.

WATTS. Could you explain that?

BHANDARI. Well . . . sometimes the overlookers were difficult about ladies and their calls of nature.

WATTS. I'm sorry to press, but could you give an example?

BHANDARI. There was one occasion when one of the Pakistani girls was using the toilet and something had gone wrong with a loom, and the overlooker went and banged on the door and said what are you doing. So the lady replied, go home and ask your wife what she does in the toilet. Little things like that.

CHAIR. I must intervene here, Mrs Watts, because Mrs Bhandari is being, if I may say so, almost icily calm and reasonable about all this. But, as everyone knows, feeling among the Asian women was very high, and I feel that calling these matters 'little things' is something of a euphemism.

BHANDARI. Euphemism?

CHAIR. I can't immediately think of another word. Perhaps Mr Lateef –

LATEEF. I'm afraid I don't speak Gujerati, Madam Chairman.

CHAIR. Oh, of course, I apologise. I shall have to rephrase.

WATTS. Perhaps you're asking, Madam Chairman, if these matters were as trivial as Mrs Bhandari seems to indicate, why did the Asian women take them so seriously?

CHAIR. I could not have put it better myself. We shall now let Mrs Bhandari answer the question.

BHANDARI. I think the answer is that these things add up. I think Asian women like to look up to their elders. It is traditional. They give respect to people in authority, and they expect respect to be returned. When it is not, by the overlookers, they don't understand. They get upset and then they get angry.

CHAIR. I have heard rumours that you yourself get quite

angry, Mrs Bhandari. I have heard lurid tales about umbrellas on picket lines.

WATTS. I should now like to ask, Mrs Bhandari, about the situation on the 28th May, when the strikers returned to work. I'm referring to the time-weaver position.

BHANDARI. Oh, yes. Well, as Mr Hussein said, we had thought the agreement meant that time-weavers would be selected from everybody. When we got back, we found two new time-weavers on the Dobcross day-shift. White.

CHAIR. I am going to ask Mr Clifford how the vacancies came about.

CLIFFORD. I am afraid I am not quite sure. I could take –

JOWETT. I can answer that. One man left for a job elsewhere in the industry, for rather better pay, I gather, and the other had a heart attack and was advised to take early retirement.

CHAIR. Thank you. The point was, presumably, that the strikers felt the vacancies should not have been filled while the strike was on.

WATTS. Yes. This undermined their faith in the agreement generally.

CHAIR. And Mrs Bhandari felt that there were Asians who were as or more experienced than the people who were appointed?

BHANDARI. Yes. Not me, of course. But a couple of Asian girls and of course, the Asian men on nights, a lot had worked for many years.

CHAIR. Yet, I suppose as most of the dayshift was white, there could be a language problem?

BHANDARI. Well, it was said. But, a time-weaver's job is to look after machines. It is true that Dobcross looms speak neither Urdu nor Gujerati. Nor do they speak English.

WATTS. Madam Chairman, my last witness is Hameed Faruqi, who is the nightshift shop steward. Unlike a weaving loom, Mr Faruqi speaks fairly good English, but feels he would be

at a disadvantage, so I would like to take his evidence
through the interpreter.

CHAIR. I am quite content with that, but I would like to hear
Mr Faruqi's evidence after a short adjournment.

Blackout.

Scene Four

Canteen.
*Two tables. At one, WATTS, FARUQI, BHANDARI and
LATEEF. KITCHEN at the other.*
Enter JOWETT to KITCHEN. He has two coffees.

JOWETT (*sitting*). So, how's it look out front?

KITCHEN. Oh, smashing show.

JOWETT. Ay, well, you've had your entertainment. I want
you up with me from now on, round that table. Might be
needed.

KITCHEN. D'you know where Joan is?

JOWETT. No.

KITCHEN. She said she'd be along.

JOWETT. Ay, well, the longer out of it the better, with Mrs
Dawson, in my opinion.

KITCHEN. What d'you –

JOWETT *hushes* KITCHEN, *having noticed* WATTS *and the
strikers coming past.* JOWETT *stands.*

JOWETT. Well, hallo, Mrs Watts.

WATTS. Mr Jowett.

JOWETT. And what do you think of it so far?

WATTS. Well, I can't come back with the usual reply to that,
Mr Jowett. We haven't had your evidence yet.

JOWETT. I like it, Mrs Watts. You met Frank Kitchen?

WATTS. No, I haven't. How are you?

KITCHEN. Fine. Yourself?

WATTS. Oh. Wonderful.

JOWETT. I must say, Mrs B, enjoyed your crack about machines not speaking English.

BHANDARI *a slight shrug.*

WATTS. I think, conversely, we enjoyed your crack about de-womaning.

JOWETT. Oh, now, Mrs Watts, can't fault me there. I'm one hundred percent on women's lib. After all, without it, not be up against a charming lady like yourself. It's such a pleasant change.

WATTS. Ah, well, Mr Jowett, it's even worse than lady lawyers now, you know. Next year, there's equal pay.

JOWETT. Well, glory be. All this and Maggie Thatcher too. Well, I'll see you back there, Mrs Watts.

He drains his coffee, exit. KITCHEN *follows.*

WATTS. I think our Mr Jowett's what they call a trouper.

FARUQI. Pardon?

WATTS. Trouper, entertainer, joker, you know –

LATEEF *says a word to* FARUQI *in Urdu.*

FARUQI. Oh yes, very true. He likes a joke.

WATTS. Though I rather fear, it's not the trouper but his troops we need to be concerned with. Mr Kitchen.

FARUQI. Oh, no, Mr Kitchen, he's OK. Comparative.

WATTS. Comparative to what?

BHANDARI. You have not yet acquaintance with our Mrs Dawson, Mrs Watts.

WATTS *looks at* BHANDARI. *Blackout.*

Scene Five

The Court.
  CHAIR, WATTS, BHANDARI, LATEEF, FARUQI,
JOWETT.

WATTS. So, Mr Faruqi. You had come out on strike again,
  because of the appointment of the white time-weavers. You
  had been sacked by the company and on the 16th of June
  your strike had been made official. And then, two days later,
  the white workers voted for a new transfer scheme that had
  been presented to them by management, a scheme that would
  probably mean that a number of strikers would not be re-
  employed at the mill. What was your reaction to this decision?

  LATEEF *translates the question to* FARUQI, *who replies in Urdu
  to* LATEEF. *Note:* FARUQI's *English is good enough not to need
  a full translation of every question; indeed, sometimes, he gives his
  Urdu reply without any translation.*

LATEEF. He says that the strikers felt very bad about this.
  They felt it was evidence of racial prejudice. The white
  workers were not interested in the victimization of the
  strikers.

WATTS. In short, the strikers felt betrayed by their fellow
  trade unionists?

  Translation. Some chatter and laughter.

CHAIR. Yes? What is the answer?

LATEEF. The phrase is untranslatable, I'm afraid, Madam
  Chairman. The nearest I can get is 'To put it mildly'.

WATTS. Finally, Mr Faruqi, we have taken your evidence
  through an interpreter, and I think it might be asked if you
  have made any attempts to learn English.

LATEEF. He says he did take some lessons in Pakistan, and
  tried to continue them in England, but he was unable to do
  so.

WATTS. Why ever not?

LATEEF. Because he found it impossible to take lessons while
  working permanent nights with compulsory overtime.

WATTS. Thank you. That, Madam Chairman, is the case for the strike committee. But I should say that other members of the strike committee are available and can be called on later if the need arises.

CHAIR. Thank you, Mrs Watts, they are here if we need them. I have, however, just one further question for Mr Faruqi. It's a matter that has not yet arisen, but we can deal with it now. Mr Faruqi, I believe that before the strike began, you made a complaint to the Race Relations Board about the position of the night-shift workers?

FARUQI. Yes, I did.

CHAIR. When did the Board report?

FARUQI. 17th of June.

CHAIR. That was two days before the non-strikers accepted the transfer deal, which Mr Faruqi considered was evidence of racial prejudice?

FARUQI. Yes.

CHAIR. What did the Board conclude?

LATEEF. They said that no discrimination had taken place.

CHAIR. I'm sorry, you said *no* discrimination?

FARUQI. Yes.

WATTS. The strikers dispute that judgement, Madam Chairman.

CHAIR. I'm sure they do. Nonetheless, that was the Board's decision.

WATTS. Yes, it was.

CHAIR. Thank you, Mr Faruqi. I now ask Mr Jowett to put the case of the National Union of Weavers.

Lights change.

Scene Six

The Court.

CHAIR, JOWETT, KITCHEN.

JOWETT. Madam Chairman, I'd like to start by saying this. I am the General Secretary of the National Union of Weavers. Now this organisation possesses a rule-book. This in fact is it. It has 28 tightly-printed pages, and the purpose of each one of them is to keep the 9,000 members of the union as far as possible from each other's throats.

The second thing I want to point out is that there is also an agreement with the employers as to procedure on grievances. This again is it. It has a mere 18 closely-typed pages on the last of which is my signature. And that wouldn't be there if I hadn't intended to stick with it. And I am employed by my union to implement this and if I don't I am liable to lose my job.

Throughout this case I and my colleagues have been trying to resolve the contents of these two documents with the demands of the strikers at Darley Park Mill.

Now I should like to run through the events. First of all, there's the allegation that the union ignored the problems of the night-shift, until, as one of their leaders put it, the problem leapt up and bit us. Now Mr Kitchen, the senior steward, is here and can speak for himself. But all I'd say is that at the time we were moving into highly complex negotiations on the Sultzer transfer, and most of the stewards' time was taken up with that. But once we got on to it we did draw up a case, we did present it, and all of this – like writing to me and so on – flew in the face of procedure, but we did it.

Now, the actual grievances that were presented. I would like to make it plain, after Mr Hussein's evidence, that the union's view was that this was a dispute about the nightshift bonus. These other matters, promotion and the overlookers and so on, were not part of the case we presented, and this was clear in our submission to management, a copy of which went to Mr Faruqi. Now we might very well have presented these matters to management, had they been put to us before the strike began. And we did indeed talk about promotion when this appeared on the strikers' list of demands during the first strike. But it was not part of their original case, and I make that point because it explains why we were surprised when the strike began that other people, dayshift people and non-weavers came out as well. Another confusion concerns whether strike notice was given, after management rejected the claim. The strikers say I advised them not to strike, and this is right. I did that, because strike notice had not been given because it's against the rules of our union to give such notice without an executive decision. It was made plain in a letter to management and personally clear by Mr Kitchen. Now it's in that context that subsequent events should be viewed. I've said that various horses, followed by carts, had been driven through procedure. But, notwithstanding, we negotiated for the strikers during the first strike. When they came out again, we didn't wash our hands, we tried to help and when management sacked them we made the stoppage official. And, then, when management presented the new scheme for phasing out the Dobcrosses, we advised the workforce not to take a decision till the strike was over. Now, we didn't persuade them, but we tried.

CHAIR. Forgive me, Mr Jowett, but I think it's worth asking, what were the new proposals?

KITCHEN. If I could –

CHAIR. Certainly, Mr Kitchen.

KITCHEN. They weren't, I mean, they weren't quite the same as the ones we'd rejected in 1973. There was a new item in the package, which was that a few dayshift jobs'd be preserved, on Dobcrosses, for special, short-run work. It's happened elsewhere in the industry.

CHAIR. However, there still had to be some compulsory redundancies?

KITCHEN. Yuh.

CHAIR. What was the voting on the package?

KITCHEN. Virtually unanimous.

CHAIR. Despite what Mr Jowett said.

KITCHEN. Despite what Mr Jowett said.

JOWETT. I think, to intervene myself, the workers felt that with the grant-aid money running out, and, frankly with the industry in a dip again, I think they felt they'd played out all the rope.

CHAIR. I see.

JOWETT. That's really it, except to say, we think we've proved that the question isn't why we didn't push hard enough, but the reason why we pushed so hard. And the reason was, we felt that here we had a group of people, most new to the industry, they didn't all speak English, and they had a grievance, so we said, OK, we'll bend the rules a bit, and we did. That's all.

CHAIR. Thank you. We will now break for lunch.

Blackout.

Scene Seven

Canteen.
   DAWSON *sits reading a magazine and eating an apple.*
FARUQI *and* BHANDARI *cross the stage. She watches them pass.*
Enter JOWETT.

JOWETT. Well, hallo, Mrs D.

DAWSON. Hallo, George.

JOWETT. Mite delayed, eh?

DAWSON. Ay. A bit of upset.

   DAWSON *pats her stomach. She's pregnant.*

JOWETT. All right now?

DAWSON. They say the little bastard's shifting to the left.

JOWETT. I'm saying nothing.

DAWSON. So, what's she like?

JOWETT. The Baroness? Oh, think she's what you'd call, well-meaning soul. A coffee-morning type, you know. The sort donates her mink to Oxfam.

DAWSON. Well, George, see our case doesn't go the same road, eh?

JOWETT. Oh, don't you worry, Joan. It's in safe hands. We'll win.

DAWSON. Ay, well, that all depends, dunnit.

JOWETT. All depends on what?

DAWSON. On who you mean by 'we'.

JOWETT. We is our members, Joan. We is the union. (*Looks at his watch.*) Well, better go.

DAWSON (*stands*). OK, what happens now?

JOWETT. Well, now I've done my case, it's them.

DAWSON. Who's them?

JOWETT. Them's who them always is. Them is the employers. Joan.

Blackout.

Scene Eight

The Court.
   CHAIR, CLIFFORD.

CLIFFORD. Madam Chairman, there have been a number of allegations flying about to the effect that the company has been tardy or laggardly in its attempts to reach a settlement of this dispute.
Madam Chairman, like all other weaving companies, Darley Park has contractual arrangements with clothing manufacturers who in their turn have commitments to the wholesale and retail clothing trades. At the other end of the operation, the firm is committed to spinning mills who had arrangements with carding and combing concerns who have contracts with raw material suppliers.
In short, we are in the middle of a long process of getting wool off the back of sheep and on to the backs of people in the shortest possible time, and any part of that process which

disrupts the smooth running of the whole will quickly lose its confidence.

Now, having said that, Madam Chairman, I would like to move on to the Sultzer transfer. Madam, Darley Park Mill has a number of responsibilities, but it believes that its over-riding duty is to stay in existence, to continue to provide employment for its workers, a service to its customers and dividends to its shareholders.

CHAIR. I trust the company's priorities are in that order and not the reverse.

CLIFFORD. I think the company would view all three as mutually dependent, Madam Chairman.

CHAIR. I am not convinced that everyone here would agree with that, Mr Clifford, but do go on.

CLIFFORD. Thank you. The point I was making was that the company has determined that the only way for it to remain competitive is to complete the transfer, and it's in that context that I'd like you to consider the management's actions. First of all, there is the claim presented by Mr Jowett on the 5th of May.

Now, despite some controversy about what was being claimed, it is agreed that the main demand was on the night-shift bonus on the Dobcrosses, and I'm sure it's obvious that the management had to turn it down, precisely because it would have had the effect of delaying the phasing out of the Dobcross looms. Now, the next –

CHAIR. I'm sorry, Mr Clifford . . . Are you saying that the company refused to improve the conditions of the Dobcross workers in order to encourage them to accept the phasing out?

CLIFFORD. That's more or less right, Madam Chairman. I'm sure you understand their point of view.

CHAIR. It's certainly understandable, Mr Clifford. It also sounds to me like blackmail.

CLIFFORD. I'm sure the company would not accept that word.

CHAIR. Can it think of an alternative?

CLIFFORD. I think it would prefer the word 'incentive'.

CHAIR. Yes. I see.

CLIFFORD. This desire to conclude the transfer speedily was also the reason why the company accepted what has been called the Ridley Agreement, which did propose a small increase in the nightshift bonus, but in the context of a commitment by all sides to a rapid recommencement of the phasing out, in the interests not only of the company, but also those of racial harmony.

Now the company has been criticised for pressing ahead with its new scheme during the second strike. There are really two points here. The first is that the company, despite the fact that the strikers had demonstrably broken their contracts of employment, stayed its hand a week before issuing termination notices, in the hope that wiser counsels would prevail.

But, and this is the second point, there was no question that, whether or not the strikers returned, the Scheme would have to be implemented. Negotiations were already in progress. They then received Mrs Ridley's blessing. I think you will understand that the company, who had advocated this scheme for so long, had no choice but to seize with both hands the chance of implementing it.

Finally, Madam Chairman, I would like to state quite unequivocally, that there is no question in the company's mind of any distinction between its employees on the grounds of race, colour, creed or national origin. It would be foolish to deny, however, that there are those within the mill for whom this is a question. The company has not in any way given into these pressures, but has tried, by a process of gradual persuasion, to allay what it regards as a groundless fears.

That is all I want to say for the moment, Madam Chairman. I should say that Mr Eric Harper, the Managing Director, is here if there are any questions that go beyond my brief.

Lights change.

Scene Nine

The Court
  CHAIR, CLIFFORD, HARPER, WATTS, LATEEF,
FARUQI.

CHAIR. Ladies and gentlemen, having concluded the initial
  statements, we now enter a general questioning session. As
  Mr Clifford's case is fresh in our minds, it would be best to
  start with him and/or Mr Harper. My first question concerns
  the whole question of the new two time-weavers, over
  which, if I may say so, Mr Clifford managed somewhat to
  slide. Now, perhaps Mr Harper could help us here. These
  two vacancies, first, one was someone who'd left the firm,
  the other had suffered a coronary, is that right?

HARPER. Yes.

CHAIR. And how were the replacements selected?

HARPER. They were selected from a list of people who
  applied when we posted the vacancies. I should point out that
  none of the applicants was an Asian. They were appointed in
  accordance with our normal procedures, procedures that
  everyone had been perfectly happy with until –

CHAIR. I beg your pardon, Mr Harper, but Mrs Watts is
  making semaphore signals at me. I haven't been in the navy,
  but I think she means 'stop'.

WATTS. Madam Chairman, with respect, it is hardly
  surprising no Asians applied, as most of them were on strike
  at the time.

HARPER. With respect, that was not a situation of the
  company's choosing.

WATTS. Well, with great respect, it is possible to argue that
  the company might have waited until the strike was over and
  the Asians were back at work before filling the vacancies.

HARPER. Well, with the greatest respect, it was not the
  company's fault that most of the dayshift was still working.
  Had they *all* been on strike, there would have been no need
  to fill the vacancies. As it was –

WATTS. With the greatest of all possible respect, Mr Harper –

CHAIR. Mrs Watts, and Mr Harper, I may not be alone in
thinking that if we have much more respect in this Inquiry,
mutual or otherwise, we shall suffocate.

WATTS. I'm so sorry, Madam Chairman.

CHAIR (*smiling*). There really is no need. I was merely . . .

LATEEF. Um, I think Mr Faruqi has a point here.

CHAIR. Yes?

A little translation.

LATEEF. He is wondering if management seriously argues that
the vacancies that occurred were as they say coincidence.

CHAIR. I am sure that Mr Faruqi is not suggesting that a heart
attack is anything but coincidence.
I think we had better leave that there. I wish now to ask the
company about the sacking of the strikers in the second
stoppage. Mr Clifford, do you or Mr Harper wish to deal
with this?

CLIFFORD. I can deal with this, Madam Chairman; it's a
matter on which my brief is quite comprehensive.

Lights change.

Scene Ten

The Court.
CHAIR, WATTS, LATEEF, FARUQI, BHANDARI,
CLIFFORD.

CLIFFORD. Madam Chairman, the company's argument on
this has nothing to do with whether strike notice was or
wasn't given and at what stage. The point is that, in law,
workers are employed to work and if they do not do so, if
for example they simply decide to stay away, they are in
breach of their contracts of employment. There is no
contractual right to give notice of an intention to stop work,
and then to say, 'We have stopped work, but we have not

broken our contracts because we told you we were going to do it seven days ago.'

CHAIR. Are you saying that any strike is a breach of contract of employment?

CLIFFORD. I am saying that unless there are specific agreements that is the case. There are agreements between employers and trade unions which say something like 'there shall be so many days' strike notice', in which case it's possible to say that a bona fide stoppage of work is provided for. There is, however, no such clause in any agreement that I can locate between the employers' organisations and the National Union of Weavers.

CHAIR. But surely, Mr Clifford, there must be custom and practice on this.

CLIFFORD. Indeed there could be, Madam Chairman. But in this case there is none because this is the first official strike organised by the NUW in the last 40 years.

BHANDARI *laughs*. LATEEF *whispers to* FARUQI. FARUQI *laughs*.

CHAIR. Um, I would point out to the Strike Committee, Mrs Watts, that having a strike-free record is not necessarily a matter for scorn.

WATTS. Well, I'm sure they take your point. It could be argued however that this strike demonstrated that the union's procedures are inadequate.

CHAIR. It could be argued, Mrs Watts, that the best test of a country's defences is a war, but it's not necessarily the best excuse for waging one.

CLIFFORD. Madam, the only thing I'd say on this is that it could be asked, under these circumstances, why the company delayed as long as it did before terminating the strikers' contracts.

CHAIR. Yes, I suppose it could be asked.

CLIFFORD. The answer, Madam Chairman, is that the company was then, as it has always been, throughout this dispute, giving every benefit of every doubt, and bending over backwards to be fair.

Lights change.

Scene Eleven

CHAIR, WATTS, JOWETT, FARUQI, LATEEF, BHANDARI, DAWSON.

CHAIR. The next question I want to ask concerns the strike Committee, but I think it would be useful before that to establish one or two things about the union organisation and the grievance procedure. Mr Jowett, I'm sure you'll want to comment on what Mr Clifford has just said, but I wonder if you could circumvent the right-to-strike question at this moment?

JOWETT. Well, yes, Madam Chairman, I'm glad of that, because it's something on which I would have waxed somewhat lyrical, at some length and in some passion, and my doctor would protest most strongly at the likely effects on my blood pressure.

CHAIR. Heaven forbid, Mr Jowett. Perhaps you could begin by outlining the union structure at the mill.

JOWETT. Well, the basic unit is the factory committee, which consists of shop stewards from each section, including warp-preparation, mending, and so on. In weaving, there are four stewards, one for Dobcross, one for days, and two for the Sultzers.

CHAIR. I dislike these questions, but could you tell me the racial breakdown of the stewards at the moment?

JOWETT. Well, there's nothing sinister about this, they reflect the composition of the sheds. The two Sultzer stewards are English, Mr Faruqi represents the nightshift, and the dayshift is looked after by Mrs Dawson, who is also with us, and seems to be a light pinkish colour.

CHAIR. Can I ask, as Mr Faruqi is on permanent nights, if there are any problems about attending meetings and so on?

JOWETT. Well, yes, there are obvious problems there, unfortunately.

CHAIR. Peculiarly so, I would have thought, under the circumstances. And the grievance procedure?

JOWETT. Well, I won't go through it all, but the first step is for a person to see the shop steward and then go with him to the senior overlooker in the shed.

CHAIR. Yes. Of course, in this case, the shop steward is 'her', and I would like to ask Mrs Dawson a question or two.

JOWETT. Please go ahead.

CHAIR. Mrs Dawson, were you aware that there was discontent among the Asian women on the Dobcross dayshift?

DAWSON. Well, I think I overheard things, ay.

CHAIR. Did you receive any official complaint?

DAWSON. No, I didn't.

CHAIR. When the Asian women came out on strike, did they talk to you about it at all?

DAWSON. They did not. They had a meeting, with their nightshift people, and next thing I knew, they was all on a picket line.

CHAIR. So really, it would be fair to say that neither the union procedure nor the grievance procedure had been followed correctly.

DAWSON. No, I'd disagree with that.

CHAIR. You would?

DAWSON. It weren't a matter, procedure not followed correctly. It were a matter, procedure not followed at all.

CHAIR. Thank you. Can I ask Mrs Bhandari if Mrs Dawson is correct in saying that no complaints were presented to her?

BHANDARI. I do not recall if any were.

CHAIR. You mean, as far as you recall, they weren't?

BHANDARI. Yes.

CHAIR. Second, can I ask who told you or asked you to come out on strike?

BHANDARI. We were asked by the nightshift men at a meeting.

CHAIR. Third, did you at any time, before the meeting or after it, ask Mrs Dawson her opinion or consult her in any way?

BHANDARI. We did not consult her in any way.

CHAIR. In any way at all?

BHANDARI. In any way at all.

WATTS. I think, Madam Chairman, that there is behind this a whole legacy, which I would like with your permission to deal with as a piece as it were –

CHAIR. Well, I'm sure you will deal with it, Mrs Watts, but before you do so I would like to clear up one further matter. Can I ask Mr Faruqi. Did he in fact think that the union had given strike notice?

LATEEF. He says that the workers made it clear what they wished the union to do.

CHAIR. Yes, but having made it clear, did he think the union responded to their wishes?

LATEEF. He says that the management had refused to give in to the demands.

CHAIR. Well, again that's not the question I asked. Whatever the workers thought, does he think that the union in fact gave notice to strike?

LATEEF. He says yes.

CHAIR. That is what I wanted to establish because I have read Mr Jowett's letter to management and I must point out that it seems quite clear that strike notice was *not* given.

WATTS *finds letter.* FARUQI *finds another copy in his pocket.* LATEEF *looks over* FARUQI's *shoulder.*

I quote: 'We have advised the workers against industrial

action, but I must inform you that feeling is so strong that they have pressed us to give you seven days' strike notice.' Now, that must mean, despite the Asians' feelings, that the union did not –

LATEEF (*looking at the letter*). Oh, no.

CHAIR. Mr Lateef?

LATEEF. Oh, no, it mustn't mean that.

CHAIR. I'm sorry?

LATEEF. I mean, it needn't mean that. It's ambiguous. I mean, it could mean something else.

WATTS. Madam, can I consult a moment?

CHAIR. Yes, I think perhaps you should.

Lights change.

Scene Twelve

The Court.
  CHAIR, WATTS, JOWETT, DAWSON, KITCHEN.

WATTS. Madam Chairman, you quoted the relevant passage of the letter of the 8th of May, and pointed out that it could be interpreted as meaning that strike notice was not given.

CHAIR. Yes?

WATTS. Now, what Mr Lateef noticed, which I must confess I hadn't spotted, was that sentence could mean two opposite things.

CHAIR. Go on.

WATTS. It could of course mean, as you said, that the phrase 'they have pressed us to give strike notice' is presented merely as evidence for the strong feeling among the Asians, and, indeed, there is the phrase 'we have advised the workers against industrial action' to confirm that view. However, I maintain that it could also mean that, despite the union's advice, the workers were insisting on industrial action, and the phrase 'they have pressed us to give strike notice' means 'we are giving strike notice, and this is it'.

JOWETT. Madam Chairman, of course the former view is the correct one, we were telling management that we were under pressure, and frankly, I think this could be a case, this isn't a racial point, but as we know some of the people don't have perfect English –

CHAIR. Mr Jowett, I must interrupt you. It is Mrs Watts who finds the letter ambiguous, and her command of English appears to be exemplary. Also, I hope I'm reasonably fluent in the language, and I must confess that now I look at it, it seems ambiguous to me.

JOWETT. Well, all right then, forgetting that I can't speak English –

CHAIR. Come now, Mr Jowett, you speak it splendidly. I've heard it whispered it's your mother tongue.

JOWETT. You haven't met my mother, Madam Chairman.

CHAIR. I'm sure it would be a pleasure and a privilege.

KITCHEN. Look, I'm sorry, Madam Chairman, but whatever's in the letter, I did make the position clear to a member of the strike committee, on the 8th of May.

CHAIR. Who was that?

KITCHEN. It was Abdul Kadir.

CHAIR. I'm sorry, who is –

JOWETT. Abdul Kadir worked in the warehouse, Madam Chairman. He was not a permanent worker, in fact, but a student. He was one of the main spokesmen for the strike committee.

CHAIR. Mrs Watts, is Mr Kadir here?

WATTS. Madam Chairman, I'm afraid that Abdul Kadir isn't here.

CHAIR. But is it possible to –

WATTS. He's unable to attend the hearing, I'm afraid.

CHAIR. Well, I suppose we must accept that.

WATTS. Nonetheless, and whatever meetings may have taken place, it is quite clear the letter is ambiguous.

CHAIR. I think we can agree, the only thing that is clear is the manifest unclearness of that letter.

DAWSON. Madam, can I make a point?

CHAIR. Yes, of course.

DAWSON. It does seem blind obvious.

CHAIR. I'm sure we'd all welcome a blind obvious point.

DAWSON. Surely it's obvious that if these people knew procedure, they'd have known that Mr Kitchen, even Mr Jowett, couldn't give strike notice without going to the union executive. I mean, that's lesson one.

CHAIR. Well, I take that point, but we have already established that for various reasons the Asians were not fully aware of procedure.

DAWSON. Ay, well, a person might not know there's a law against murder, but don't stop him going to prison if he kills someone.

CHAIR. Well, I'm not convinced that that's a very helpful analogy –

JOWETT. Madam Chairman, can I come in. I think the point Mrs Dawson's making is that if the letter can be taken in two ways, then knowing what the rules are and all other things being equal, the strikers couldn't –

WATTS. Can I point out to Mr Jowett, that if all other things were equal, then we wouldn't be here.

A pause before lights change.

Scene Thirteen

The Court.
  CHAIR, WATTS, DAWSON, BHANDARI, SANDHU, HUSSEIN, JOWETT, KITCHEN.

WATTS. Madam Chairman, a few moments ago, it was revealed that the strikers had not followed correct union procedure. With your permission, I would like to probe the reasons for that a little with Mrs Bhandari.

CHAIR. Certainly.

WATTS. Mrs Bhandari, you said earlier that you didn't trust Mrs Dawson and, by implication, the union. I'd like to try to discover why. First, are you a member of the National Union of Weavers?

BHANDARI. Yes.

WATTS. Did you join immediately you started work at the mill?

BHANDARI. No, it was about a month later.

WATTS. Who invited you to join?

BHANDARI. Mr Hussein.

WATTS. Who is not on your shift, and indeed is not a shop steward?

BHANDARI. No.

WATTS. And had you been approached at all by Mrs Dawson or any other shop steward?

BHANDARI. No, I had not.

WATTS. Now, I believe elections for shop steward take place in March. Am I right in thinking you decided to stand for election this year?

BHANDARI. Yes, I did.

WATTS. Now we know you didn't win, because Mrs Dawson is still your shop steward. But how well did you do?

BHANDARI. I didn't.

CHAIR. Sorry, you mean you didn't do well?

BHANDARI. I didn't do at all. I was not allowed to stand.

WATTS. What reason was given for that?

BHANDARI. Because I had not been a member of the union for two years. Apparently there is a rule.

JOWETT. Madam Chairman –

WATTS. I would be grateful if I could finish with Mrs Bhandari before Mr Jowett comments.

CHAIR. Would you mind, Mr Jowett?

JOWETT. Not at all.

WATTS. Now can I ask why you feel people did not make use of the grievance procedure.

BHANDARI. Well, part of the problem is that you go first to the senior overlooker, and a lot of the girls don't want to do that.

WATTS. Why not?

BHANDARI. Because it was mostly him they had a complaint about.

WATTS. Yes. Is there any other reason?

BHANDARI. Well, it's hard to say. But, let me . . . Say you have a little grievance. And you don't, it seems so silly, make a fuss. And then your friend, she has another silly grievance. And her friend another. And together, they stop looking so silly. But, of course, you cannot put them together.

WATTS. So what you're saying is that the procedure can't by its nature cope with grievances that are as it were cumulative and collective. That a worker is not going to nit-pick over a small thing, which on its own looks trivial, but which taken together with other things add up to evidence of something else.

CHAIR. Perhaps Mrs Bhandari could hazard what that something else might be.

BHANDARI. I suppose, that someone, somewhere, is prejudiced against you.

WATTS. Thank you, that's all.

CHAIR. Mr Jowett?

JOWETT. Well, all I want to say is that there is indeed a rule that elected people have to be financial members of the union for two years. But that applies to everyone.

WATTS. But I'm sure Mr Jowett would agree that in effect –

JOWETT. This rule was adopted in October 1953.

WATTS. Look, no-one's suggesting that this rule was *intended* to discriminate –

JOWETT. Well, thanks –

WATTS. – but it's my argument that in the context of all the other factors, that is the effect of that rule. Madam Chairman, I would like to discuss a couple of those factors with Mr Ranjit Singh Sandhu, who works in the Sultzer shed.

CHAIR. This is still your reply to the union?

WATTS. Yes, it is.

CHAIR. Then, very well.

WATTS. Mr Sandhu, how long have you worked at Darley Park?

SANDHU. From leaving school. Seven years.

WATTS. And because of that relatively long experience, you were moved to the Sultzers two years ago.

SANDHU. That's right.

WATTS. And it's also fair to say that you're good at your job?

SANDHU. Well, I suppose . . . I used to earn good piecework. I think I'm good at it.

WATTS. And in the normal run of events, you'd expect to get promotion, I mean, you might see yourself becoming a time-weaver?

CHAIR. Not now, surely, Mrs Watts? Mr Sandhu is only 22.

WATTS. No, I'm not suggesting that. Mr Sandhu, do you think you will become a time-weaver at some stage?

SANDHU. I very much doubt it.

WATTS. Why not?

SANDHU. I think promotion for Asians became a dead duck two years ago.

WATTS. Why then?

SANDHU. Because it was then that a white was put in as a time-weaver on the nightshift.

CHAIR. We have had this before. Wasn't an Asian subsequently appointed as well?

WATTS. Yes, but what I wanted to ask Mr Sandhu was what the reaction of the white workers on the Sultzers was to this incident.

SANDHU. They were, one could say, not too chirpy.

WATTS. But couldn't you see the point? They were worried that the man who had been appointed might be demoted to make way for the Asian.

SANDHU. But he wasn't demoted.

WATTS. Yes, but I was suggesting –

SANDHU. And still, that was not what bothered them.

WATTS. What did bother them?

SANDHU. What bothered them was the Asian being promoted.

WATTS. I see. And it was the memory of this incident, and the white workers' attitudes, it was because of this that you were so concerned when, in this dispute, you came back off strike and found the two new time-weavers on the dayshift?

SANDHU. I think that's called a rhetorical question.

CHAIR. Could you answer it nonetheless.

SANDHU. Of course we were, as you say, concerned.

WATTS. Finally, there has been criticism of people not concerned with the dispute, coming out on strike. You work on the Sultzers. Why did you join the strike?

SANDHU. The question is the other way round. Why did the

whites not come out with us. Why, even when it was made official, did the union allow them to keep working. That's the question you should ask.

WATTS. All right. Will you answer it?

SANDHU. The whites did not come out because they are so racialist that they are prepared to destroy their union rather than let us get promotion. You asked why I came out. I came out when my people came and asked me to.

JOWETT. Right. I'm going to answer that. I'm actually quite pleased that Mr Sandhu's said what he has said. I'm pleased because at last you're hearing the real voice of this dispute. What's actually been happening. The kind of things, been hearing on the picket line. You mentioned Mrs Bhandari seeming calm and cool. You haven't, with respect, been through a picket-line and had her shriek abuse at you.

CHAIR. When you say abuse?

JOWETT. Well, I don't know, Madam Chairman. One thing they shout's a word that sounds like cha-cha. Don't know if, it's s'posed to be a joke about the way I walk –

WATTS. The word is chancha, I'm informed. Roughly translated, it means a lackey of the management.

JOWETT. Oh, well, I thought it might be on those lines. And I think if we're flinging words like lackey and racialist around, then we might as well say some other things, and admit for starters that for all this talk about machines not speaking English, there are language problems and experience problems and they're not the only problems that face us and we'd best be straight on that and all.

CHAIR. Go on.

JOWETT. Well. It's just – a fact. There are fears. P'raps I don't quite share them. But I'm not going to deny them.

CHAIR. What do you mean?

JOWETT. I mean, there's fears, among the English workers, that in three years time, won't be a white face left.

SANDHU. Oh, yes, now he –

JOWETT (*mostly at* SANDHU *now*). Cos there's people there who've worked their lives –

CHAIR. Mr Jowett –

JOWETT. And it wouldn't matter if you were all Germans, Japanese or Buddhist monks –

CHAIR. Mr Jowett, I'm afraid you can't have it both ways. You implied a moment ago that the Asian workers are incapable of doing the job, and that could be true. You've just said they might be so good that they'll take over the mill, and that could be true as well. But they can't both be true, and I'd suggest in fact that neither –

JOWETT. All I'm saying is you've got to understand –

WATTS. All you're saying is, you won't support your –

JOWETT. Look, you, we've bent over backwards, and I know that you're not used to how we –

SANDHU. Not used? Not used to being used as slaves!

DAWSON *laughs loudly*.

CHAIR. What's funny, Mrs Dawson?

DAWSON. Oh, dear me. Oh just you hear him. We're not used to being slaves. We're not like British workers, not prepared to graft all hours for lousy wages. We are proud and dignified.

CHAIR. I'm not quite sure . . .

DAWSON. They came. Eight year ago. They came and they did nights and they did overtime. Don't ask me, ask George Jowett. Ask how long he'd fought, get rid of people being forced to do nights overtime. And nearly won it too. And then they came, and yes sir, no sir, eight hours, ten hours, twelve hours full sir.

SANDHU. So why when we go on strike to get rid of it –

DAWSON. Oh, ay, and you'll hear all about union solidarity and black and white unite and fight and brotherhood of man. You heard him? What he said just then? It's when *my* people said come out, he came out. We are not his people.

SANDHU. No, you are not my people.

DAWSON. But when we say, we stand up for our own kind, that is racialist. When we protect our own jobs, oh, that's racialist. When we say –

SANDHU (*to* CHAIR). Now, you listen. Listen. Now you're hearing all this filth that we have had throughout this –

DAWSON (*she makes to go*). Well, I'm not stopping here to get abused, I think I'll –

CHAIR. No, you will *not* go, Mrs Dawson. You will sit down, as will Mr Sandhu.

After a pause, they sit.

Ladies and gentlemen, I had hoped that this Inquiry would serve to bring together the parties in a calm and reasonable atmosphere. I had feared, however, that if these proceedings became uncalm and irrational, then they might tend to exacerbate the tensions that gave rise to this hearing. I'm very sorry that my fears should have been so amply confirmed. It is not yet five o'clock, but I see no alternative at this time but to adjourn for the day.

WATTS. Madam Chairman, I would like to say one thing before this session closes.

CHAIR. Well, you may, Mrs Watts, but I would ask that it be brief and a great deal more temperate than the statements we have just been hearing.

WATTS. It is brief and I hope it is temperate. It's just that earlier in the day, it was claimed that there were, I think the word that Mr Clifford used was pressures, racist pressures, from the workforce, on the company. I think it should be pointed out that what Mrs Dawson and, to a certain extent, Mr Jowett have said might be seen to confirm that point of view. (*Pause.*) That's all.

Lights change.

Scene Fourteen

The Court.

WATTS *clearing up her papers*. BHANDARI, HUSSEIN *waiting for her*. DAWSON *stands there. The* OTHERS *have gone*.

DAWSON. Eh. Mrs Watts.

WATTS. Yes, Mrs Dawson.

DAWSON. Where d'you live?

WATTS. In London. Why?

DAWSON. Where, London?

WATTS. Highgate Village.

DAWSON. Highgate Village. Ay, well, that explains it.

WATTS. What?

DAWSON. There's plenty of them there.

WATTS. I'm sorry?

DAWSON. Just wait till one moves in next door.

WATTS *picks up her papers to go.*

Eh, Mrs Watts. Your kids go 'way to school?

WATTS. We haven't any kids.

DAWSON. Oh, see. I have. Two. And this one on the way. You ought to see their school.

WATTS. Why?

DAWSON. Cos more Mohammads there than there are in bloody Mecca.

Pause.

WATTS. I'm sorry, Mrs Dawson . . .

DAWSON. Eh – Not that – Not, 'sorry, Mrs Dawson' – after what you said just now.

WATTS. What did I say just now?

DAWSON. You said it. Not me. You said you was on the bosses' side.

DAWSON goes out.

WATTS. I didn't . . .

HUSSEIN. Um, well . . . in a way, you did.

WATTS looks at HUSSEIN. WATTS looks at BHANDARI. Blackout.

Scene Fifteen

Pub.

SANDHU and HUSSEIN leaning on the bar with their pints.

HUSSEIN. How d'you think it's going?

SANDHU. Better. Better than this morning.

HUSSEIN. Yes.

SANDHU. Things coming out.

HUSSEIN. Things coming out.

Pause.

Hey, want a game of darts?

SANDHU. I didn't know you played.

HUSSEIN. I'm in the team. Pub team.

SANDHU. I don't play darts.

Pause. Something amuses HUSSEIN. He smiles.

HUSSEIN. Hey. You remember that bloke, who got arrested. Something Khan.

SANDHU. Haider.

HUSSEIN. Yuh. And he was up in court and the magistrate said, 'Can you speak English', and he said, 'No, no English.'

SANDHU. Mm.

HUSSEIN. Cos he'd been told by someone you did better if

you have no English. You know, poor old bugger, speaks no English, being crippled, got to make allowances. And the guy said, 'Very well', and so has the interpreter. (HUSSEIN *is beginning to laugh at his own story*.) And then the magistrate said, asked, 'It has been established', this was what he said, 'it has been established that Mrs Khan was among the most forceful of the picket leaders. Can you inquire of Mr Khan' this was the question, see, 'can you inquire if Mr Khan's behaviour can be explained by the influence of his wife?' You remember Mrs Khan?

SANDHU. Indeed I remember Mrs Khan.

HUSSEIN (*laughing*). And, before the interpreter has a chance, Khan leaps straight in and says: 'Well, your lordship, I don't know if that kind of thing happens in your house, but it certainly doesn't happen in mine.'

HUSSEIN *laughs merrily*. SANDHU *is not sure he has followed*.

You see, he said he spoke no English, and so the magistrate, of course, went quite bananas. And he got three months.

SANDHU *now sure he hasn't followed*. HUSSEIN *laughing like a drain*. *To explain*:

Suspended, you know.

He laughs.

'But it certainly doesn't happen in mine.'

SANDHU *taps* HUSSEIN's *arm*. *He's noticed that* KITCHEN *has appeared further down the bar*. HUSSEIN *stops laughing*. *A* BARTENDER *appears with a drink*. *He stands there*.

SANDHU. That Khan went back of course.

HUSSEIN (*sips his beer*). Yes, well. They did. Can understand. They want a quiet life. Just make a little money, then go home.

SANDHU. You going home?

HUSSEIN. I s'pose I think I'm going to go home.

KITCHEN *goes over to the* ASIANS.

KITCHEN. I didn't know you drank in here.

HUSSEIN. Oh, yes. I'm in the darts team.

KITCHEN. Oh, ay?

HUSSEIN (*glances at* SANDHU). Yes. We drink in here.

KITCHEN. It's not against your faith?

HUSSEIN. Oh, I'm not a good Moslem. In fact, I'm a
    terrible Moslem. And Ranjit here's a Sikh, and they do
    anything.

Pause.

KITCHEN. Hey, thought, right funny, all that stuff, we
    haven't got the right to strike. George Jowett turning blue.

HUSSEIN. Oh, yes.

KITCHEN. A man of moderation, George. The quiet life.

HUSSEIN. Well, some of us, as well, quite like the quiet life.

KITCHEN. No, I meant, he's not, for me, not militant
    enough.

HUSSEIN. I see.

Slight pause.

KITCHEN. He better get in quick, though, with a claim, when
    this lot's over.

HUSSEIN. Why?

KITCHEN. Well, you know, the Common Market
    referendum, now we lost that, moving Tony Benn and all.
    I'll bet you, TUC'll cave in, and we'll have bloody wage
    controls.

HUSSEIN. Didn't they say they wouldn't –

KITCHEN. Oh, they always *say*.

Slight pause.

So, slap our claim in double quick.

SANDHU. Our claim.

KITCHEN. That's right.

Pause.

She is, Joan, she's a good militant. A damn sight better than George Jowett. Just, she's got a blind spot. Her uncle got shot, in Calcutta, in the Army, 1946.

SANDHU. My uncle got shot too. In Burma. 1943.

KITCHEN. Oh, ay. I know 'bout that. Sikh regiments. The best of all.

Pause.

Where d'you actually come from?

SANDHU. Me? I come from Bradford.

KITCHEN. Sorry, no I mean before that.

SANDHU. Oh for a bit I was in Leeds.

KITCHEN. Sorry, I didn't, meant, where did you come from.

SANDHU. Oh, sorry, see what you mean. Where was I *born*.

KITCHEN. That's right.

SANDHU. Southall.

Pause.

HUSSEIN. I'm from Lahore. My mother came in 1961. To be a nurse. In answer to a Government advertisement. The Ministry of Health, they wanted people for the hospitals.

KITCHEN. Yuh, well –

HUSSEIN. The Minister at that time was a man called Right Hon Enoch Powell.

Pause.

KITCHEN. I'm not a Powellite. I don't think you should all go back.

SANDHU. Look. OK. It's very nice, you come and drink with us. We're very touched. But, really, don't tell us, you do not wish repatriation. Go and tell your Mrs Dawson.

KITCHEN. Look, I'm not –

SANDHU. Cos we are not the problem. She's the problem. And she's not our problem. She is yours.

Pause. KITCHEN shrugs.

KITCHEN. Play it your way.

He's about to say something else. Changes his mind, takes his pint and exits. Pause.

HUSSEIN. You know, you want to find the biggest racialists of all, you to to India and Pakistan. Oh boy.

SANDHU. I've never been to India or Pakistan. I live in England.

Long pause. HUSSEIN starts chuckling.

What?

HUSSEIN *chuckling.*

HUSSEIN. 'Well, your lordship . . . I don't know if that happens in your house . . .'

SANDHU *smiles.*

'But it certainly . . .'

HUSSEIN*'s laughter is infectious.*

'It certainly doesn't happen in mine . . .'

HUSSEIN *laughing fit to burst.* SANDHU *picks it up. The two men laugh and laugh. Blackout.*

Scene Sixteen

DAWSON*'s house.*
    DAWSON *and her* VISITOR *sitting facing each other. They are drinking tea. Pause before* DAWSON *speaks.*

DAWSON. I mean, you'd not believe the things they're saying. Think we owe them everything. That everything that's done to them's our fault. It's us to blame, that they're cheap labour.

Pause.

I mean, I know what's going to happen. Everybody knows. If they get this, then every time a job comes up, if they don't get it, it's discrimination. Three year, all be gone. Why shouldn't we stand up to stop that happening? We've got rights too.

Slight pause.

D'you want another cup?

The VISITOR *shakes her head.*

OK.

Slight pause.

See, take a place like this. And what it used to be. It's all gone rusty. Not just them. The state of things. The shops all full of mucky magazines. The whole thing tarnished. Mouldy.

Pause.

We know what happens. Area like this. I mean, it's just the facts of life. They come in, and a place just drops apart. It's just a fact of life.

Slight pause.

Dunno where John is.

Slight smile.

Never do.

VISITOR *smiles sympathetically.*

I sometimes feel split off. Detached from things around. All look the same. Same streets, and full of people. But it's like you're in a perspex box. Can see, but reach out, you can't touch them. Don't know who you are.

Pause.

Why should I? Feel guilty? They're the ones as should feel guilty. What they done to us. To me. It's not me should feel guilty.

Slight pause.

Got a cigarette?

The VISITOR *shakes her head.*

Good. I shouldn't, really, now.

Slight pause.

I mean, I don't, don't blame them. Personally. Think they're just as much the victims. Blame the people let them in and blame the people who inflame them once they're here.

Pause.

You've got to ask what is behind all this. You've got to ask *why* people let them in.

Slight pause.

I mean. How can I bring a person into this, when I don't know the reason for what's happening, and who's behind it all. What can I say?

Pause.

VISITOR. We think we've got an inkling of what's happening. And who's behind it all.

Slight pause.

DAWSON. You know –

VISITOR (*stands*). Well, look. The time.

She takes a newspaper and books from her bag.

I've got your copy of the paper. And a book or two you might have time to read.

She gives them to DAWSON.

You'll tell me what you think?

DAWSON. I will.

The VISITOR *turns to go.*

You know, before you came, I didn't . . .

VISITOR *looks back.*

You know, I really didn't have, before I joined . . .

She doesn't say anything else. The VISITOR *smiles.*

VISITOR. I'll see myself out, now. Good night.

She goes. DAWSON *sits holding the books and newspaper.*

DAWSON. You see . . . I've grown up since you came.

Lights fade.

ACT TWO

Scene Seventeen

Hotel.
    CLIFFORD *and* HARPER *are finishing breakfast.*
    CLIFFORD *has had croissants and coffee.* HARPER *has had cooked breakfast and tea.*
    CLIFFORD *offers a cigarette to* HARPER.

CLIFFORD. Cigarette?

HARPER. No thanks.

   CLIFFORD *lights his cigarette.*

CLIFFORD. I'm always full of admiration, people who can eat their way through all that flesh first thing. Sure it's a sign of moral fibre.

HARPER. Well, I –

CLIFFORD. Coffee, croissants and the crossword, 'bout my limit.

   Slight pause.

HARPER. Well, I don't, I mean, at home. Just porridge or some cornflakes.

   He gestures at his breakfast.

   Treat.

   CLIFFORD *smiles.*

CLIFFORD. Well, it's a filthy Yankee habit, breakfast meetings, but I thought . . . Worthwhile.

   Slight pause.

HARPER. So what's your view, the score so far?

CLIFFORD. 'Bout equal. Union and strikers. P'raps the latter, just ahead on points. Since all the rumpus.

HARPER. Us?

CLIFFORD. We're where I wanted us to be.

HARPER. Which is?

CLIFFORD. Not on the field at all. Observers. Watch the game. Or, p'raps a better way of putting it, a kind of referee.

HARPER. That's how you want it?

CLIFFORD. Yes.

Slight pause.

Do you?

HARPER. Not sure. No, I suppose, in this, you're right.

CLIFFORD. In this?

HARPER. In this affair. I'm thinking really . . .

CLIFFORD. Yes?

HARPER. About the wider thing.

Pause.

CLIFFORD. What wider thing?

Pause.

HARPER. You know, Nick, in this area, the textile business, twined around its heart. Defines the place. What's good for worsted, so they say, is good for the West Riding. Mean, they treat the going rate for wool tops like the weather forecast. Even now.

CLIFFORD *smiles.*

You know, there was a time, this industry, when bosses knew their workers, all of them, by name. That's when that didn't mean a working grasp of Arabic.

HARPER *smiles.* CLIFFORD *half-smiles.*

You know, there's – in the boardroom, there's these portraits, of these stern old gentlemen, my grandfather, great grandfather. All rich and heavy.

And there's my uncle, and my father, he took over, when my uncle died in Normandy, in 1944. And he, p'raps not so stern – benign. Still firm, still very much in charge, but more benign.

Slight pause.

Then at the end. A kind of afterthought. There isn't really room for it, wedged in between my uncle and the window frame, there's me.

Slight pause.

And when you look at it, it's got a sort of silly smile. Kind of apologetic. S'if the painter knew – my picture was the last.

CLIFFORD *embarrassed.*

CLIFFORD. Isn't your son – ?

HARPER. My son's at LSE. He's reading Economics. Wants to be a teacher. Hates the north. He wants to teach, in somewhere proletarian, like Bethnal Green.

Pause.

That's not the point. Not what my son . . . The point is that my industry is dying.

Pause.

It's difficult, therefore, to stand back and observe.

Pause.

I better go. I want to slip up to the works. I'll see you there.

He stands.

There's only one way for this business to survive, you know. Only one way.

CLIFFORD *looks up, questioning.*

The new technology, of course. And something else. Secure and stable workforce. Not people work a year or two and

bugger off for better pay. Or leave it altogether. Need . . .
Commitment. Discipline . . . And any firm who's got that,
will survive.

Slight pause.

The rest of us . . .

CLIFFORD (*quietly*). Oh, come on, Eric . . .

HARPER. You know, I welcome this Inquiry. Actually. Not
cos of what's been said. So far, I mean. What could be said.
About the real, facts of life.

Slight pause.

Perhaps . . . it's after all, your job, to stop me saying them.
I'll see you there.

He goes out. CLIFFORD *puzzled. Then he shrugs, picks up his
paper. Then he pours another coffee, but the pot is empty. Calls*:

Um, waitress – ? Miss?

Pause. Lights change.

Scene Eighteen

The Court.
    CHAIR, JOWETT, WATTS, SANDHU, HUSSEIN,
RIDLEY, CLIFFORD.

CHAIR. Ladies and gentlemen, I would like to begin this
morning with Mrs Anshuya Ridley of the Manchester
Community Relations Council, but before that, I have been
told by Mr Jowett that he wishes to make a short statement.

JOWETT. Thank you. I think it's obvious what this arises
from.
Madam Chairman, we in the National Union of Weavers
have an inter-racial membership. We have a lot of white
people, some brown people and one or two black people. In
the winter we have blue people and in summer some of our
members lie on beaches and turn bright red. Now we could
pursue a policy of unequal treatment of any of these hues, but
we believe that a worker is a worker is a worker, and we

reject discrimination against any members, wherever that discrimination may come from. As far as humanly possible, we have been, are now and intend to remain a colour-blind organisation. That's it.

CHAIR. I'm sure everyone here will welcome that, Mr Jowett. I wonder whether at this point there is anything Mrs Watts wishes to say on behalf of the strike Committee.

Slight pause.

WATTS. Well, I would say . . .

Her eye catches SANDHU's.

That on this side we agree with your statement that an atmosphere of reason is preferable to one of irrationality.

Pause.

CHAIR. Yes. I see.
Let us move on. I had hoped, in view of Mr Faruqi's complaint, that we would have a representative of the Race Relations Board of the Inquiry. However, sadly, the officer concerned is overseas at the moment. Mrs Ridley has agreed, however, to comment on the role of the Board in a general way, and in a broad sense to represent what is known in the jargon as the Race Relations Industry. Mrs Ridley, I am afraid you can have had no more than a cursory glance through yesterday's transcript, but I wonder if there's anything you'd like to say?

RIDLEY. Well, I don't think I wish to make any general statement. There are however a couple of specific points I'd like to touch upon.

CHAIR. Please.

RIDLEY. They both concern the matter of my feeling that the move to an integrated production situation would remove many of the potential areas of tension and division. While this appears to have been accepted, there seems to be an impression that I was unmindful of the redundancy implications. I must state unequivocally that this is not so. It was made quite clear to me that an additional element – the retention of some dayshift jobs – would be part of any new

package, and it was also made plain that the choice was either
a new package or the firm's collapse.

The second point is an obvious one. It was not of course in
my mind that the new scheme would be presented while
most of the Asian workforce was on strike.

CHAIR. Thank you. Are there any comments on this?

CLIFFORD. Yes, a couple, Madam Chairman. The first is to
repeat that while the second strike may not have been in Mrs
Ridley's mind, it was not, of course, in the company's mind
either.

The second point is that there was a proposal raised at one
point that the company should introduce some kind of quota
system for Asian promotion. This was not considered
appropriate and I wonder if Mrs Ridley could comment on
this.

RIDLEY. This is answered simply. It is not, to use counsel's
words, inappropriate to introduce a quota system. It is illegal
under the terms of the Act.

CLIFFORD. I see.

CHAIR. Mr Clifford, do you have anything else?

CLIFFORD. Well, only to hope that Mrs Ridley will comment
on the fact that the company was found not guilty of
discrimination under the Race Relations Act.

RIDLEY. Yes. Can I preface this by explaining that there are
two statutory bodies concerned with Race Relations. One is
the Community Relations Commission, which I represent,
and which has no legal powers. The Race Relations Board,
on the other hand, has the job of implementing the 1968 Race
Relations Act. I have worked for the Board in the past, and
have read its report in this case.

CHAIR. I can ask you to comment, but I cannot press you to
do so.

RIDLEY. I can make a comment, in a general way. There are
three reasons, I think, why this complaint failed. The first,
frankly, concerns the very nature of the legislation, which
stipulates that no investigation can take place unless there has

been a complaint from an individual. Obviously, in a case like this, there are a larger number of individual grievances, which built up into a general pattern for the minority group, but the Board is only empowered to deal with the individual matter brought to its attention, which may, in isolation, not appear so grave.

CHAIR. This is really the point made yesterday about the company's own procedure.

RIDLEY. Yes, I think I spotted that. The second point is more specific. According to the Board, the main complaint was about compulsory overtime. Unfortunately, this was held not to be discriminatory because the workers had accepted it voluntarily.

CHAIR. Mrs Ridley, are you saying that if a racial minority as it were agrees to be put in an inferior position, then that is not discrimination?

RIDLEY. Under the terms of the Act, no. It is a general deficiency of this type of legislation. Another vivid example is recruitment. Obviously, many black and coloured people do not apply for certain jobs when they have been told, or fear, that they will meet prejudice. In such a case, they are, of course, victims of discrimination in a very real sense. But if they do not actually face concrete rejection, then, in legal terms, it does not exist.

CHAIR. Let me get this clear. If there was a situation where a racial minority – or even a majority – were as it were prevented by entrenched custom and practice from work in certain areas, and therefore never bothered to apply, knowing there'd be no chance of getting a job, then that would not be held to be discrimination?

RIDLEY. I see exactly where you're heading, Madam Chairman. Yes. It is true, that on the face of it, the Race Relations Act 1968 would find it extremely hard to find racial discrimination in the Republic of South Africa.

CLIFFORD. Madam, this is all highly instructive, but it does not alter the fact that the Board found that no discrimination had occurred in this case.

RIDLEY. Well, it found that no discrimination had occurred under the Act. It's really a reverse of the old joke that the only person who can prove they are sane is the person who has a certificate of dismissal from a mental hospital. Now, the company has a kind of certificate saying that it has not contravened the law. This doesn't mean that it has not discriminated. This is another reason why people tend to be circumspect about using the law in these cases.

CHAIR. Mrs Ridley, do I detect a point of inter-departmental rivalry here?

RIDLEY. Of course you detect no such thing, Madam Chairman. It is, however, true that I now work for an organisation that muddles along quite happily without recourse to statutory powers.

CHAIR. You said there was a third reason for the failure of Mr Faruqi's complaint?

RIDLEY. Oh, indeed. From the report it is clear that the Board received a marked lack of cooperation from one of the parties involved.

CHAIR. This was the company?

RIDLEY. No, the company was quite helpful. The party concerned was the strike committee. They refused to see the Board.

CHAIR. But it was a member of the strike committee who made the complaint in the first place.

RIDLEY. Yes.

WATTS. Madam Chairman, I think what has emerged in the last few minutes demonstrates quite clearly why the Asian workers were unwilling to cooperate with the Board.

CHAIR. Well, yes, but that doesn't explain why Mr Faruqi made the complaint in the first place.

WATTS. May I consult a moment?

CHAIR. Of course.

WATTS *talks to* HUSSEIN *and* SANDHU.

WATTS. I think the best way of putting it would be to say that there was a disagreement on tactics. Mr Faruqi made his complaint, of course, before the strike began. By the time the Board got round to investigating it, the strikers felt themselves to be, using an Americanism, in a whole new ball-game.

DAWSON *laughs.*

CHAIR (*sharply*). Mrs Dawson, do you have a comment?

DAWSON. No, I have no comment.

CHAIR. Mrs Ridley, is there anything you'd like to say in conclusion?

RIDLEY. Yes, briefly.
I think that anyone who works in what you called the Race Relations Industry is aware that there are no easy panaceas for the problems of communities living together. There are wide cultural differences, which it is foolish and not a little romantic to deny.
But, having said that, I think the revelation of disagreement within the Asians themselves is, in a paradoxical way, rather encouraging. Because it shows that the minority workforce is a group of people with individual concerns and priorities, just like any other group. In the same way, the fact that a largish number returned to work during the second strike, while this might seem regrettable in some ways, is at least an indication that the mill is not irreversibly divided on racial lines. It is, I am sure, our hope that the indigenous workforce will not feel that they must act like a tribe in defence of their interests, and one way to prevent that is for the minority communities not to operate in a tribal fashion either.
I think that's all I have to say.

CHAIR. Thank you . . . I wonder, before you go, if you could repeat one point you made.

RIDLEY. Yes?

CHAIR. Did you say a large number of Asians returned to work during the second strike?

RIDLEY. Well, I was not involved at that stage, of course, but I had gathered that that was the case.

CHAIR. This I think is new.

WATTS *whispering with the strikers.*

JOWETT. Perhaps I could . . .

CHAIR. Yes of course.

JOWETT. Broadly, what happened: it was during the second week of the second stoppage. The Asians had come out on Thursday the 29th May. The following Tuesday and Wednesday, the third and fourth of June, a largish number, I mean, 20 or so, came back.

CHAIR. Were these perhaps people not directly involved?

JOWETT. Well, some. But a lot were nightshift workers. It was this, frankly, led us to think there might be, shall we say, external influences at work.

CHAIR. People like Mr Kadir?

JOWETT. People, like that, yes.

CHAIR. Can I ask why you didn't mention this before?

JOWETT. Well . . . I think . . . I don't agree with this strike. I never have. But, on the other hand I'm not one to volunteer the fact a strike's not solid. You could say it goes against the grain.

CHAIR. Mrs Watts, there must be some comment on this.

WATTS. I am instructed that what Mr Jowett says is more or less so. A number did return.

CHAIR. Why?

WATTS. Well, to be frank, one reason was that there were families, extended families, whose only breadwinner worked at the mill, or whose only source of income was perhaps two or three family members working. In these cases, the committee did let a few people continue to work, on compassionate grounds.

CHAIR. Yes, I see that, but we're not talking about people continuing to work. We're talking about people returning to work, if I may say so, in droves.

I had gathered that that was the case.

WATTS. Another factor, of course, may have been the issue of dismissal notices. This precipitous act –

CHAIR. Well, I'm sorry, that doesn't work either. Mr Jowett said the return was on the second and third. The dismissal notices weren't sent out till the fourth.

WATTS (*after a pause*). Madam Chairman, I'm afraid I am going to have to take further instructions.

CHAIR. Do I take it that there is another factor in all this?

WATTS. I'm afraid I have to take instructions.

CHAIR. Very well. I was planning a short adjournment. We will take it now.

Lights change.

Scene Nineteen

Canteen.
Enter WATTS followed by HUSSEIN and SANDHU.

WATTS. Well, I'm sorry, but I think you're berserk.

SANDHU. So you keep saying.

They sit, as:

WATTS. What on earth will we gain?

SANDHU. What do you think?

WATTS. Tell me.

SANDHU. We'll gain by making clear why we will not work with the Race Relations Industry. We'll gain by making clear why Mr Jowett's white and black and blue and crimson workers is just –

WATTS. Ranjit. We're talking about what is, I mean, don't get me wrong, I'm dead opposed to it, but we are talking now about a criminal offence. Offences.

SANDHU. Oh dear.

WATTS. Yes? Oh dear what?

SANDHU. Oh dear you're all the same. This fetish with the law. You're all the same.

WATTS. When you say 'you' –

SANDHU. White liberals.

HUSSEIN. Ranjit.

Pause.

WATTS. I can't stop you. You employ me. And whatever you may think of how I'm doing this, or what I am, I will do what you want.

Pause.

HUSSEIN. We think that this thing must be brought out.

WATTS. I disagree with you, but we will do it. Right?

SANDHU. And there's the other matter.

WATTS. Oh, yes. That. Well, once again, I must say my advice is –

SANDHU. Look, we know about it, it's quite common knowledge, been on all their marches, been –

WATTS *stops* SANDHU *with a gesture. She has noticed* KITCHEN *and* DAWSON *have entered.*

WATTS. Shall we adjourn, find somewhere quiet?

HUSSEIN. Yes, let's do that.

WATTS, HUSSEIN *and* SANDHU *go out.*

KITCHEN. What's it all about d'you s'pose?

DAWSON. Well, I dunno, do I?

Pause.

KITCHEN. I see them two last night.

DAWSON. Oh, ay?

KITCHEN. I talked to them.

DAWSON. That's nice.

KITCHEN. No, weren't. Bloody edgy. Fact, they was bloody rude.

DAWSON. You shatter me.

Slight pause.

KITCHEN. Just wondered why, that's all.

DAWSON. What d'you mean, you wondered why?

KITCHEN. The tone of voice, you know, the style of talking. Déjà vu.

DAWSON. Frank, I don't speak foreign languages. S'why I find working Darley Park so –

KITCHEN. Sounded just like I do when I'm locked in some great barney with the management. A kind of, sullen. Sarkey. Clever. And distrustful.

Slight pause. Laughter.

Just don't expect to hear it used at you. I'll go and get some coffee.

He goes out.

DAWSON. Frank –

DAWSON *looks after for a moment. Then she looks at the table where the strikers were sitting.*

You go ahead.

Blackout.

Scene Twenty

The Court.
 CHAIR, WATTS, DAWSON, SANDHU, HUSSEIN,
JOWETT, KITCHEN.

WATTS. Madam, I asked for time to consult on this question, and the reason was that I felt that certain matters involved would be counter-productive to the strikers' case. I have put this point of view, but have failed to convince those who are instructing me. I must therefore ask you to let Mr Hussein make a statement. I should also say that Mr Hussein will shed light on why, as I said yesterday, Abdul Kadir is unable to assist this Inquiry.

CHAIR. Mr Hussein.

HUSSEIN. Um, Madam, the position is this. Although most of the picket line trouble occurred recently, a few arrests did happen during the first strike. One of the people arrested was Abdul Kadir, on the 23rd May. He was, um –

WATTS. Remanded.

HUSSEIN. He was remanded on bail to appear in court some time in early June, charged with threatening abuse or some such charge.

Slight pause.

However, on 1st June, a Sunday, Mr Kadir was arrested at his home for a different offence. He was taken in custody and was later transferred to a prison in the south of England. To await deportation.

CHAIR. Deportation? Why?

HUSSEIN. Because he was, it was claimed he was an illegal immigrant. A student overstayer. Stopped his course, should have gone back. Under the Immigration Act he can be – well, the word's not even deportation. He can be 'removed'.

CHAIR. Mr Hussein, I'm still not quite sure how this connects with –

HUSSEIN. Well, I think it is not too hard to comprehend. There is a strike. There are pickets and they are stopping things going in and affecting the company's operation. And then a Pakistani is arrested and he faces being removed. Two or so days later, other Pakistani strikers, in a body, break the strike, go back to work. I think it's not impossible to understand.

CHAIR. You're saying, in effect, that some or all of these strikers were fearful that they too might be arrested as illegal immigrants?

HUSSEIN. Of course.

CHAIR. Then can we conclude that some or all of them are in fact living illegally in this country?

HUSSEIN. Under the 1971 Immigration Act or the Pakistan Act, yes.

CHAIR. Under the law of our land?

HUSSEIN. Yes, under the law of your land.

CHAIR. Thank you. I must say I can understand Mrs Watts' reticence, under the circumstances. But there we are. Before we move on, I must ask a couple of questions. I did detect, I think, an implication that the company had been involved with, had somehow provoked, the arrest of Mr Kadir. As I'm sure this was not the case –

SANDHU. Oh, no, of course, they had nothing to do with it.

CHAIR. I'm glad to hear that, Mr Sandhu.

SANDHU. Cos they don't need to. Any immigrant will tell you. This, machine, it operates without the touch of human hand, it works quite automatically. As it is designed to do.

Pause.

CHAIR. Yes. I'd now like to ask, I think we ought to know, if Mr Jowett and/or Mr Kitchen knew about this?

JOWETT. I think it's fair to say I had an inkling. It's not, again, the sort of thing I'd volunteer.

CHAIR. And Mr Kitchen?

KITCHEN. No.

CHAIR. You mean you –

KITCHEN. I'd no idea at all.

CHAIR. Thank you. I think, now, we must leave the matter there. I now wish to proceed –

SANDHU. But there is another point.

CHAIR. Mr Sandhu, I think unless –

SANDHU. A different point. From Mrs Watts.

CHAIR. Perhaps then she could tell us what it is.

WATTS. Yes, Madam Chairman, there is a further point. It is in fact another point I advised the Committee not to pursue, in this case on the grounds that you might find it inadmissible. But once again, I have been over-ruled. The argument, the point is really that, as, already we have moved, or been dragged, into what you could call a more political situation . . .

CHAIR. Mrs Watts, I think it would help your point if you came to it.

WATTS. Well, it concerns, in brief, the political affiliations of a member of the factory Committee.

CHAIR. Then your advice was correct. I would be most unhappy –

WATTS. Yes, well I must put their argument, and say that in this case the matter is of relevance.

CHAIR. And I must disagree with you.

WATTS. Then I must ask, if you would be prepared, perhaps, to admit this evidence in camera.

CHAIR. Well, even then, I would be most –

DAWSON. Don't bother.

CHAIR. What?

DAWSON. Don't bother, go in camera. I'll tell you what she's on about.

CHAIR. Well, I'm –

DAWSON. She's on about me being in the Front.

Pause.

CHAIR. By 'Front', you mean, the National –

JOWETT. Madam Chairman, I'm not a lawyer, and I don't know how you're supposed to make objections, but –

DAWSON (*interrupts*). Cos I have sat here for two days and heard everyone being very polite and very reasonable and very friendly. And no-one's been so vulgar as to say there might be sides, and some on one and others on the other. Now, perhaps, it's time that things came out, a bit, into the open.

And I won't be long, promise. Cos she's already said it. Far as I'm concerned, Mrs Highgate Village said it. The employers and the coloureds on the same, same side. Well, begin to ask some questions. Don't you? Then.

Cos far as I'm concerned, she's right. They are the other side. We are our side.

Slight pause.

But, of course, aye, can't be. Cos they are the oppressed. And bosses are oppressors. How they stop you seeing. That the people called exploiters and exploited are the same. They say, the bosses and the communists are locked in struggle for the world. They stop you seeing that it's bankers and financiers who give the money to the communists. See how it's them encourages this lot to come here. Live here. Breed. And inter-breed.

It's a conspiracy. No doubt in my mind. It's a conspiracy, to undermine our race. By bringing them. By other things. The unemployment. Common Market. Mucky magazines. The general . . . rot. Pollute our nation from within.

It's all connected. Seems quite clear to me. Destroy the nation. Then take over everything. You see?

Slight pause.

I hadn't seen it, quite that . . . Hadn't seen before.

Pause.

Well now, if you'll forgive me. Suddenly, don't feel too good. As may be obvious, I'm in what you could call a pregnant situation.

DAWSON *stands and goes out.*

CHAIR. Well –

KITCHEN. Madam Chairman, I'd like to ask something.

CHAIR *waves him on.*

I think – I'd like to ask, Mr Hussein or Mr Sandhu. What I want to ask is, why they told us. 'Bout their people being illegal immigrants. I'd like to ask them that.

CHAIR. Would – one of you . . .

HUSSEIN. Well. Mr Jowett said earlier that a worker is a worker is a worker. White or black or brown or green with yellow stripes. Mrs Ridley said earlier that we should be the same as other workers. Don't be a tribe and they won't be a tribe.

Slight pause.

But we are not the same as other workers. Because white workers do not have to take their passports when they go to work. That is the point.
We are not like whites because they are not working side-by-side with people who desire to put them all on boats to go back where they did or didn't come from. That's the point.

Pause.

We are not over here because of some great conspiracy. We are over here because you wanted us to come here. We are over here because, dear Mr Kitchen, you were over there.

SANDHU. And if they divide us, they're dividing you.

Blackout.

Scene Twenty-One

Canteen.
    DAWSON *sits.* BHANDARI *and* SANDHU *cross the stage. They look at* DAWSON, *she doesn't look back. At exit,* SANDHU *goes out, but* BHANDARI *stops and turns back. She gives a little cough. No reaction. She tries again.* DAWSON *looks up.*

DAWSON. Want something?

BHANDARI. No.

DAWSON. Right.

BHANDARI. Wondered, you might want something.

DAWSON. Like what?

BHANDARI. Some dinner, something.

DAWSON. Being got some, thanks.

BHANDARI. You OK now?

DAWSON. I'm wonderful.

Slight pause.

Well. Don't let me detain you. Sure you've got lots to be getting on with. Planning tactics with your friend the whirling dervish.

Slight pause. BHANDARI *smiles.*

BHANDARI. Dervish? You mean Ranjit Sandhu? Oh, he's OK. Şhows off, you know.

DAWSON. You what?

BHANDARI. He likes to think he's tough. But underneath, no way.

DAWSON. Oh, ay?

BHANDARI. He once – he saw us, women on the picket line, it scared the pants off him. He said.

DAWSON. Oh, did he?

BHANDARI. Yes.

Slight pause.

DAWSON. I doubt that many of your menfolk were that shot on your activities.

BHANDARI. Now that is true. That's very true.

DAWSON *looks in some surprise as* BHANDARI *continues chattily.*

A lot of them, you know their husbands said, when they said they were on picket duty, said, oh you can't do that. With all those men. Stay home, my girl, and catch up on the laundry. Can't have you going on all hours striking. What about the cooking and the home? And, even worse, we went collecting and a lot of husbands, fathers, they said: that's begging. And of course that's very bad. Oh, no, a lot of them said, they don't approve at all.

Slight pause.

I s'pose your husband, might react the same, if you came out on strike.

DAWSON. I doubt it. Rather different, i'n't it, Asian women. Subjugated. Kept in purdah. Kept behind locked doors. I wonder, what they thought of Madam Ridley. Married to a white. I bet that went against the grain. I bet that went down like a cup of sick.

BHANDARI. Well, surely, it's the same the other way.

DAWSON. Keep them locked up. Don't want them, get polluted by our filthy Western ways.

BHANDARI. Oh, not just Western ways. In fact, it's happening in India and Pakistan. Women campaigning. 'Gainst arranging marriages. Fighting for rights. In fact, it's not just here.

Slight pause.

But it is harder here. Because if you do not belong inside your own community, there's nowhere else you can belong.

DAWSON. Go home then. If it's harder here. Go back to where you came from.

BHANDARI. If I go back where I came from, I get shot.

DAWSON. You what?

BHANDARI. Uganda.

Slight pause.

DAWSON. Hm. You know, funny, i'n't it. Any place you got two races. Never mix. The blacks don't want the Asians in Uganda, and now I come to think of it, round here there's one or –

BHANDARI. Uganda, it was not the blacks who made divisions.

DAWSON. Who, then?

BHANDARI. Was the British. Put the Asians in, to run the blacks. Because Uganda is a little bit too hot for white men. So they put the Asians in, to run things for them. No surprise, what happened, don't you think?

Pause.

DAWSON. Well, you're all right now, aren't you? Now we've welcomed you with open arms.

BHANDARI (*smiles*). They didn't look that open in the camps. They didn't look that open for the husbands without British passports, shuttled round the world.

Pause.

DAWSON. Well, this is most illuminating, but –

BHANDARI. D'you mean that, what you said in there? About an international conspiracy?

DAWSON. Of course I mean it. Said it, didn't I? There's people who would like to see our race destroyed.

BHANDARI. Bankers, you said. Financiers.

DAWSON. That's right.

BHANDARI. You know, that's very interesting.

DAWSON. Why?

BHANDARI. Cos that is just what is said by our own President Amin. Only he's a little more specific. Says it is the Jews.

Slight pause. DAWSON moves to stand. KITCHEN has appeared with DAWSON's dinner, stands behind her.

Don't you, really . . . You say the race. You are not, p'raps, before you are an English person, first of all a worker? Or perhaps a woman?

DAWSON. First, I'm a white woman. First, I'm a white worker.

BHANDARI. Mm. Sometimes, you know, I think . . .

DAWSON. Yuh? What d'you think?

BHANDARI. That they give you whiteness so that you can put up with the rest. They give you such a dreadful life, but say, at least you're white. At least, in that, you are superior. You know, if you're the bottom of the pile, the real dregs, black woman . . . We've grown up, through this strike. We won't put up with dreadful things, now, any more. From overlookers. Husbands. Foremen. Fathers. You.

DAWSON. Well, I'm very sorry, love, but frankly I can't give a toss about your home-life or your strike.

BHANDARI (*suddenly hard*). Then we were right. You are a chancha.

DAWSON. Sorry, don't speak Urdu.

BHANDARI. Gujerati. Scab.

She makes to go.

KITCHEN. You should have –

BHANDARI *turns back.*

You should have said that in there.

DAWSON. So what?

BHANDARI. We're not brought up to say too much out loud.

She goes out.

DAWSON. Frank? Frank?

KITCHEN (*giving her the food*). Your dinner.

DAWSON. Ta. Where's yours?

KITCHEN. Not hungry. Got to have a word with someone.

DAWSON. Someone being who?

KITCHEN. You'll see.

DAWSON *puts down her dinner, stands.*

DAWSON. Frank, for Christ's sake, not getting sentimental?

KITCHEN. Sentimental?

DAWSON. Brotherhood of man. That lot.

KITCHEN. Oh no. Not brotherhood of man. Far from it. Naked, crude self-interest. Not just mine and all.

He makes to go.

DAWSON. Eh, Frank. Is this your bloody déjà vu?

KITCHEN. I'm sorry. Don't speak Urdu. Love.

Blackout.

Scene Twenty-Two

The Court.
CHAIR, WATTS, KITCHEN, HARPER, DAWSON.
WATTS *is reading a hastily scribbled piece of paper.*

CHAIR. Ladies and gentlemen, we are now approaching the stage of final speeches. I have asked Mr Jowett and Mr Clifford if they have any further questions or comments before they sum up, and they have said they are satisfied. Mrs Watts, is there anything else from you at this point?

WATTS. Well, I'm afraid there is, Madam Chairman. It's a matter, or shall I say a perspective, that has only just, as it were, sprung to my notice.

CHAIR. Then you must spring it on us.

WATTS *is not quite sure what she is doing, but she begins confidently.*

WATTS. What I have to say relates really to what has become something of a hardy perennial in this Inquiry: the history of the various Sultzer transfer schemes. Now we have here three events. The first is the initial agreement of 1971, which, as you said, was a splendid deal from management's point of view. We then had what was described as the union's much more belligerent line in 1973 and their final acceptance a month or so ago of the deal they'd rejected in 1973, compulsory redundancies and all.

CHAIR. But with the promised retention of some Dobcross dayshift jobs.

WATTS. Yes.

WATTS looks at KITCHEN, who is looking sepulchral.

As you will remember, the reason given for the change in the workers' attitude was that in 1973 the industry was in a buoyant state, whereas in 1971 it was fairly depressed.

CHAIR. I recall Mr Jowett said, you win some and you lose some.

WATTS. Indeed. But I would point out, that it is possible, indeed it is really much more likely, that those economic factors would in fact operate in a different way. It is when an industry is in recession that workers can be expected strenuously to protect their jobs, whereas in a time of expansion, there are wider job opportunities in general, and they may regard redundancy less seriously. In other words, it could be argued that the union's reaction to the question of redundancy on these two occasions was, in theory, precisely the wrong way round.
I wonder, now, could I ask Mr Harper a question?

CHAIR. Yes, of course . . . Mrs Watts, are you quite sure where you're going?

WATTS. Oh, I hope so, Madam Chairman . . . Mr Harper, I wonder if you can remember when in 1973 the transfer negotiations occurred? I mean, the month?

HARPER. Well, they started in late September, broke down in early November.

WATTS (*unsure of herself*). Now, we know, of course, that something else happened in the same year, which was the white worker being appointed as a time-weaver on the nightshift, and the protests, and your having to promote an Asian; can you tell me when that happened?

HARPER. To the best of my recollection, that chain of events occurred in mid-October.

Pause. WATTS clicks.

WATTS. Oh, I see.

Pause.

Oh, I see. There must have been . . .

CHAIR. Uh, Mrs Watts . . .

KITCHEN *has had his finger raised for a few moments.*

WATTS. I'm so sorry, Madam Chairman, but I've only just, um . . .

KITCHEN *coughs.*

CHAIR. Yes, Mr Kitchen, you have caught my eye, but unless your point's germane –

KITCHEN. Oh, it's germane all right.

WATTS, *with a knowingly expansive gesture towards* KITCHEN, *sits.* DAWSON *looking at* KITCHEN *in alarm.* CHAIR *sizes up.*

CHAIR. Go on.

KITCHEN (*slow and cool*). What Mrs Watts's come up with, not before time, is that things broke down, two years ago, cos the company had broke their side of the agreement.

CHAIR. Sorry, which agreement?

KITCHEN. The 1971 agreement.

CHAIR. Oh, yes, you mean they broke their side of it by asking for compulsory redundancies? You mean that bit?

KITCHEN. Well, no, not quite that bit. The bit about promotion.

CHAIR. What bit about promotion?

KITCHEN. The bit that said, we'd buy the transfer, with no strings, if we could have it guaranteed there wouldn't be no Asians made time-weaver.

CHAIR. Sorry?

KITCHEN. Cos, 'course, the transfer happens, and we're all together, i'n't we. On the Sultzers. Spread throughout the mill, our sunburned brethren. And there's bright lads, 'mong the Pakkies, sooner, later, bound to get the leg-up. So we said, no guarantee, no deal.

And everything were fine. Till two year ago. We're
renegotiating. What they do? Promote a darky, don't they.
OK, on the nightshift, and that's as black as ink. But once
they set a precedent . . . D'be the Sultzers. One. And then
another. Then another. So we says, no way. The transfer
stops, right now.
That's all.

CHAIR. I had been under the impression that it was something
to do with preventing redundancies among the women
weavers.

KITCHEN. Oh, ay, and that as well.

CHAIR. Now let me get this straight –

KITCHEN (*slightly impatient*). There was a deal. No black
time-weavers. Deal, with management, so they could get
their precious Sultzers in. Not written down. Not formal.
Shall we say, a gentleman's agreement.

Pause.

CHAIR. Can I ask why you've said this now?

KITCHEN. Oh, yuh. A reasonable question. Cos it was a
lousy deal. Because of what we lost. Because the thing was
bad right through.

CHAIR. You mean, ethically?

KITCHEN. Practically. Bad, for us.

*He looks to DAWSON. He stands. As he speaks, he writes
something on a piece of paper.*

Well, I don't know if you was planning breaking this, but I
need a cup of tea.

He gives WATTS the piece of paper and goes out. Pause.

WATTS. Um, Madam Chairman, the fact that members of the
white workforce are opposed to Asian timeweavers is not
news.

CHAIR. No, it isn't. Perhaps, Mr Harper . . .

During some of the following, WATTS puzzles over the piece of paper KITCHEN *has given her. She gradually realises what it means, and makes a few notes.*

HARPER. Well, Madam Chairman, really, none of this is very new.

CHAIR. In what way, Mr Harper? It seems quite novel to me.

HARPER. Well, I mean, this atmosphere of, shall I say, melodrama and dénouement. We've acknowledged all along that there would be reistance to promoting Asians.

CHAIR. But the point is, Mr Kitchen said you were party to a deal –

HARPER. I wouldn't say a deal.

CHAIR. What would you say?

HARPER. More, an acknowledgement of the facts of life.

CHAIR. But there is a difference between acknowledging a fact, if fact it is –

HARPER. Oh, it's fact all right –

CHAIR. And making it part of an agreement.

HARPER. I wouldn't say it was entirely part of our agreement.

CHAIR. Mr Harper, was there, or was there not, a deal, arrangement, understanding, what you like, that if you didn't promote Asians, that then and only then would the white workers accept the transfer scheme?

Pause.

HARPER. If we'd promoted Asians, as we wished, on merit and experience, then we'd have had a walk-out. Now I don't like that, any more than you, but it was just accepting an accomplished fact.

CHAIR. Mr Harper, 50 Asians walked out seven weeks ago. That was accomplished and it's still a fact. Now you have said you gave into white pressure to avoid disruption. Now there does seem to be some kind of double-standard operating here. To put it mildly.

Slight pause.

Now I must ask you once again, if there was what Mr Kitchen calls a gentlemen's agreement on promotion to which you as management were party?

HARPER. I'm saying we acknowledged what the situation was. That's all.

WATTS has worked everything out.

WATTS. Madam Chairman, just one point.

CHAIR. Yes?

WATTS. It's about the final offer, the new scheme, accepted on the 18th of June, the one that was explained by Mr Jowett as the workers running out of rope.

CHAIR. Yes?

WATTS. I'd just like to ask Mr Harper to remind us how many jobs will be retained for Dobcross dayshift workers.

HARPER. There will be eight jobs retained.

WATTS. Then can I ask, if voluntary redundancy were to continue at an expected rate, would you expect there would be enough natural wastage to reduce the dayshift from its present twenty-five to eight?

HARPER. No. I'd say, we'd need actually to dismiss around, say, ten. But this was made quite clear –

WATTS. Madam Chairman, the white workers, including, for it was a virtually unanimous decision, the white women, accepted on the 18th of June a deal that would, we've heard, require about ten compulsory redundancies on the Dobcross dayshift alone. It seems very odd that they should accept that, rope or no rope, until you remember that six days earlier eleven Asian women, who otherwise would have competed for those eight jobs, were sacked for having gone on strike.

CHAIR. Yes. I see the point.

WATTS. No I am tempted, I am very tempted, to ask Mrs Dawson a question or two about that.

She picks up KITCHEN's piece of paper.

But I shall refrain from doing so, because I have another
question for Mr Harper, which may put the matter in a
different perspective. I wonder if Mr Harper has the actual
text of the new scheme to hand.

CHAIR. Mr Harper?

HARPER (*finds it*). Yes.

WATTS. And could he read the actual clause about the eight
Dobcross jobs.

HARPER. Well, I think this is the one. 'It is further agreed that
a minimum of eight dayshift jobs shall be preserved on the
remaining Dobcross looms.'

CHAIR. When you say a minimum?

HARPER. I must confess that also means a maximum.

CHAIR. Yes, I see. Mrs Watts, I'm sorry, what exactly is the –

Click.

Mr Harper, read that again.

HARPER. Um . . . 'It is further agreed that a minimum of
eight dayshift jobs shall be preserved on the remaining
Dobcross looms.'

CHAIR. It doesn't say jobs for women.

Pause.

HARPER. So it doesn't.

CHAIR. It could mean men? Male jobs?

HARPER. Well, yes, it could.

CHAIR. Does it?

HARPER. Eventually.

Pause.

CHAIR. Can I ask why?

HARPER. Well, you of all people should know that, Madam
Chairman.

CHAIR. Continue.

HARPER. I mean, you're going to be on it, so I read.

CHAIR. On what?

HARPER. The Equal Opportunities Commission.

Pause.

WATTS. It's now July 1975. The transfer takes, say, a year. On the first of January 1976, the Equal Pay act comes into force.

CHAIR. Mr Harper, you said, or implied, that you hoped to see an all-male weaving workforce, I think you said 'eventually'. How soon is eventually?

HARPER. Eventually is, frankly, as soon as possible. A year at most.

Pause.

Look, it's just the facts. That if you've got to pay the same . . . You lose the flexibility, they can't be moved to shifts . . . And, frankly, it does cost to train them. And then, they do, get married. Pregnant.

Slight pause.

Nothing I can do, to change the facts of life.

DAWSON *stands and quickly goes out.*

CHAIR. Mrs Watts, curiosity has got the better of me. What was on the piece of paper Mr Kitchen gave you?

WATTS. Oh, just . . . what he wrote was: 'Glory be. All this and Maggie Thatcher too.'

CHAIR. I'm sorry.

WATTS. Just a private joke.

Lights change.

Scene Twenty-Three

The Court.
  The final speeches.
  Spot on CLIFFORD.

CLIFFORD. Madam Chairman, the company believes that this
  Inquiry has shown it to be, in many ways, the pig-in-the-
  middle of this affair, crushed between the irresistible force of
  the Asian workers' demands on the one hand, and the
  immovable object of the indigenous weavers' fears on the
  other.

Spot off CLIFFORD. *Spot on* JOWETT.

JOWETT. Madam Chairman, the union takes the view that
  events of the last couple of days show it to have been the
  ham-in-the-sandwich in all of this. It is the union that has
  been trying to mediate between the Asians' insistence on
  better pay and conditions, and the company's refusal to yield
  to those demands.

Lights change.

Spot off JOWETT. *Spot on* WATTS.

WATTS. Madam Chairman, I think it is now clear, whatever
  the Race Relations Board may have concluded, that there has
  been a legacy of systematic and conscious racialism at Darley
  Park Mill. It is up to you to decide on the causes of this, but I
  would like to suggest a possible perspective.
  In the late 1960s, like many other companies, the
  management of Darley Park took on immigrant labour to
  perform jobs that indigenous workers were unprepared to
  do. These jobs involved low pay, bad conditions and unsocial
  hours. While the immigrants were prepared to acquiesce in
  this, it was in the company's interests to preserve divisions
  between the immigrant and indigenous workforces.
  Specifically, the company was sure that if certain privileges
  were preserved for the white workers, then those workers
  would be content to allow the continued exploitation, or I
  might say super-exploitation, of the Asian workforce,
  whether or not this undermined agreements and practices that
  the union has struggled over many years to secure. This was,

I would submit, the background of the shabby, and aptly-named gentlemen's agreement that Mr Kitchen had the courage to reveal to us earlier today.

However, this kind of arrangement was only satisfactory to the company while the Asian workforce was prepared to accept its situation. Two years ago, the Asians as it were gave notice that it was no longer prepared to be super-exploited, and in the last seven weeks it has confirmed its new militancy in no uncertain terms. The advantages of continued racial division between the workers, from the company's point of view, disappeared at the moment when the Asians insisted on their right to be promoted equally with whites, and demonstrated its willingness and capacity to fight. From that point onwards, it was in the interests of the company to support a liberal and progressive policy against the shopfloor racialism that it had itself created. In short, the company had built a monster which then went way beyond control, and it is now denying its own creature.

The consequences of this seem clear. The victims of this sorry saga are not going to be white men, or even, probably, Asian men. They are going to be white and Asian women. The divisions between white and black – which the union allowed to grow and then insisted be retained – have in their turn allowed the firm to drive a further wedge, a wedge affecting black and white, between the men and women in the company.

Madam Chairman, I have one final point, and, if you'll forgive me, this does go back quite far into history. Over a hundred years ago, during the American Civil War, Lancashire textile workers refused to work cotton that had been imported from the Southern States. The workers were in many cases starving, and were offered high wages to spin the cotton, but they refused to do so as an act of solidarity with black slaves fighting for their freedom. This is not, of course, an isolated case. The British Labour Movement has always had a strong and noble tradition of support for the liberation of all people, black and white, from exploitation and oppression. It's my hope that this Inquiry will see that fine tradition brought on home.

Lights change.

Spot off WATTS. *Spot on the* CHAIR.

CHAIR. Thank you, Mrs Watts. It is now my task to produce
a report on the evidence that I have heard and to present it to
the Secretary of State. I would thank you all for your
attendance and your contributions. I declare this hearing
closed.

Blackout.

Scene Twenty-Four

Various.
  In the darkness.

LOUDSPEAKER (*ting tong*). Flight announcement. Will
passengers for TWA Flight 301 for Washington please
proceed to Departure Gate 21. Passengers for TWA
Washington please proceed to departure gate 21. Thank you.
(*Ting tong.*)

*Lights on a young Pakistani sitting on one of the short row of plastic
chairs. His hand luggage is beside him. He is reading a Government
report.*

LOUDSPEAKER (*ting tong*). Passenger announcement. Will
Miss Susan Palmer, passenger recently arrived from Sydney,
please report to the Qantas desk in the main concourse. Staff
announcement. Will Mr Ramesh Desai please go to the
catering managers' office. Thank you. (*Ting tong.*)

Lights fade a little on the Pakistani. Light on CLIFFORD *at the
desk, on the telephone. The same Government report is open before
him.*

CLIFFORD. Mr Harper please, Nicholas Clifford calling.

Pause.

Eric. Nick. Hallo. Have you seen it? Oh, well, you should
get it today. In general, from your point of view, it's fairly
predictable. Um . . . . 'The company in my view showed
insufficient courage . . . Unduly timid . . . occasionally
unthinking and precipitous . . . errors of judgement . . .'

Slight pause.

Oh, money? Well, I'm afraid she wants an interim bonus and piecework changes. Not all they demanded, but . . .

Pause.

Oh, yes, of course, that hadn't struck me, yes, as you say, since yesterday, a whole new ball-game, with this six pounds limit thing, agreed. Presumably that means that even if you wanted to . . . Yes, indeed. You couldn't break it. After all, it's more or less the law.

Lights off CLIFFORD.

Lights back up on the Pakistani. He lights a cigarette.

LOUDSPEAKER (*ting tong*). Flight announcement. Will passengers for Pan American Flight 313 for New York please proceed to departure gate 12. Gate 12 for Flight 313 for New York. Thank you. (*Ting tong.*)

Immediately:

(*Ting tong*). Staff announcement. Will Mr Ramesh Desai and Mrs Sukhdev Kaur report at once to the catering managers' office. Flight announcement. Will passengers for British Airways Flight 308 for Johannesburg please proceed to departure gate 17. Gate 17 for passengers to Johannesburg. This is your final call. Thank you. (*Ting tong.*)

Lights down a little on Pakistani. Lights on JOWETT *and* DAWSON, *round a table, at a meeting. It is clear that there are others present.* JOWETT *has the report open in front of him.*

JOWETT. Right, brothers and, sister. I hope you've had a chance to cast your eyes across the oracle. I think its general conclusions are what we'd have thought. We are, for instance . . . um . . . 'sometimes unmindful of our overall responsibility . . .' um, 'unwise counsel . . . poor communications that perhaps could have been . . .' cetera etcetera, 'misjudgement rather than a conscious ill-intention'. I should point out that the strike committee is accused of being irresponsible, and outside militants, and all that kind of thing. As far as what's been recommended . . . We are told, as if we didn't know, that, um . . . 'unions have tended to resist overt outside interference in their affairs . . .' and we're left with, shall we say, a rather vague exhortation to see that everyone is represented equally.

Slight pause.

To which we shall genuinely respond.

Pause.

So. All in all, I think we've come through this quite well. Any comments?

Pause. DAWSON *raises her hand.*

Yes, Joan?

DAWSON. Well, I just wondered, George . . .

Slight pause.

When you say, we've come through this, I just wondered . . .

Slight pause. Change of tack:

What you mean by, 'genuinely respond'?

Lights off DAWSON *and* JOWETT. *Lights up again on the Pakistani.*

LOUDSPEAKER (*ting tong*). Staff announcement. Will Ramesh Desai or Mrs Sukhdev Kaur or any other members of the Terminal Three Catering Division please report without delay to the catering managers' office. Repeat, any members of the Catering Division report to the catering managers' office without delay. (*Ting tong.*)

Lights fade a little on Pakistani. Lights on WATTS, HUSSEIN *and* BHANDARI, *who are also discussing the report.*

WATTS. Well. I think the first thing to say is that in general this is excellent. It accepts almost all our arguments. Although it does make predictable remarks about irresponsible advice and so on, it is much more critical of the other parties than of you.

HUSSEIN. Specifically?

WATTS. Well, there's a problem. You see, she recommends that the choice of which workers are or aren't to be retained during the redundancy should be made on the basis of merit and experience, regardless of race colour creed etcetera. The problem is the word experience. Because, the legacy, what's happened in the past, has brought about a situation in which the Asian workers are, in general, inexperienced on Sultzer looms. So, in effect, what's bound to happen is, the whites will get first pick. And the only way to stop that would be some kind of quota system, which –

BHANDARI. Which is illegal.

WATTS. Yes. It's not her fault, of course. Law of the land.

HUSSEIN. Of course. The law of the land.

Lights off WATTS, BHANDARI and HUSSEIN. Lights back up on the Pakistani.

LOUDSPEAKER (*ting tong*). Flight announcement. Will passengers for Air Pakistan Flight 321 for Karachi please proceed to Departure Gate 19. Gate 19, Air Pakistan Flight for Karachi. Thank you. (*Ting tong.*)

An immigration OFFICIAL stands by the Pakistani. He consults his clipboard.

OFFICIAL. Kadir?

The Pakistani looks up.

Abdul Kadir?

The Pakistani nods. The OFFICIAL nods towards the loudspeaker.

Your flight. It's time to go.

The Pakistani puts the report down on the next chair. He stands and picks up his hand baggage. The OFFICIAL picks up the report and glances at it. Then tossing the report on the chair.

OFFICIAL. OK, Kadir. Wave goodbye to England. Sorry, can't be au revoir.

They are about to go when the LOUDSPEAKER intervenes.

LOUDSPEAKER (*ting tong*). Ladies and gentlemen, this is a special announcement to all passengers. We regret to announce that due to unofficial industrial action by catering staff, all Terminal Three refreshment facilities are temporarily suspended. We apologise to all passengers for any inconvenience caused. Thank you. (*Ting tong.*)

OFFICIAL. Bloody hell. Ask me mate, you're well out of it.

ABDUL KADIR *smiles. He stubs out his cigarette.*

ABDUL KADIR. OK. Let's go.

Scene Twenty-Five

The stage.
  The company.

1st PERFORMER. What you have just seen is a piece of fiction. There was no such place as Beckley, no such union as the National Union of Weavers, and no such firm as Darley Park Mills. None of the characters is real.

2nd PERFORMER. However, most of the events described in the play are based on things that have really happened, in different industrial disputes, in different places, at different times.

3rd PERFORMER. At a firm in Nottingham called Crepe Sizes, for instance, Asian workers founded a TGWU branch. When five workers were sacked, the Asians came out on strike, but their white colleagues remained at work.

4th PERFORMER. At Standard Telephones in North London, white workers refused to train a West Indian machine setter. The AUEW made the consequent strike official, but allowed its white members to work normally.

5th PERFORMER. At British Celanese, a plastics factory in Derby, the union took four months to recognise the credentials of an elected Asian shop steward. In eighteen months, he saw the works convenor once.

6th PERFORMER. At Harwood Cash Mills, Mansfield, the Race Relations Board ruled that there was no discrimination when Asian workers were paid the same wages for a compulsory 60-hour-week as white workers were paid for 48.

7th PERFORMER. During a strike by Asian workers at Imperial Typewriters, Leicester, the National Front organised a march in which many white workers participated. In their journal Spearhead, the Front described the white workers' actions as a racial struggle against both communism and international capitalism. A year later, the American owners of the firm closed down their Hull and Leicester factories. At Hull there was an occupation, but at Leicester, the divided workforce just caved in.

8th PERFORMER. At Mansfield Hosiery Mills, Loughborough, the National Front was also active during an Asian strike against discrimination in promotion to high-paid knitters' posts. During the strike, the white knitters accepted a productivity and redundancy agreement that they had previously rejected, and the company appointed a number of white knitters brought in from outside. During a subsequent Court of Inquiry, it emerged that the company had entered into a covert agreement with the knitters not to promote black workers.

1st PERFORMER. After the Inquiry, the Hosiery Workers' Union President commented: 'We helped the Asians far more than we helped our own people. This is what stuck in my craw all the time we were trying to get a settlement.'

2nd PERFORMER. It all depends on who are whose own people.

Chronology of the Dispute at Darley Park Mills Ltd, Beckley, summer 1975.

April

Mon 21: After a series of unsatisfactory meetings with senior steward Frank Kitchen, Asian nightshift workers write to the General Secretary of the National Union of Weavers, George Jowett, to press their demands for an improvement on the nightshift bonus and the piecework rates on the old (Dobcross) looms.

Wed 23: Hameed Faruqi, nightshift shop steward, complains to the Race Relations Board about the fact that Asians at the Mill are forced to do overtime on the nightshift.

Thurs 24: Following the receipt of the letter to Mr Jowett, Frank Kitchen meets the Asians to discuss their grievances.

Mon 28: A further meeting is held between Mr Kitchen and the Asians, with George Jowett in attendance. A case is drawn up.

Tues 29: The union writes to management, presenting the case of the nightshift workers.

May

Mon 5: Mr Jowett and Mr Kitchen meet management and present the Asians' case. Management turns down the demands.

Wed 7: Mr Jowett and Mr Kitchen meet the Asian workers and report back on the meeting with management. The Asians ask that seven days' strike notice be given.

Thurs 8: The union writes to management informing them of the Asians' reaction.

Thurs 15: The Asian workers meet Mr Kitchen and enquire about progress on the claim. Mr Kitchen informs them there has been no progress, and the Asians tell him they are going to take strike action. Mr Kitchen advises them to delay until they have seen Mr Jowett.

Fri 16:   At a meeting with the Asians, Mr Jowett advises them not to strike. However, the Asians set up their own strike committee and come out on strike.

Thurs 22:   Mrs Anshuya Ridley of the Manchester Community Relations Council is called in to assist in resolving the dispute. She has a preliminary meeting with the union and management.

Fri 23:   Violence flares on the picket line and two arrests of Asian strikers are made.

Tues 27:   After a second meeting involving Mrs Ridley, proposals for a return to work are agreed. That evening, the terms are put to the strikers and accepted.

Wed 28:   On their return, the Asians find that two white time-weavers have been appointed on the old loom (Dobcross) dayshift, in apparent breach of the Ridley agreement. That evening, the strikers meet and decide to resume strike action.

Thurs 29:   The strike restarts.

June

Wed 4:   The management sends letters to all strikers giving seven days' notice of termination of their contracts of employment.

Thurs 5:   The management issues a new scheme for phasing out almost all the Dobcross looms and for a transfer to a three-shift operation on new weaving machines (Sultzers).

Wed 11:   The strikers are dismissed from employment by the company.

Fri 13:   A delegation of strikers meets George Jowett to demand that the strike be made official.

Mon 16:   The union executive meets and makes the strike official.

Tues 17:   The Race Relations Board makes its report on Mr Faruqi's complaint of discrimination.

Wed 18:   The non-striking workers meet to discuss the management's new scheme for a transfer to the Sultzer weaving machines. Against Mr Jowett's advice, the workers accept the scheme.

Thurs 19:   The union meets management to attempt to secure
            an agreement to end the strike. Management refuses
            to guarantee that no redundancies among the Asian
            strikers will take place.

Fri 20:   The strikers meet and reject the terms for a return
            to work, demanding a 'no victimization' clause.

Mon 23:   Violence again flares on the picket line and fifteen
            arrests are made.

Thurs 26:   Further violence and more arrests on the picket line.
            The Secretary of State for Employment sets up a
            Court of Inquiry to consider the case.

Teendreams

Written with Susan Todd

Monstrous Regiment was formed in 1975 as a touring theatre company with a majority of women members, whose work was intended to explore the experience of women past and present, placing that experience in the centre of the stage, instead of in the wings.

Teendreams was the company's sixth production and its first venture into working with a male writer. The form of the work was, initially, a discussion of possible themes between David Edgar and Susan Todd as collaborators. The company then undertook a workshop/discussion period which included sessions with women who had special areas of expertise (including Angela McRobbie, Liz Whitman, Beatrix Campbell and Eve Brook). The content, form, structure and progression of the play was then assembled by David and Susan into a detailed synopsis, which was then discussed by the whole company. David then wrote the play from the sum of this work.

Teendreams began its first tour in Bristol in January 1979. Eight years later, the opportunity arose to rework the play for a production by drama students in the same city. The text in this book emerged from considerable work between the authors, director Martin White and the Bristol University Drama Department Third Year performance group in early 1987.

Teendreams was first presented by the Monstrous Regiment at the Van Dyck Theatre, Bristol, on 25 January 1979, with the following cast:

TRISHA/CATHY/SANDRA	Chris Bowler
FRANCES	Gillian Hanna
ROSIE/DEBBIE	Susan Todd
RUTH/SHARON/LYNNE	Jenifer Armitage
DAVE/HOWARD/TONY/BREWER	Clive Russell
COLIN/KEVIN/GARY	David Bradford
ANNE/MARIA/DENISE	Mary McCusker

Directed by Kate Crutchley
Designed by Di Seymour
Lighting by Meri Jenkins

The revised version of the play was first presented by the Department of Drama of Bristol University in the same theatre, on 11 March 1987, with the following cast:

TRISHA/CATHY/ANNE	Julia Selby
FRANCES	Justine Midda
ROSIE/DEBBIE	Sara Fleming
KEVIN/COLIN/GARY	Tim Dynevor
HOWARD/DAVE/TONY/BREWER	Mark Ravenhill
RUTH/SHARON	Alexandra Saint
SANDRA/DENISE	Colette Wrigley

Directed by Martin White
Assisted by Dot Peryer
Set Design by Jennie Norman
Stage Managed by Juliet Fox

The play is set in England. The main action takes place in 1975, with flashbacks to 1968, 1972 and 1961.

Scene One

Music: 'Will You Still Love Me Tomorrow' by the Shirelles.
     *FRANCES' flat, summer 1975. A sofa, in front of it a coffee table.
On the table a big 60s political poster book. Nearby a record-player
and tape-deck. A glass of whisky on the same table.*
     *TRISHA, who's 15 and dressed in an approximate school uniform,
sits on the sofa. A moment. Then she leans forward, as if to open the
book. But FRANCES enters, and TRISHA recoils. FRANCES is
26, dressed at present in a T-shirt and jeans.*

FRANCES. Well, hallo there, Trisha.

TRISHA. 'Lo, miss.

FRANCES. Oh, heavens. Frances, please.

     *She goes out the other side. ROSIE enters after a moment, from the
     same side. She's the same age as FRANCES, but dolled up. She
     smiles at TRISHA and goes out the other side. Pause. TRISHA
     reaches for the book again, but again is interrupted by FRANCES,
     who enters buttoning a blouse.*

FRANCES. Now, do please make free with the kitchen. And
     there's the record player and some stuff on tape.

     (*As she goes.*) Doubt if they'll be to your taste. All classical
     and golden oldies, I'm afraid.

     *She goes out. Once again, ROSIE crosses the stage in the opposite
     direction. Then FRANCES re-enters, zipping her evening
     trousers.*

FRANCES. Hey, wasn't it your last?

TRISHA. Beg pardon?

FRANCES. Last exam.

TRISHA. Oh, yuh.

FRANCES. So, how d'you do?

TRISHA shrugs.

TRISHA (*doubtfully*). OK.

FRANCES. OK.

She goes. Pause. This time, TRISHA has time to open the book. ROSIE enters as TRISHA reads.

ROSIE. Dead to the world.

She switches off the tape. Cut the Shirelles.

TRISHA. Uh – sorry?

ROSIE. Kids.

TRISHA. Oh, good.

ROSIE. Dead right. What's this?

TRISHA shows her the book. ROSIE reads:

'Wherever death may surprise us, let it be welcome, provided that this, our battle cry, may have reached some receptive ear, and another hand may be extended to wield our weapons, and other men be ready to intone the funeral dirge with the staccato chant of the machine gun and new battle cries of war and victory.' Phew.

FRANCES has entered. She carries a mac.

FRANCES. It's Che Guevara.

Slight pause.

Murdered by the forces of reaction in the jungles of Bolivia when you were six. Or seven.

Slight pause.

Is there anything damper than yesterday's dreams?

Pause.

ROSIE. So, are we ready?

FRANCES. Yup.

ROSIE. Their names are Damion and Sophie.

FRANCES (*gives a piece of paper to* TRISHA). Here's the number where we'll be.

ROSIE. So, then. Bye bye.

FRANCES (*as they go, with her mac*). I decided that it looked like rain.

FRANCES *and* ROSIE *go.* TRISHA *puts down the book. Pause. She stands, goes to the tape deck and puts on the tape. It's Julie Driscoll, 'This Wheel's on Fire'.* TRISHA *stops and fast forwards and plays. It's Grace Slick, 'White Rabbit'.* TRISHA *stops, fast forwards and plays. It's Suzi Quatro, 'Your Momma Won't Like Me'.* TRISHA *lets this play a little, but it clearly distresses her. Then she stops it. She puts on the record player. The record on the turntable is Carole King's 'It Might As Well Rain Until September'. She plays it from the beginning.*

TRISHA *picks up the whisky, and takes it to the sofa. She sits, takes out a bottle of pills. She starts to take the pills, washed down by the whisky. The music swells.*

Fade to blackout.

Scene Two

FRANCES' *flat. A day or two later. The poster book is shut on the table.* FRANCES *sits on the sofa. A suitcase is nearby.* ROSIE *stands near her.*

FRANCES. You know, when *I* was 15, I remember, was the same as poor old Trisha. Yes, I used to think, like she did, when I met him at the candy store, and when he whispered sweet and secret nothings in my ear, and when we walked off hand in hand into the sunset, that in that very moment, suddenly my whole life changed. But, still, the thing was, I did know, p'raps unlike Trisha, deep down, that the whole shebang was so much shit. It wouldn't last. The blissful moment was, by definition, just momentary.

But when I was 19, and went to college, 1968, the dawn in which of course 'twas bliss to be alive, and when I met him at the demo and he whispered sweet and secret dialectics in my ear, and when we walked off hand in hand into the sit-in, and in *that* very moment suddenly my whole life changed . . .

I thought it had.

And even more, I thought *that* tatty teenage fantasy was going to be a blueprint for the Changing of the World.

You know?

It's simple. Thought we could change people.

We were wrong.

And so, friend Rosie, I am going home.

ROSIE. Frances. Don't go.

FRANCES *stands and goes to her suitcase.*

FRANCES. Back home. Where I'll be safe.

ROSIE. Stay here. At least a day or two.

FRANCES *picks up her case.*

FRANCES. Returning back, where I belong. Back to the past. Because I liked it there.

She remembers she's forgotten something. She snaps her fingers. Puts down her case, goes out.

ROSIE. Speak for yourself. Friend Frances.

Lights fade to a spot on ROSIE.

Scene Three

As the scene changes, play the Wedding March and bells. Hold the spot on ROSIE, fade up spots on HOWARD and KEVIN. ROSIE is watching, respectively, her husband and his best man, at her wedding in 1968.
  Fade music.

KEVIN. Right then, first of all thanks to the bridesmaids and the pageboy, Tracy leave Lee alone, I always said little girls should be obscene and not heard.

Never tell an Irishman a joke on Saturday in case he laughs in church.

Howard, wanted by the police. Mum says, no accounting for taste.

Howard, if all the birds he's had laid end to end, I wouldn't be at all surprised.

Sorry Rosie, had to slip it in. As the Art Mistress said to the postman. Speaking of which.

He unfolds a telegram.

First telegram. 'Note merged accounts stop future products filed in pending query hope not triplicate congrats from all at office.'

Filed in pending. Triplicate. It's the way I tell 'em.

Number two. 'The Students' Union'. 'The University'. To Rosie. 'Dont' – I s'pose that's 'Don't', 'don't forget your promises love Frances.' Well.

You tell em, gel. Reality is just an escape for people who can't cope with drugs.

Well, onward to the revolution. Next –

Snap blackout on KEVIN *and* HOWARD.

We see FRANCES, *dressed as she will be in the next scene, watching* ROSIE. *Darkness.*

Scene Four

Music: 'Those Were the Days', by Mary Hopkin.
   It is broken into by a metallic TANNOY, *over the hubbub of many voices*
   During the TANNOY, *fade up lights on the scene.*
   It is the summer of 1968. We are in a corner of a Victorian-Gothic University Hall, which is presently under occupation. A few sleeping-bags lie around.
   Left, a table, at which a student, RUTH, *is typing a leaflet on a stencil.*
   Centre, and facing upstage, is the kneeling CATHY, *who is*

*making placards with a red magic-marker on pieces of card. She has
already completed two, which read:*

*'Don't Demand – Occupy' and 'Revolution is the Festival of the
Oppressed'.*

CATHY *wears a short skirt.*

TANNOY. Well, good morning, campers, this is your friendly
neighbourhood occupation organising committee, and first of
all, for any new occupants, breakfast of a sort is being served
in the Registry reception, recently acquisitioned for the
people – oh and agitprop wants to know, if anyone can work
a Gestetner could they go to the agitprop desk which I
believe is situated in the Bursary like pronto. Thank you and
have just a wonderful day.

The hubbub fades up again. CATHY *picks up her third placard. It
reads: 'Death to the Plastic Culture'.*

CATHY. Hey. Ruth.

RUTH (*not looking round*). Mm?

CATHY. Hey, Ruth, you suppose this is all right?

RUTH *turns and looks.*

RUTH. Lovely. What's it mean?

CATHY *reads her placard.*

CATHY. Well now, there I think you have me.

RUTH *back to typing.*
CATHY *checks a list and starts work on another placard.*
Enter DAVE, *a student leader, wearing a red armband and carrying
papers. He strides over to* RUTH.

DAVE. Colin?

RUTH. I'm sorry?

DAVE. Where's bloody Colin.

RUTH. I don't know, Dave. Ask Frankie.

DAVE. Where is Frankie?

RUTH. Dunno, Dave. She's been around.

DAVE (*glances at his watch*). That's great.

He drums his fingers.
Then, for something else to do, he reads the top of the stencil
RUTH *is typing.*

What's this for?

RUTH. It's a leaflet, Dave.

DAVE. Oh, yuh?

RUTH. What d'you think of it?

DAVE. Yuh, well . . .

He looks round, vaguely.
Sees CATHY *at her work and looks at her short skirt.*

Yuh, well, at this precise moment I'm not that concerned
with the politics of the transitional programme in late
monopoly capitalism. Like at this precise juncture I'm a bit
more bothered about why the Halls of Residence weren't
leafleted, what's up with the Gestetner and why we appear to
be minus one bloody hero.

To RUTH:

If you see what I mean.

RUTH. Oh, sure.

DAVE *decides to go. He passes* CATHY *and glances at her skirt*
and then her work.

DAVE. Hey, Cath.

CATHY (*kneels up*). Yes? What?

DAVE. Two 'C's' in 'consciousness'.

CATHY. I see.

FRANCES *has entered left.* DAVE *notices.*

DAVE. Ah. Frankie.

FRANCES. Yes.

DAVE. You know if Colin's coming in?

FRANCES. I think so.

DAVE. Think so.

FRANCES. Well, he said –

She's interrupted by the TANNOY.

TANNOY. 'Tention Comrade Robertson. Please go to the admin desk. Comrade D. Robertson to the admin desk. Oh, sorry, scrub that, Dave, I mean the Soc Soc desk.

DAVE. I try to run a revolution.

DAVE goes out.
CATHY is looking at her finished placard. It reads: 'Freedom is the Consciousness of our Desires'. The second 'c' of 'consciousness' is inserted.

CATHY. Well, that'll have to do.

To FRANCES:

Well, will he speak?

She gets up, collects up her placards.
During the following, unnoticed, COLIN enters. He is 20, dressed with informal elegance, and a sense of the drama of the events about to take place.

FRANCES. Well . . . I think he's worried about his dad.

CATHY. His *dad*?

FRANCES. You know, the family thing. His having worked his way up, getting here. The family pride thing. You know, throw it all away.

RUTH. What do *you* think?

FRANCES. Well . . .

Pause.

COLIN. What *do* you think?

FRANCES (*turns*). Oh. Colin.

RUTH. Colin, Dave was after you.

COLIN. I'll bet he was.

CATHY *picks up the placards and manages a clenched-fist sign at* COLIN *as she goes out.*

CATHY. Good luck.

COLIN. Well, ta.

CATHY *takes her placards out right.* RUTH *decides to leave as well. She gets up, picks up the typewriter, and takes it out.* COLIN *and* FRANCES *left there.*

FRANCES. Well, then.

COLIN. Well.

Pause.

The solicitor informs me that I am about to put him in what he calls an impossible situation.

Being realistic, I suppose I ought to demand the impossible.

FRANCES. Them having all the guns, but us the numbers.

COLIN. Well, exactly.

Slight pause.

I'm not sure, the technicalities. Whether I get arrested here and now. I brought my toothbrush, just in case.

Pause. COLIN *smiles.*

Well, here's looking at you, kid.

FRANCES *goes to* COLIN *and they embrace and kiss.* *Enter* DAVE.

DAVE. Ah, Colin – Oh.

DAVE *stands there. He scratches his ear. Finally,* COLIN *turns to him.*

COLIN. Comrade.

DAVE *looks at his watch.*

COLIN (*with a shrug*). I self-criticise with all humility.

DAVE. So, are you proposing to harangue the throng?

COLIN. I thought I might try and catch the Chairman's eye.

DAVE. Then let the spectacular commence.

He gestures COLIN out. COLIN kisses FRANCES again and follows. DAVE gives FRANCES a grin and a wink as he goes. FRANCES looks off right towards the meeting. RUTH enters behind her. She is smoking.

RUTH. Friends, Romans, Comrades?

FRANCES. What? Oh, yes.

RUTH (*to herself*). So are they all, all honourable men.

But FRANCES doesn't hear. The two WOMEN look offstage right at the meeting, which we hear:

DAVE. Comrades. Can we start the meeting.

Hubbub.

Comrades. Can we have order.

Hubbub fading.

Right. Comrades, the meeting has been called, specifically, because of the University's action in taking out a court injunction against five comrades who they regard as being ringleaders of the occupation.

Buzz of reaction. Hisses. During this, CATHY re-enters and nods at RUTH and FRANCES before leaning up against the table to smoke a cigarette and watch.

Sadly, two of the five comrades concerned are unable to comply, or indeed not to comply with the order, as they graduated from the University last summer.

Laughter.

One of those who hasn't graduated however is Colin Cook, secretary of Soc Soc. He's still very much around, in fact he's here, and I call on Comrade Cook to speak to the meeting.

Applause.
FRANCES *a smiling glance at RUTH.*

COLIN. Comrades, I have in my hand a piece of paper, issued

in the High Court of Justice, which restrains me from entering or re-entering this building, and particularly from inciting or encouraging others to enter, re-enter or remain in the aforesaid building, upon pain of further legal action of a character unspecified.

A sound of ripping.

I now have in my hand two pieces of paper. And I'd like to incite and encourage you all to remain in this building.

Applause. It grows.
FRANCES *turns to* RUTH.

FRANCES. Magic. I mean, it's magic.

Mean, you read the history, the Paris Commune, Russian Revolution, mighty moments, everything is changed.

But for it to be happening now. To see it. Be it. And for me, to be with it, me, to be happening, too.

RUTH. Yes.

FRANCES *turns back to look at the meeting. Applause going on. Perhaps even people singing the Internationale.*

Yes, it is indeed 1968. And everything's in question. Everything is challenged, everything is new. We don't demand, we occupy, because the plastic culture's melting on the stove of history.

Slight pause. FRANCES *has turned to her.*

So one does just wonder . . . Why the fuck we're still doing the typing and making the tea.

FRANCES *a little shrug.*

FRANCES. Now there you have me.

Blackout.

Scene Five

Immediately, in the darkness, the Gloria from Bach's 'B Minor Mass'. This scene takes place in ROSIE's *kitchen.* ROSIE *is at her worktop, between the hob and the fridge. On the worktop are a bottle of oil, a pepper grinder, a chopping block, a knife, bags of mushrooms and courgettes, a tin of baked beans and a tin opener.*

We are going to see a kind of culinary ballet in which ROSIE *prepares three meals. On three occasions during this, her husband* HOWARD *will enter with the phone on a long lead. He will wander back and forth with the phone, and go out again. He is wearing a business suit, though in his second entrance he has taken off his tie.*

He looks what he is, a highly motivated, upwardly mobile young junior manager.

It is January 1972.

ROSIE *puts two saucepans on the cooker. Then she takes a baby's bottle from the fridge, and puts it in one of the saucepans. Then she takes a third saucepan from the cupboard, opens the baked beans, and puts them in the saucepan and on the cooker.*

Enter HOWARD *with the phone.*

HOWARD. Uh huh. Uh huh. No, sure. No problem.

Yuh, mate, just off the plane. First port of call.

He winks at ROSIE.

Look, mate, I've just cleared them 20 grand. The least they can do is read a fucking memo.

He looks to ROSIE, *realising he's said 'fuck' in front of her. She smiles. He carries the phone out.*

So?

He's gone. ROSIE *takes two frying pans, puts oil in one and butter in the other, and puts both on the hob. She takes two steaks and a packet of fish fingers from the fridge.*

She puts the fish fingers in one of the frying pans.

She expertly chops the mushrooms.

Re-enter HOWARD.

HOWARD. No, no, I don't think that's a problem but we'd need to talk it through.

Hey, yuh. Why not. No hassle.

Well, I think we were going to a show or something, but it's nothing we can't shift.

He looks at ROSIE *and mouths 'Thursday'. She nods.*

Yuh. Sure. It's eminently changeable.

He goes.

ROSIE *grinds pepper on the steaks and pops them in the other frying pan with the mushrooms. She takes the baked beans off the cooker, stirs them, puts them back. She chops the courgettes.*

Slight panic – she's forgotten the fish fingers.

She takes their frying pan off the cooker and turns them over.

She finishes the courgettes and puts them in the third saucepan.

She goes out, re-enters with a bottle of wine and a corkscrew. She is opening the bottle as HOWARD *appears with a Lufthansa bag. As he speaks, he takes out a bottle and a jewelry case and puts them on the worktop in front of* ROSIE.

HOWARD. No, mate, I told you. Just back from Heathrow.

Yuh, well, I tell you, Frankfurt's better than Cologne.

Yuh, apparently the lights were out here too. All afternoon.

Right on, mate. What a bloody country.

He blows a kiss at ROSIE *and goes out.* ROSIE *puts down the bottle, opens the jewelry case, takes out a necklace and smiles.*

The Bach swells.

Scene Six

A baroque trumpet fanfare in the darkness. Not very well played. After the fanfare we hear a song and a fragment of an agit-prop play by RUTH, ANNE *and* TONY *(who played the trumpet). During it, the lights come up on a bare room in a squatted house. It is the spring of 1972. The play is being rehearsed in the next-door room. In this room,* SANDRA, *a nineteen-year-old working-class woman, is feeding her baby with a bottle. She is sitting on the floor, next to a primus on which is a saucepan of water.*

A placard leans up somewhere. It reads 'Fuck the Family'. The play goes as follows:

VOICES. Onward Christian housewives
          Marching to the sink
          Providing what our husbands
          Demand to eat and drink
          We milk their sunshine breakfasts
          Bake our humble pie
          We are drowned in fairy liquid
          Raped by what we buy
          Onward Christian housewives
          Marching to the store
          The image of the Master
          Going on before.

TONY (*full ecclesiastical works*). And so, wilt thou, man –

RUTH. That's me?

TONY. That's you, have this Woman for thy wedded wife –

A knock at the outside door.

– wilt thou beat her, exploit her and scorn her, in her sickness and your wealth, and forsaking all others –

Knock knock.

– except of course for those bits of stuff, crumpet, skirt, arse and cunt on the side –

SANDRA. Hey. DOOR.

TONY. – that are every man's due and right, for as long as you feel inclined?

RUTH. I certainly will.

SANDRA. Hey, DOOR.

TONY. And wilt thou, woman –

Knock knock knock.

SANDRA. Hey someone. DOOR.

ANNE. All *right*.

SANDRA *feeds her baby.*
ANNE *crosses the stage.*
She is dressed in a parody wedding gown, festooned with pots, pans,

*chains and symbols of degradation. She goes through the set and out.
Offstage, we hear her answer the door.*

ANNE. Yes? What is it?

FRANCES. We wondered if Ruth is about.

ANNE. What d'you want her for.

FRANCES. Well, we're from a thing called the Fight the Rent
Act Campaign. We're building for a meeting.

ANNE. Oh, I see.

ANNE, COLIN *and* FRANCES *come into the room.*

ANNE. Right. Hold on.

She goes out the other side.
SANDRA *clocks* FRANCES's *and* COLIN's *look to each other.*

SANDRA. They're practising a play.

COLIN. I see.

FRANCES. D'you squat here?

SANDRA. Yuh. That's right.

Pause.

You're going to have a meeting?

FRANCES. Yes. D'you want to come?

SANDRA. What's it about?

FRANCES. It's about the fight against the Tory Rent Act.

SANDRA. Ah. I don't pay rent.

FRANCES. Well, still . . .

Slight pause.

The reason people have to squat, is rents. Bad housing,
speculators shoving up the prices, so that they can make a
million out of empty office blocks like Centre Point. I mean,
you have to squat because you've nowhere else to live.

SANDRA. Well, uyh, that's not exactly why I –

But she's interrupted by the entrance of TONY, *a young man carrying a trumpet and dressed as an Abbess. He walks across the stage. As he goes:*

TONY. Good afternoon.

And out.

COLIN. Oh, hi.

SANDRA (*standing with her baby*). That's Tony. He's a Mother Superior.

SANDRA *smiles, and goes out with her baby as* RUTH *enters. She is dressed as a Victorian employer.*

RUTH. Hallo, Fran.

FRANCES. Don't tell me, let me guess. The Ruling Class.

RUTH. Dead right in one.

Enter ANNE. *She sits on the floor to do something to her costume. Pause.*

COLIN. The reason, looked you up, was cos we got a meeting planned, to fight the HFA, and thought perhaps –

RUTH. The HFA?

COLIN. Housing Finance Act.

RUTH. Oh.

COLIN. And we wanted someone from the squatting movement. Speaking. And we hoped it might be you.

RUTH. Well, I . . .

COLIN. We got a leaflet. It explains what's going on.

He hands RUTH *a leaflet.*
She reads it.
TONY *comes in, without the trumpet. He leans against a wall, waiting.*

FRANCES (*to* ANNE). What's the play for?

ANNE. Oh, it's the Festival of Light. Cliff Richard's lighting up a bloody beacon in the park. We're an alternative attraction. Kind of, powers of darkness.

COLIN *and* FRANCES *smile.*

Bit scary, really.

Slight pause.

It's a marriage play. Tony's the Church and State, and I'm the little woman wedded unto Capital.

COLIN. Oh, so you're kind of, the working class as well?

ANNE. Um . . .

RUTH *gives the leaflet to* COLIN.

RUTH. Thank you.

To ANNE *and* TONY.

Right. We better move.

ANNE (*standing*). Right then.

RUTH. Tony, have you got your bloody horn?

COLIN. Uh . . .

TONY. In the car.

RUTH. OK.

COLIN. Um . . .

RUTH. Yes?

COLIN. About the meeting –

RUTH. Meeting? No. Not interested. Sorry.

COLIN. Why?

RUTH. Oh, I just don't think that it's of much concern to us.

COLIN. But of course it's of concern –

RUTH. Otherwise, you'd be discussing wife-battering, and instead of big guns from the NUM and Parliament, you'd have a woman on the platform.

Pause. COLIN *thrown.*

FRANCES. That is why we're here. We obviously think that women should be mobilised. That's why we're here.

RUTH. They should be mobilised.

FRANCES. That's right.

RUTH. Them forming half the working class.

COLIN. Of course.

RUTH. The bottom half.

COLIN. Indeed.

RUTH. You having, as it were, the big guns, us the numbers. So. A token pussy on the platform. Add a little feminist appeal. Attract the cannon fodder.

COLIN. No, that's not –

RUTH. Met Sandra? She's got housing problems. Notably, the owner of her house keeps laying into her.

FRANCES. The landlord beats her up?

RUTH. Her husband.

Slight pause.

COLIN. Well, you could always bring – that up –

RUTH. Look, Colin, are you just naturally stupid or are you being deliberately obtuse?

COLIN. You tell me.

RUTH. Oh, I really don't think I can be bothered.

Pause.

FRANCES. This meeting's about housing. It's about taking on this Tory Government. It's about continuing what started with the miners and the fight against the Industrial Relations Bill. And I personally don't think it's possible to emancipate our sex without emancipating the working class. I don't think you can just change your lifestyle and the rest follows. I don't think you can change the insides of people's heads without changing what's outside them first.

COLIN *decides not to say anything.*

ANNE. Hey, Ruth, does she mean we're going to have to wait until after the revolution?

RUTH. I think that's right, Anne. After which, of course, the family and all its works just melt away.

ANNE. You mean, like Engels thought, when women went to work, and had a boss, that male supremacy would just, kind of, collapse?

RUTH. That's right, whereas in fact, of course, what's happened is that working women have two jobs, one paid and one unpaid –

COLIN. Well, I think that's oversimp –

TONY. You know, what really gets right up my nose about Fred Engels?

Pause.

COLIN. No?

TONY. It's that his view of my lifestyle was summed up in the phrase 'degrading and perverted'. And what really does extend my nostrils about blokes like you, is when you say my way of living's alienating to the working class, it doesn't strike you that the working class is fucking alienating to me.

Pause.

COLIN. What did I say? When did I say that?

RUTH. Hey. I've got a wonderful idea. Why not let Tony address the meeting. Or Anne. Or all of us. We'll all of us go 'long and speak. Or sing. Much better. Do a little turn. We'll really turn them on. Or p'raps they might be worried that we'll really turn them off?

COLIN. Do you want to talk about it seriously?

RUTH. No, not a lot. I'm bored. I really haven't got the energy, you know, to talk to you. In fact, I think I want to go.

Slight pause.

ANNE. Yuh, sure. Let's go.

She goes out. RUTH picking up the placard.

TONY. Right then.

TONY goes out.

FRANCES. Good luck.

RUTH. The same to you.

She goes out. Pause.

FRANCES. Well.

Pause. COLIN's not going to say anything.
FRANCES feels she ought to say something.

I mean, I'm not opposed to the demands, I mean of course
there should be equal pay and free abortion. I just do find it
difficult, to take that seriously a group of people arguing that
the Queen's exploited by her footmen and her stable boys.

You know?

COLIN *a smile and a wink.*

COLIN. Well, here's looking at you, kid.

They are about to go when SANDRA enters with another bottle.
She kneels by the primus, to put it on to boil. She realises
something. She looks up to COLIN and FRANCES.

SANDRA. Hey, you got a match?

Blackout.

Scene Seven

In the darkness, 'Stand By Your Man' by Tammy Wynette.
*After the change, fade under a burst of laughter and lights fade up on
the scene. It is a small meeting of WOMEN, in May 1975. They sit
in a kind of circle. It is important that the focus of this scene is in the
centre of it, directed from the WOMEN to each other, not at all out
front, and even slightly excluding the audience.*
*The WOMEN are RUTH, SANDRA, ROSIE (who has her
back to us) and CATHY who is now a college lecturer. She wears an*

abortion campaign badge. RUTH *wears a Women's Movement badge.*
ROSIE *and* RUTH *are smoking. The* WOMEN *are laughing. The*
laughter subsides, but whatever's just been said sparks one or two to
revive the laughter, and the humour still bubbles through the first few
lines.

CATHY. You know, I really think we ought to talk about
doing something.

SANDRA. Oh, ar. Voice of reason.

CATHY. I thought, perhaps what we were saying,
nurseries . . .

ROSIE. I'm sorry, what was that?

RUTH. Last week, we talked about the lack of nursery
facilities. We thought of doing something.

ROSIE. Doing what?

CATHY. Well, I did have some thoughts, in fact.

She finds a piece of paper.

SANDRA. Course, they might not need a nursery.

CATHY. I thought we might consider a three-pronged
approach. First, we could raise a petition, for a nursery.

RUTH. Whereas, they might want something else.

I mean, this is quite a well-off area. A lot of women don't go
out to work. They sit at home. Don't meet. Don't use the
launderette.

They sit at home, just going quietly bonkers.

Perhaps they just need a place to meet. Perhaps we should
think about a place for women to meet.

Pause.

CATHY. Well, I'm not sure where that would get us. I mean, I
know a lot of women who'd love not to have to work. I feel
there's things that are much more politically important.

RUTH. It's not politically important, then, that women sit at
home going bonkers?

CATHY. No, that's not –

RUTH. In fact, I know, this woman. What you'd say, I s'pose
   you'd call, an unimportant, bored . . . And she has, I mean,
   this woman's made so bonkers by the role that unimportant
   way of life has forced her into, that she spends her day, her
   whole day, mind, just cooking, separate meals, for all her
   family. The baby's mush. The five-year-old's fish fingers.
   The eleven-year-old subsists on hamburgers, she's into haute
   cuisine and hubby's just gone vegan.

And that, of course, is leaving out the bloody dog.

And I do, frankly, feel –

ROSIE *jumps up. She's dropped her cigarette into the folds of her
   dress.*

ROSIE. Oh, God –

SANDRA. What's the matter?

ROSIE. Lost a fag. Oh, here . . .

She finds it. Sits again.

Ruin more frocks that way.

Pause. The incident has changed the atmosphere.

RUTH. I think, I mean, I think we're still not starting from
   ourselves. I think we're still frightened of confronting *our*
   wants, *our* fears, *our* rage, the way that we're oppressed by
   men, emotionally, intellectually, physically, day by day.

SANDRA. Oh, speak for yourself.

RUTH. What do you mean?

SANDRA (*parody*). 'What do you mean?'

Slight pause.

I just get a bit fed up when you talk as if the things you think
   and feel are what all women think and feel.

And I think in fact, sometimes, getting heavy and
   aggressive's just as – well –

ROSIE. I'd like –

They turn to her.

I'd like to know.

Slight pause.

Bit more about the woman cooks five meals a day.

Pause.

RUTH. You mean, 'bout who she –

ROSIE. Why she does it. How a person could.

Pause.

RUTH. Well. S'pose.

Slight pause.

She hasn't got a life. Life of her own. She's stored it, packaged it out, between her husband and her children. And she does it well. Her life is comfortable. Painless. Tranquil. Numb.

Pause.

Oh, it isn't easy. I don't find it easy. In the pub, a good time being had by all, and some bloke calls someone a cunt, or cracks a sexist joke, or peers at some girl's bottom. And it ain't easy, take him up on it, be heavy and aggressive, lay your scene on him, and he says, oh beg pardon but for Christ's sake I don't *mean* . . . And you've fucked up the good time. Ruined it. That really don't come easy.

SANDRA. No. No, I can see that.

Everyone except RUTH picks up the joke. Then RUTH picks up the joke. The tension eases.

RUTH. Liberated? I don't feel liberated. I feel like I just jumped off a cliff without a parachute.

CATHY. That's Germaine Greer.

Pause.

SANDRA. Right on.

Pause.

CATHY. But don't you think . . . don't you really think we should decide . . .

Pause. SANDRA suddenly finds this the funniest thing in the world. It's completely infectious. All the women collapse laughing.

Blackout.

Scene Eight

In the darkness, 'Black Jack Davy', from the LP, 'All Around My Hat', by Steeleye Span.
The lights on FRANCES's flat.
It is later the same night.
COLIN is listening to the record which is on the record-player.
He drinks a glass of wine and is reading a copy of International Socialism. In front of him, on the floor, is a two-litre bottle of red wine, another glass, and a tray with coffee things.
A full ashtray also on the floor.
COLIN's coat over the back of the sofa.
FRANCES comes in, and COLIN takes off the record.

FRANCES. She's putting the kids to bed.

COLIN. Where's she putting them?

FRANCES. Oh, one's in the study and the little girl'll sleep with Rosie in the spare room.

COLIN. Anything to help?

FRANCES. Don't think so.

FRANCES sits on the sofa and fills her glass.

Well, what a thing.

COLIN. So, what happened?

FRANCES. Well. Apparently she'd been to a women's meeting, some consciousness raising thing, and got home late, and he was furious, and made a crack about bra-burning and capow. She walked out. There and then. The kids and all.

COLIN. That is amazing.

FRANCES. I haven't seen her for years. Not properly, since she was married.

Pause.

Just like that. I think it's bloody marvellous.

Enter ROSIE.

Hi. Have you got them settled down all right?

ROSIE *crosses her fingers and sits. She's tired.*

Rosie, you met across a crowded pile of suitcases and children, but this is Colin.

ROSIE. Yes. Hallo.

COLIN. It's nice to meet you.

FRANCES. Colin was round. For dinner.

Pause.

COLIN. Speaking of which, I'll . . . go and do the kitchen.

FRANCES. Right.

COLIN *stands and goes out. During the following, we hear him whistle as he washes up.*

D'you want a glass of wine? Or coffee? Or, indeed, I think, somewhere some scotch?

ROSIE. No thank you. Later, p'raps.

FRANCES. OK.

Pause.

ROSIE. I have just left my fucking husband.

Long pause.

FRANCES. D'you want to talk about it?

ROSIE. Sorry?

FRANCES. Oh, that sounds as if you've just had a bereavement. I meant –

ROSIE. No. Not a bereavement. The reverse.

FRANCES. That's right.

Pause.

How did he take it?

ROSIE. Howard?

FRANCES. Yuh.

Pause.

ROSIE. Looked lost. Last thing of him I saw, just standing in
the kitchen, looking at the rows of gleaming things. I really
don't think, that he knew, what they were for.

I've got this odd contraption, dices onions. He just stood
there, gazing at it, trying to work it out.

Enter COLIN *in what is obviously* FRANCES' *pinny. He has
plastic gloves on. He is whistling. He puts down a clean ashtray,
puts the dirty one on the tray and takes it out.*

FRANCES. He wasn't angry, then? Just lost?

ROSIE. Oh, he was wild with rage. Was like, you know, you
lost things, lose a purse, a chequebook, and you're in a hurry,
and you can't believe it's gone. You stand there, trying to
think. You get a kind of, furious inertia.

He was standing, staring at my autochop, like that.

Pause.

FRANCES. Colin and I were saying, it's quite marvellous. To
do it, just like –

ROSIE. No, not marvellous. Don't think. Not marvellous.

Pause.

I feel as if I've been asleep. A soft-down slumber. All these
years. Faint voices, in the distance, through the doze. Half-
heard. The world outside.

And then to wake up, find yourself, the middle of a
nightmare, carnage all around, bits of your body ripped up
on the bed . . . You want to shut your eyes again, turn over,
pull the blankets tight.

You can't. But it's not, marvellous.

FRANCES *smiles*.

FRANCES. No. Sure.

A warm pause. Enter COLIN, without the pinny and gloves. He sits, lights a cigarette.

COLIN (*to* ROSIE). Do you want some wine?

ROSIE. No thanks.

COLIN *gestures to* FRANCES *with the bottle.* FRANCES *nods, so* COLIN *pours them both wine.*

What do you do?

COLIN. Well, for a living, I'm a teacher. But my main thing's postgraduate research.

ROSIE. What into?

COLIN. The British Labour Movement during World War Two.

ROSIE. I see.

Pause.

FRANCES. I don't know if you saw, there was a series, on Granada, last year, 'bout wartime Liverpool. Colin did a lot of the research.

ROSIE. I didn't see it, no. Sounds wonderful.

Pause.

COLIN. What was this meeting that you went to?

ROSIE. Oh, it was a group of women. Met one of them through Damion's school. Asked me to come along.

COLIN. What was it about?

ROSIE. Well, it wasn't, really, quite *about* anything. I mean, it was about day nurseries, but not *about*.

Slight pause.

I'm sorry . . .

FRANCES. Know what you mean.

COLIN. I used to be very suspicious of all that.

ROSIE. All what?

COLIN. Oh, small group politics. In fact, the Women's Movement. Fran will tell you.

FRANCES. Fran will tell you.

COLIN. Yes. I mean, I used to think it was, just therapy. Trying to find individual solutions to problems that were essentially collective.

FRANCES *grins at* ROSIE.

I think, in fact, it was a kind of reaction, to the sixties, you know, all that free your head stuff, and we all reacted very strongly, in the opposite direction, kind of bend the stick, particularly with the Tory Government, the revival of industrial militancy, and so on.

COLIN *is warming to his theme.*
ROSIE *is looking at* COLIN, *trying to concentrate, a fixed and nervous smile on her face.*

But I think that was a great mistake, or anyway, mistake to *keep* that kind of prejudice. Because the kind of politics, the Women's Movement's into, small group, consciousness, particularly, I think, the concern with raising consciousness, can make a major contribution to the wider struggle, as a whole, and –

ROSIE. Excuse me, would you shut up please?

Pause.

COLIN. Beg pardon?

ROSIE. Would you, please, mind shutting up?

Slight pause. She's nearly crying.

I'm sorry . . .

COLIN (*looks to* FRANCES). Uh . . .

FRANCES. Colin, Rosie has just . . .

COLIN (*to* ROSIE). Look, I'm –

The phone rings.

FRANCES. Shit.

She looks at her watch.

Oh, who the fuck.

She stands and goes out to the phone. COLIN *and* ROSIE *don't know what to say, so they listen to the conversation.*

FRANCES (*off*). Hallo, Frances Lockett.

Oh, Steve.

Yes, they said at the branch they hadn't arrived.

Well, of course it's urgent. It's also your fault.

Look –

Look, Steve . . .

Look, Steve, can I get this straight . . . That's right, can I get it straight that you are seriously . . .

You're seriously ringing me at two a.m. To ask me to get up at six, drive thirteen miles and meet a fucking train?

I mean, you are of course joking. I mean, you are pulling my leg.

Oh, fuck off, Steve.

That's right.

Slam of phone. FRANCES *re-enters.*

COLIN. Who was it?

FRANCES. Oh, some creep from rank and file. He wanted me to get up in four hours and go and get some leaflets off Red Star.

COLIN. Now, look, I hope you told him –

FRANCES. Yes, of course I told him.

Pause.

Blokes. The bloody nerve.

Pause.
COLIN *glances at his watch.*
FRANCES *seizes the time.*

Uh, Col, I know it's late, but you wouldn't mind not staying, would you?

COLIN. Sorry?

FRANCES. See, I think it might be . . . Mean, I'd put you up, but Rosie's kids and all.

COLIN. You'd Put Me Up?

FRANCES. I think it would be simpler if you went.

Pause.
COLIN *stands.*

COLIN. Fran, could I have a word? outside?

Pause.

FRANCES. Oh, all right. If you want to.

They go out.
ROSIE *left there. She picks up the* International Socialism, *but is really listening – as are we – to the conversation from off.*

COLIN. So what's all this about?

FRANCES. Well, I'd just rather if you didn't stay.

COLIN. Why not?

FRANCES. Well, just, it's difficult.

COLIN. What's difficult about it?

FRANCES. Well, you –

COLIN. And I would point out that usually when I stay the spare room doesn't come into it.

FRANCES. That's not the point.

COLIN. What is the point?

FRANCES. It's just . . . I want to talk to Rosie.

COLIN. Well, who's stopping you?

FRANCES. Oh, *Colin.*

COLIN. Have I said something wrong? Look, of course I'm sorry if I . . . Look, I did get out of your way. That's why I did the washing up.

FRANCES. Well, thanks a lot.

COLIN. Oh, for heaven's –

FRANCES. Colin, go away.

Pause.

I'm sorry. But please go away.

Pause.

COLIN. I'll get my coat.

He comes into the room. He decides not to ask ROSIE for his magazine back. ROSIE realises she's sitting on his coat. She gets up. COLIN is trying very hard not to show his anger.

COLIN. Nice to meet you, Rosie.

ROSIE. Yes. And you.

He meets FRANCES coming in.

FRANCES. Night–night.

COLIN *goes.*
ROSIE *pours herself a glass of wine.*
FRANCES *sits.*

ROSIE. I'm sorry, if I . . .

FRANCES. No.

Pause.

ROSIE. I thought, to start with, that he lived here.

FRANCES. Nope. We stopped all that two years ago.

Now we have this, well arrangement. You know, dinner and

a fuck from time to time. Just as and when the inclination grabs us.

Sadly, like all informal, non-coercive, liberated and relaxed arrangements, it's extremely difficult to de-arrange.

ROSIE. I see.

FRANCES. It's tricky, cos he's given me so much. Well, in a way, he gave me everything.

Pause.

Look. An example. At the NUT, the teachers' conference, a year or two ago. And I proposed this motion. And I had to force them, put it on the agenda. And I did. And won it.

Quite a triumph. You know, points of order, citing precedent, procedure, challenging the chair. A mighty victory. But I came off shaking. Really shaking. Blubbering. Quite awful. And, well, Col was there, and did his stuff, and rallied round, and pulled me back together. Generously giving. As he always is. And does. But, still . . . (*Pause.*) I'm sorry, it's not –

ROSIE. Go on.

FRANCES. It's just . . . That Col is Peter Pan. He doesn't alter. Oh, the words, the ideas even, change. I mean you heard him, and I may say on his attitude to feminism in the early days, the half he did not tell you, but he . . . Underneath it all, he's still the little boy who got arrested at the sit-in and was marched off, all white-faced and brave, to jail.

ROSIE. He went inside?

FRANCES. One night. Then he got fined a hundred and we raised it and they let him go.

Not that it wasn't, in its way, quite brave . . .

But always, on his terms. And never, if it threatens anything, inside.

And what is even worse, is that I look at him, his busy-ness, routine, unchanging and unbending energy, the lack of any kind of pain or challenge, and I see myself.

See Me.

Pause.
ROSIE *laughs.*
Not inquisitorially:

So what's funny?

ROSIE. Well. Must tell you. Speaking of, changes.

She leans forward to FRANCES. *For the first time, she's relaxed.*

Was the other day. Was playing pantomimes with Sophie. It's a game, to guess the end. And I was doing Sleeping Beauty. And I had done the bit about the curse, and how the princess fell asleep, and years and years passed by and then I asked her, do you know what happened next.

And then she looks at me – you know the way they do, that effortless superiority – and says, oh yes, mum, know *that* one. This prince turns up, he finds the princess, kisses her, she wakes up and he turns into a frog.

FRANCES *laughs.*

My darling, let me press your cherry lips to –

ROSIE *turns into a frog.*

Rivet rivet rivet.

FRANCES *laughs.*
The two women frog away at each other.

FRANCES. Rivet rivet rivet.

ROSIE. Rivet rivet.

FRANCES. Oh that they all would.

ROSIE. What?

FRANCES. Turn into frogs.

They laugh.

Now look, comrade person, for the sake of the international

proletarian struggle, you've just got to go and – rivet rivet rivet.

ROSIE. Hello Rosie How's Yerself You Burnt Yer Bra Yet How About A Bit Of Liberation Huh Know What I – rivet rivet rivet.

FRANCES. Yes of *course* I'll do the dishes darling but I'll do them when *I* – rivet rivet rivet rivet.

ROSIE. Oh now come on petal come on tulip after all it's Saturday oh come on flower why not – rivet rivet.

FRANCES. Oh come on sweetheart, mean, all very well, but after all it's hardly real politics, now is it?

Pause. That's slightly too close to the bone for a second. But then:

Rivet. Rivet. Rivet.

The laughter again. And this time the frog imitation gets out of hand, and mutates into a kind of game, with much thrashing of arms, which provokes a memory of a similar game long past and the following lines:

FRANCES. Hey – hey – I must –

ROSIE. You must –

FRANCES. – improve . . .

The laughter finally dies.

The time. I teach at nine.

ROSIE. Please miss you know your stocking's got a great big – rivet rivet rivet.

This sets them off again.
Eventually, the laughter dies.

Look. Is it OK if I stay.

FRANCES. Oh, yes, of course. You must.

ROSIE. I mean, I'll pay you rent.

FRANCES. Now, come on, what d'you use for money?

ROSIE. Ah.

Slight pause.

For money. Use.

She taps the side of her nose in a conspiratorial fashion. She goes out and returns with a cardboard box. She sits and takes out a necklace.

Gifts.

She drops the necklace. Picking out another couple of trinkets:

Gifts from my man to me.

She drops the trinkets. Finding more:

Hundreds of glittering gifts. Gifts of his love. Generously given.

She drops more trinkets, picks out more.

Given so much. Given me everything.

She upends the box on the floor.

I'm going into trade.

Blackout.
'It's In His Kiss', by Linda Lewis, covers the change.

Scene Nine

The music fades as lights come up on a school classroom.
   It is the next day.
   The cloakroom is represented by a bench, about six feet long, underneath which are two vertically divided shelves for shoes. Above the bench is a row of pegs on which overcoats, hats, lacrosse and hockey sticks, etc. hang.
   There are two SCHOOLGIRLS on the bench.
   One is TRISHA, who sits, facing out front, adjusting her make-up in a small mirror.
   DENISE lies on her tummy, her head cupped in her hands, smoking.
   A magazine lies on the bench in front of her, though it is not immediately clear, when she speaks, that she is quoting from it.
   A few moments, then:

DENISE. Hey, Trisha.

TRISHA. Yuh?

DENISE. It's happened.

TRISHA. Yuh?

DENISE. You've met the Boy Of Your Dreams.

Pause.

TRISHA. Oh. Right.

DENISE. Are you first attracted to him . . .

TRISHA. Yuh?

DENISE. By his brooding good looks and exotic air of mystery?

TRISHA. Um . . .

DENISE. Or his sentimental, old-world habits, buying flowers, always opening the door for you?

TRISHA. Tt, well . . .

DENISE. His line in witty and sophisticated chat –

TRISHA. Oh, I dunno . . .

DENISE. Or p'raps his friendly cheerful manner turned-up nose and happy smile?

Pause.

TRISHA. Don't think his turned-up nose.

DENISE (*finding a pencil to mark the score in*). No way his turned-up nose.

TRISHA. I s'pose, on balance, brooding good looks and exotic air of mystery.

DENISE. OK.

She pencils it in.

I think I'm going for the witty chat.

TRISHA. Oh, yuh. What's next?

DENISE. OK you've caught your fella and the big night comes. Your date is –

TRISHA*'s noticed someone coming.*

TRISHA. Hey –

DENISE. What is it?

TRISHA. It's The Droop.

DENISE *looks off, quickly, stubs her cigarette out in one of the shoes in the shelves beneath her, turns and catches* TRISHA *who is trying to hide behind the coats, pulls her back.* DENISE *sits up, her feet on the bench.*
TRISHA, *checking with* DENISE, *sits too.* MR BREWER *comes in. He is a schoolmaster in his mid-thirties.*

BREWER. Ah. Here we are. Patricia and Denise. Playing hookey in the changing room. Again.

Pause.

DENISE*'s tactic is to sit still, ignoring* BREWER.
TRISHA *follows this tactic, but with less assurance, and the occasional glance at* DENISE *to confirm what she's supposed to do.*

Yesterday morning it was geography we skipped. Somewhat to my surprise. Seeing as how Denise likes geography. Insofar as she finds anything of interest, geog is it. Strange people from strange lands. Some of them stranger, even, than herself.

Pause.

And yesteraft we missed our maths. On this occasion, was a little shaken by Patricia. Cos Patricia's good at mathematics. Even very good. Her little chums, Denise included, wouldn't recognise a logarithm if one slid up and bit them, but Patricia can square a root and map a matrix like there's no tomorrow. So we must just hope and pray that she recalls how few of them she's got before she's thrown upon the tender mercies of the Joint Matriculation Board.

Pause.

And today, right now, in fact, it's metalwork. Fought long
and hard for, metalwork. So we would not be stereotyped.
Demeaned, by being forced into traditional roles.

Pause.

Why are we not in metalwork, dear pupils? Why, despite all
the efforts of our struggling sisters, have we cut our class?

DENISE *turns very slowly and looks at* BREWER. *It is a stare of
not inconsiderable contempt.* TRISHA, *after a glance, tries the
same. Hold. Then*:

All right. I'll get your tutor. She will talk to you. Who
knows, and work a miracle, and make the dumb to speak.

He walks out.
DENISE *puts her legs down, picks up the magazine and reads*:

DENISE. (a) Boating on a lily-covered lake and listening to the
nightingales. (b) Ten pin bowling at your local alley with his
gang of madcap friends. (c) Quiet dinner in a wayside
country inn with old oak beams above a roaring fire. (d)
Rave-up at the trendy highclass London disco where you sip
champagne and dance till dawn.

TRISHA. The lily-covered lake.

DENISE. The rave-up.

Pencils in.

Right.

TRISHA *stands, biting her lip, clearly worried by the* BREWER
incident.

S'only Lockup.

TRISHA. Yuh.

She sits down again.

What happens next.

DENISE (*reading*). (3) Afterwards.

TRISHA. After what?

DENISE. The Date.

TRISHA. Oh. 'Course.

DENISE. He either walks you home beneath the blossom in your local churchyard. Or you ride on horseback home across the windswept moors beneath the brooding sky. Or, he buys you a chop suey at the Chinese take-away –

TRISHA. Yuck.

DENISE. Yuh, or else you speed along the freeway in his silver Lamborghini.

Pause. TRISHA *not sure. She takes the magazine, glances at it. She looks at the pop star pin-up on the opposite page.*

TRISHA. Hey. D'you think he looks a bit like Gary?

DENISE. Gary?

TRISHA. Yuh.

Pause.

DENISE. I think I fancy being driven in his silver whatsit.

TRISHA. Ooh, I think the ride across the windswept moor . . .

DENISE. You'll catch your death.

TRISHA. Safer than you are in his bloody Lamborghini.

Pause.

DENISE. Gary.

TRISHA (*slightly coy*). Yuh.

DENISE. What about Brian?

TRISHA. Oh, he's boring.

DENISE. Gary's boring.

TRISHA. Gary *isn't*.

DENISE. How do you know?

TRISHA. Can *tell*.

DENISE *looks round.*

DENISE. Here she comes.

She takes the magazine back and reads as FRANCES *comes in:*

Right, question four. Fantastic! Yesterday he said he was in love with you forever and he pledged you'd never part. You know it's true, cos he went on to say:

FRANCES. Hallo.

Pause.

TRISHA. 'Lo, Miss.

Slight pause. DENISE *a kind of wave.*

FRANCES. I was asked to have a word with you. By Mr Brewer.

TRISHA. Yes, Miss.

FRANCES. You're supposed to be in class. In metalwork.

Slight pause.

Can I ask why you're not there?

DENISE. Well –

Thinks better of it.

S'boring, miss.

FRANCES. I see.

Pause. TRISHA, *sensitively:*

TRISHA. Mean, s'no more boring than the other lessons, Miss. I mean, we think that needlework and cooking's a right pain as well.

FRANCES *smiles. She sits on the bench.*
DENISE *moves a little.*

FRANCES. What are you reading?

She picks up the magazine.

Which question are you on?

Pause. TRISHA *not sure whether to reply.* DENISE *slightly impatient:*

DENISE. The one 'bout what he says to you just after he's said he loves you and you'll never part.

FRANCES. I see.

She puts down the magazine. TRISHA *takes a decision, picks up the magazine, and reads, to* FRANCES.

TRISHA. His life's been just spent waiting for a girl like you. He lost his head to you in that first moment that you met but was too shy to say. He'd like it if this moment stayed forever and he'll never let you go. He loves you cos he needs you and his whole life's changed.

Pause.

Which would your fella say, Miss?

FRANCES (*caught out slightly*). Well, I don't know many men, who'd, well, be likely to say anything like that.

TRISHA/DENISE (*sympathetically*). Oh, Miss.

FRANCES. Not sure I'd want to.

TRISHA. Wouldn't you?

FRANCES. I mean, it's not my type of dream.

DENISE. What *is*, then, Miss?

Pause.

FRANCES. Well, I . . . I like a man who treats me as a human being, lets me be independent, and who knows how to wash his own socks.

TRISHA *and* DENISE *look at each other, deeply shocked.*

I mean, come on, you can't seriously think that any real person's going to talk like that?

Pause. The GIRLS *clam.*
Then DENISE, *quietly:*

DENISE. Think how they do talk, Miss.

FRANCES. What do you mean?

The GIRLS don't reply.
The bell goes.
It stops.

Well. There we are. I'm afraid it looks as if Mr Brewer has been denied the satisfaction of your unwilling presence in the metal –

TRISHA *and* DENISE *are giggling.*

What's so funny?

They giggle on.

Oh, come on, what's the joke?

TRISHA. Just, Mr Brewer, getting satisfaction, Miss.

FRANCES. Yes? So?

Pause.

TRISHA *glances at* DENISE.
DENISE, *with an 'in for a penny' shrug:*

DENISE. He's called the Droop, Miss.

FRANCES. Droop?

DENISE. You know, like Brewer's . . .

FRANCES. Ah.

She laughs. The GIRLS laugh as well.
The three of them are having a high old time until FRANCES notices MR BREWER standing there. He wears a tracksuit.

Ah. Mr Brewer.

She stands.
The GIRLS are having trouble.

Yes. Well, Mr Brewer, I've had a word, of course, Denise, Patricia, and it is – they say it definitely – won't occur again. No question. Of it. Happening. As you might say, again. It's all, um, sorted out, uh, Mr Brewer.

FRANCES *pushes her way past* BREWER. *Lights up on two*

chairs elsewhere on the stage – representing the staff room.
BREWER follows FRANCES to the staff room as the lights on
the changing room fade.

Scene Ten

In the staffroom, FRANCES takes out marking. BREWER takes off
his tracksuit. He wears black refereeing kit.

BREWER. I mean, don't get me wrong, Miss Locket.

I mean, I'm quite delighted you're so keen their independent
little personalities should be developed. Most impressed,
technique of yours, treating them as if they're human beings.

He goes out left.
Shouts from off:

And I quite understand, of course, and sympathise, your
problems in that project, with Denise. Her relationship with
the human race being no more than mildly coincidental.

He re-enters with a pair of black socks and football boots. He sits on
the other chair and changes his shoes and socks.

And while of course it's true the only way we could assist
Denise vocationally would be help her polish up her lock-
picking, there is the minor matter of the fact that she's
encouraging Patricia, too, into a life of crime. And while of
course it's true that dear Patricia's hardly set fair for an
Exhibition to St Hilda's, she does have a little spark, a little
talent, limited, 'tis true, but there.

He stands.

A talent which Denise, of course, is set on snuffing out.

He goes out right.
Shouts from off:

Now, I appreciate, of course, your view of things is
somewhat different. For you, of course, they are not little
girls at all, they're victims of oppression, they're exploited by
the running dogs of bourgeois ideology.

He re-enters with a football, which he puts down by his chair.

And thus are nothing more or less than willing or unwilling soldiers of the Revolution. Soldierettes.

BREWER *picks up his normal shoes, goes out left, continues shouting*:

And, consequently, what is best for them, is quite irrelevant. Or even harmful. As it might dilute their military zeal.

BREWER *re-enters, carrying a whistle, and putting a notebook in his top pocket.*

And, of course, their actual wishes, what they want, come even further down the list of your priorities.

BREWER *putting his shirt inside his shorts and his whistle round his neck.*

But, nonetheless, they are still little girls, their prospects and their visions grossly limited. Perhaps, for one of them, an 'O' or two, so she can climb, at least, the bottom rung . . . But I do quite appreciate, for you, that even that would be no more than just a sell-out to the patriarchial bourgeoisie.

FRANCES (*decides to react*). Uh, Mr Brewer –

BREWER. Miss Lockett, don't imagine for a moment, I don't understand your game.

He blows his whistle to test it, and makes to stride out.

FRANCES. But, Mr Brewer –

BREWER (*turns back*). Yes?

FRANCES. You've forgotten your ball, Mr Brewer. It would never do to go without your ball.

She picks up the ball and throws it to BREWER.
He smiles, rather more knowingly than we might expect.

BREWER. Thank you so much, Ms Lockett.

He goes out. FRANCES stands.

Scene Eleven

Music fades. Lights on the changing room. TRISHA *has gone.*
DENISE *sits on the bench. She's counting money on her lap. Her
handbag beside her.*
   FRANCES *joins her.*

FRANCES. 'Lo, Denise.

   DENISE *quickly puts her arms over the money.*

DENISE. 'Lo, Miss.

FRANCES. You're not at games?

DENISE. I got a mum's note, Miss.

FRANCES. Oh, yes, of course.

   Pause.

   FRANCES *sits beside* DENISE.
   DENISE *doesn't quite know what to do about the money.*

FRANCES. Do I assume . . .

DENISE. What Miss?

FRANCES. That we have found the mastermind behind the
   fourth form poker ring?

   Pause. DENISE *raises her arms.*

DENISE. Well . . . only 80p, Miss.

FRANCES. Only 80p.

   DENISE *puts her money into her handbag. She realises*
   FRANCES *is not going to go away. So, to make conversation:*

DENISE. D'you play cards, Miss?

FRANCES. Not with you I don't.

   Pause.

   So what was the result of the quiz?

DENISE. Eh?

   Slight pause.

Oh, yuh. Quiz. Well, um.

Slight pause.

Trisha was a one hundred per cent reality-proof romantic. She dreamt of faraway places and strange exotic experiences. She went for blokes who promised brooding mystery and just a hint of danger. Her fault was that perhaps her dreamy nature tended to like blind her to the faults of others.

FRANCES. Yes, I see. And you?

DENISE. I am not one for the simple romantic pleasures am I cos I want a life of luxury and glamour p'raps I set my sights too high. Sez they.

Pause.

F'y'ask me, it's a load of rubbish.

FRANCES. Well, there I might agree with you.

DENISE. Yuh. Well.

Pause.

Mean, Trish just buys 'em for the pinups and the beauty hints. Like me, prefer me thrillers.

FRANCES. Thrillers?

DENISE. Yuh.

FRANCES. What kind of thrillers do you like?

DENISE. Oh, you know. Ed McBain. And that.

Pause.

FRANCES. My favourite's Raymond Chandler. Have you read his books?

DENISE *looking neutral.*

The Big Sleep? Things like that?

Pause.
DENISE *decides to risk it.*

DENISE. 'I walked into the room. Neither of the people in the room took any notice of me, which was odd, cos only one of them was dead.'

FRANCES' *delighted smile makes* DENISE *think she's maybe gone too far.*

I haven't read 'em all. I mean, they're always taken out, the library.

FRANCES. You could, I mean, I've quite a selection.

Slight pause.

You could, perhaps, come round.

DENISE. Uh, well . . .

FRANCES. I don't suppose you ever babysit?

Pause.

DENISE. Uh, Miss, you got a . . .

FRANCES. No, not me. A friend staying with me.

DENISE. Oh.

Slight pause.

Yuh. Sure. Be nice.

Slight pause.

Could I bring Trish?

FRANCES. Of course. I'll have a word, my friend, and let you know, an evening.

DENISE. Fine.

Pause.

FRANCES. You like Trish, don't you?

DENISE. Yuh. Best friend.

Pause.

FRANCES. Denise, what did you mean, you said, this morning, bout the way that boys talk. What d'you mean by that?

DENISE. Eh?

She remembers.

Oh. Oh, yuh.

Pause.

Well, just. Like, humping. Having. It, an'. Getting it. And slit. An' up your hole. And shouting, come on, show's your hangers. Shouting out, she got her rags on. Scrubbers. Slags.

Slight pause.

An' all.

FRANCES. You needn't take all that.

DENISE. I don't.

FRANCES. But some girls do.

Pause.

DENISE. I don't.

FRANCES. You shouldn't.

Pause.
DENISE *looks at* FRANCES, *suspiciously.*

DENISE. Eh, Miss. You women's lib?

FRANCES. Yes. If you like.

Pause.

Because I think you shouldn't take all that. Because I think that that's a waste of you. I think you've got a better life, a life of your own.

Pause.
DENISE *says nothing.*
FRANCES *glances at her watch and stands.*

Well, p'raps I ought to go. I'll let you know about the babysitting?

DENISE. Yuh. F'you like.

FRANCES. Well, cheerio, Denise.

DENISE. Yuh. Cheers.

FRANCES goes out.
DENISE sits there.
Then enter TRISHA in hockey gear. She's dripping wet.
She goes to her peg, finds her mirror in a coat pocket, and brush and comb, sits, looks at herself.

TRISHA. It's raining. Bloody raining.

She looks at her hair.

Mean, just look. Me split ends got split ends.

She tries to brush her hair.

Met *Gary* in the corridor. Me hair, like *this.*

DENISE. Oh, *Gary.*

TRISHA turns to DENISE, smiling, as if it's a joke between them.

Oh, bloody *Gary.*

DENISE looks away from TRISHA, who stops smiling.
TRISHA decides to shrug it off.

TRISHA. Eh, that the Lockup, talking to you.

DENISE (*assenting*). Mm.

TRISHA. So what she want to talk about?

Slight pause.

DENISE. She wanted us to babysit.

TRISHA. She got a baby?

DENISE. No she got a friend.

Pause.

TRISHA. I like the Lockup. Mean, she's really smart. Them's Lotus shoes.

DENISE. You what?

TRISHA. Her shoes. What else she say?

DENISE. She talked, she said I shouldn't waste myself.

TRISHA. You shouldn't what?

DENISE. She said, like I'd got a better life.

TRISHA. What, better than –

DENISE. Life of me own.

TRISHA. Eh, Den.

DENISE *looks at her.*

Eh, Den. D'you think I'm 'shallow'?

DENISE. No. Who says?

TRISHA. Oh, just . . . A Lack of Character?

DENISE. You what?

TRISHA. The Droop said once. I'm shallow. Need, like to develop character.

DENISE. Once asked me mum, if I was pretty. And she said, don't worry 'bout it pet, cos you got character. Mean, like I think she meant, instead.

Pause.

TRISHA. I think you're pretty.

DENISE *shrugs.*

You're me best friend, Den. I hope we'll always be the way we are. I hope we'll never change.

D'you promise, that we'll always be?

Pause.

DENISE. Oh, yuh. I promise.

TRISHA. Really?

DENISE. Sure.

Pause.

Do you? D'you promise, really?

TRISHA. Yuh, I promise.

Slight pause.

Cross my heart and hope to die.

Pause. TRISHA *looks at herself in the mirror.*

Oh, just look me bloody hair.

TRISHA *and* DENISE *hold. Lights change.* DEBBIE *and* SHARON *enter. They are 15-year-old ravers.* DEBBIE *is near* TRISHA *and* SHARON *near* DENISE.

DEBBIE. She'd always been the dreamy one, forever longing for the one true love that would transport her into endless bliss.

SHARON. She'd always been the do–or–die type, full of madcap notions, wild ideas and harebrained schemes.

FRANCES *appears.*

FRANCES. But still, they were the very best of friends, and it seemed impossible that anything or anyone could come between them.

Start the music.

DEBBIE. And so little did she think –

SHARON. And who'd have thought –

FRANCES. And how could – how could she have known . . .

Swell music: Linda Lewis, 'Old School Yard'.
Lights fade.
Interval.

Scene Twelve

The flashing lights of the Youth Club Disco. Play Suzi Quatro: 'You Can't Make Me Love You' from the LP Your Momma Won't Like Me. The words of the song fit round the lines in the scene. Enter DEBBIE *and* SHARON, *looking extraordinary.*

SUZIE QUATRO. Well, you thought you got an angel
    But I tell you, it just ain't so.

DEBBIE. It was disco-night at the Youth Club, and all the crowd were there.

SUZIE QUATRO. This cherub-looking momma
Ain't no baby, doncha know.

SHARON. Sharon and Debbie and all the other girls dolled up to the nines.

SUZIE QUATRO. When you touch me you set me aglow.

DEBBIE. There was only one thing missing –

SUZIE QUATRO. And when I'm in your arms, I really don't wanna go . . .

SHARON. So where are the fellas, huh?

SHARON and DEBBIE dance to the chorus, during which, GARY makes an entrance. He is about 16, chews gum, and leers a lot. He stands there, leering.

SUZIE QUATRO. Well you can make me want you
But I ain't gonna love you
Ain't gonna be the one at home
Waiting for you
I feel the rhythm but I never gonna feel the pain

SHARON and DEBBIE stop dancing. They turn and see GARY and freeze:

SHARON/DEBBIE. Wow – It's – GARY.

GARY leans somewhere.

SUZIE QUATRO. Lady little lady
I'm an actress in your game

DEBBIE. And it had happened, there he was, standing silhouetted in the flashing lights . . .

SUZIE QUATRO. Dancing and romancing
What you trying to gain

SHARON. Gary the fifth-form heart-throb, the scrummiest guy in the school . . .

SUZIE QUATRO. Just lead me to your bed.

DEBBIE. And there was only one question:

SUZIE QUATRO. But if I stay all night
I'm gonna get inside your head.

SHARON. Which of us was to be the lucky girl tonight?

SHARON and DEBBIE, once again dance through the Chorus. GARY leans, leers and looks horrible. And, at the end, DENISE enters, looking amazing.

SUZIE QUATRO. Well, you can make me want you
But I ain't gonna love you
Ain't gonna be the one at home
Waiting for you
I feel the rhythm but I never gonna feel the pain

Same routine for SHARON and DEBBIE, though this time, they look to DENISE.

DENISE. Well hi there gang.

During the middle-eight instrumental, SHARON, DEBBIE and DENISE go into a conversational huddle as a spot fades up on TRISHA at the side of the stage. She is dressed in a dressing gown, and wears a headscarf.

TRISHA. It was dance night at the Youth Club. But for once I had chosen to stay at home and cram my math. I knew that my friend Denise was going to the hop, but I never dreamt that very night that she would take my world and dash it into little pieces.

She stays there.
The three GIRLS break huddle.

DENISE. S'Ok, you wanna try me?

DENISE marches over to GARY as:

SUZIE QUATRO. Just like the rain is falling
Tears fall from my eyes

DENISE. Hey you.

GARY. Who me?

DENISE. Yuh you.

SUZIE QUATRO. You know, the way you feel, for me
   Came as no surprise.

DENISE. You wanna dance?

GARY. I wanna what?

DENISE. You heard.

SUZIE QUATRO. I guess I'll be moving on.

DENISE. Well, d'ya wanna dance or doncha?

SUZIE QUATRO. Cos another lover's arms are
   Waiting for me to come

GARY. Well – I s'pose – yuh, l'right.

   DENISE *takes* GARY *to the floor and they go into an*
   uncomfortable clinch and freeze, as:

SUZIE QUATRO. Well, you can make me want you
   But I ain't gonna love you
   Ain't gonna be the one at home
   Waiting for you
   I feel the rhythm but I'm never gonna feel the pain

TRISHA. Oh, Denise, Denise, how could you –

SUZIE QUATRO. I feel the rhythm but I never gonna feel the
   pain.

   Backed by the staccato chords that end the song, DENISE *suddenly*
   pulls back from GARY.
   Her face is screwed up.
   She wipes her mouth with her hand.
   She looks at her hand.
   She looks, in some disgust, at the boy GARY.
   Blackout as the song ends, and at once:

DISC JOCKEY. And OK all you luscious lasses out there, it's
   turning up the tranny time, yes, yes, it's Les'n'Eric and the
   lovely boys, the b-b-b-Bay City Rollers with b-b-b-bye bye
   baby . . .

   Play the Bay City Rollers: 'Bye Bye Baby'.

Scene Thirteen

Lights on TRISHA's *room. The record goes on.*

TRISHA *sits, in a slip, pinning up a dress, on a cushion on the floor. Beside her is a Snoopy mug containing, as it happens, Pernod, and the opened-parcel which contained the dress. Also the tranny from which the Rollers are proceeding.*

DENISE *lies on the bed, smoking, reading a magazine, and also drinking Pernod from a Snoopy mug. The actual bottle is near her.*

TRISHA *switches off the radio, raises her glass.*

TRISHA. So then. The Joint Matriculation Board.

DENISE. Its tender mercies.

TRISHA. An' all that.

They drink. TRISHA *looks in her glass.*

TRISHA. What's this again?

DENISE *waves the bottle at* TRISHA.

Pernod.

DENISE. It's oh.

TRISHA. Y'what?

DENISE. Pernod.

TRISHA. I see. It's nice.

Pause.

So where you get it?

DENISE. Waitrose Winemart. Slipped it under me potatoes.

TRISHA. *Den.* One day you'll get picked up, you know.

DENISE. Well I should be so lucky.

Pause.
TRISHA's *finished pinning.*
She stands:

TRISHA. Right then. Moment, all been waiting for.

DENISE *rolls over and watches* TRISHA *as she puts on the frock.*

Well, then. What you think?

DENISE. Oh, very *nice*.

TRISHA. You're sure?

DENISE. Oh, absolutely. Highly chic.

TRISHA. It's not too short?

DENISE. Just so. I mean, just very, very chic.

TRISHA. Chic, eh.

DENISE. That's right.

TRISHA, *in pleasure, does a little swirl, singing*:

TRISHA. Bye bye baby baby bye bye . . .

DENISE *rolls over, pours herself another Pernod.*
TRISHA *takes off the frock.*

DENISE. You know, you do –

TRISHA. Yuh, what?

DENISE. Look good. Looks great, on you.

Slight pause.

You wear it well.

TRISHA *looks at* DENISE, *not sure what she's implying.*

TRISHA. Oh. Yuh.

To change the subject:

Hey, meant to ask. The disco.

DENISE. Disco?

TRISHA. Yuh. How was it?

DENISE. Oh, all right.

TRISHA. All right?

DENISE. Well, great. Was lots of reggae.

TRISHA. Who was there?

DENISE. Oh, Sharon, Debbie, people.

TRISHA (*into a monkey imitation*). Huh-uh-uh.

DENISE. What you doing?

TRISHA. Them two. Half the time can't tell they're girls or blokes.

Monkey.

Huh-uh.

DENISE. Yuh, well.

Pause.

Talking of blokes –

TRISHA. Yuh?

DENISE. Gary there.

TRISHA. You what?

DENISE. Said, Gary there.

TRISHA *turns off the radio*.

TRISHA. Mean, *Gary*?

DENISE. Yuh, mean Gary. An' –

TRISHA. An' what?

DENISE. Well, in fact, he –

TRISHA *turns to* DENISE.

He's just a washout, Trish. Mean, not worth bothering. A real pain.

Pause.

Mean, not worth running after. Fact, you're better running opposite direction.

Pause.

Mean, Trish, even weedy Brian's –

TRISHA. How d'you know?

DENISE. Know what?

TRISHA. That he's a washout.

DENISE. Oh, cos of what happened.

TRISHA. Tell me what happened.

Pause.

DENISE. Well, like it all started, kind of joke, asked him to dance. You know, a kind of dare. And he was terrible. All eight left feet.

TRISHA. A kind of dare.

DENISE. That's right, and as it happened, smoochy number, dancing, tried to kiss me. Eight left hands an' all. A bleeding octopus. All fumbly. Mean, he tried to kiss me twice, an' missed me mouth both times.

Slight pause.

You ever had a nose-full of someone's tongue? I mean, it made me want to sneeze, an' –

TRISHA. Den, you cow.

DENISE. You what.

TRISHA. You went with Gary.

DENISE. No I didn't.

TRISHA. Went with *Gary*.

DENISE. No, he went for me.

TRISHA. You cow.

DENISE. He's awful, Trish.

TRISHA. You, bloody cow.

DENISE. Stop calling me a cow.

TRISHA. Why not? It's what you are.

Pause.

DENISE. Trish, I was telling you cos of –

TRISHA. Not surprised he hit your nose.

DENISE. You what?

TRISHA. Could hardly miss it.

DENISE. Now, Trish –

TRISHA. Great big fat cow nose.

She is crying.

I'm not surprised he wouldn't kiss you properly. I mean, he probably just did it for a joke himself. Kiss Denny. Probably a bet. Kiss ugly Denny.

DENISE. What.

TRISHA. Like they all say.

DENISE *is looking, hard, at* TRISHA.
TRISHA *knocks over the Pernod bottle.*

Pernodd. Per – noh. Think you're so flash. So smart. When all they're doing's laughing cos no boy'd look at you.

Pause.

DENISE. If they're all like Gary, wouldn't want 'em to.

TRISHA (*sarcastic*). Oh, course you wouldn't would you?

DENISE. No.

Pause.

TRISHA. I think you better go.

DENISE. I will.

TRISHA. Right now.

DENISE. I will.

DENISE *stands.*
She *looks at the notice-board.*

I wouldn't want 'em to.

TRISHA. Just piss off out of it, Denise, OK?

DENISE. Them creeps. Them smutty little boys. Their gap-teeth, spots and pus. And think they're such big men, when stupid little teenies go an' scream at 'em.

She rips down a picture of the Bay City Rollers.
TRISHA *turns in horror, but doesn't dare to say anything or intervene.*

Them stupid teenies, dreaming one day one of 'em will fall for me, oh bliss, oh rapture, Love That Lasts For Ever And Your Whole Life's Changed. When all they really want's to get inside your pants and hump you.

She rips down the picture love story.

But still, spend all those hours, all that work, that *time*.

She's pulled down a beauty chart.

The money, fuck's sake, where you find it? Moisturizers, creams, mascara, powders, spotstick, lipstick, shadow, what the fuck's a blusher?, all this shit . . .

Screws up the cutting:

So an't you got a face?
Face of your own?

Slight pause.

Under all that shit, that waste, life of your own?

Pause.

TRISHA. My posters.

DENISE. Oh, your *posters*. Poor old *posters*.

Pause.

TRISHA. Den. Who's saying this to you.

DENISE. Miss Locket says it. In our conversations.

Pause.

Conversations, that we have, together.

Pause.

Says that girls like you are just a waste of time.

Mocking:

'A'nt she got lovely shoes.'

Pause.

Well. Say *something*. Dear Patricia.

TRISHA *suddenly, very fast and angry*:

TRISHA. Yuh will, true what I said. All say you can't get
boys. I can, they come here, come up here, my fellas, they all
say to me, your best friend, Denny, Trisha, all my boys say,
wouldn't touch her with a ten-foot pole. Or sometimes 20.
Sometimes 20 foot, they wouldn't touch you with, that's
what they say to me.

She screams:

MY BOYFRIENDS SAY TO ME.

Pause.

DENISE. Your boyfriends say.

She turns and goes out quickly.
Pause.

TRISHA. Oh Den.

Oh Den.

I'm sorry.

Blackout.

Scene Fourteen

*Immediately, the title track from Suzie Quatro's 'Your Momma Won't
Like Me'. During it, lights on the Youth Club. Two tables, each with
four chairs. A bowl of sugar on only one of the tables. During the first
verse and chorus, SHARON and then DEBBIE enter, each with
plastic cups of coffee.*

SHARON. Hi Deb.

DEBBIE. Hi Shar.

They look round, as the music goes on.
DENISE enters. She too has a coffee.

SHARON. Hi Den.

DENISE. Hi Deb. Hi Shar.

The three GIRLS *look round the room.*

SHARON. Well, shall we sit?

DEBBIE. Why not.

SHARON. Down here?

DEBBIE. OK.

They sit at the sugarless table, DEBBIE *and* SHARON *notice that* TRISHA *has appeared in the club, also carrying a plastic coffee.*

DEBBIE. Oh.

SHARON. Ah.

And cut the record, just before the second verse starts. DEBBIE, SHARON *and* DENISE *talk pointedly among themselves.*

SHARON. Well, see, we had this dare, a gang of us, the most could nick from Lipton's. So we all go in, and course I'm last, so get the most to nick. And I get lifted, check-out girl, they hauls me off, to see the manager.

DENISE. What happened then?

TRISHA moves nearer the table.

SHARON. Well, s'luck would have it, left alone with him. And he says, what's a nice young pretty girl like you . . . So I says, yuh, you're right, I am quite young and pretty, if you call the police I'll tell 'em that you was alone with me in here and tried a finger.

TRISHA. Hey, Den, look –

SHARON. Hey, girls, I didn't know was slag night. Did you Debbie?

DEBBIE. No, I didn't. Did you Den?

Slight pause.

DENISE. No, didn't know, was slag night.

SHARON. Shall we move?

SHARON *and* DEBBIE *stand,* DENISE *following, careful not to catch* TRISHA*'s eyeline. They go to the other table and sit.*

DENISE (*nervy attempt at assurance*). So what d'he say?

SHARON. The Manager? Well, kind of spluttered, you know, say'n as how this time he'd let it go, but next time, you know. So I says, cos now this other bloke's come in, I says Oh Thank You Mr Manager. I'll never do anything like this again, I promise. And so off I goes. An' still got half a dozen sachets of shampoo stuffed down me trousers, i'n't I.

Slight pause, during which DENISE *gives a glance at* TRISHA *which* TRISHA *picks up, and, during the following,* TRISHA, *very carefully and nervously comes over.*

DEBBIE. But that wa'nt all.

SHARON. Oh, no. See we, we thought the check-out girl, like needed something of a caution, so as how she wouldn't do that kind of thing again.

TRISHA. Look, Den –

DEBBIE. Eh, Den, you know, that Karen Whitaker. She went with Barry Craig. An' what he did, he gave her phone number to all his mates. So she thought she was really popular. In fact, of course, all *knew*.

SHARON. Tring tring. Hur hur.

DEBBIE. Tring tring. Hur hur.

DENISE. Tring –

They look at her.

'Hallo. It's 4–3–7, double–5–4–3.'

It's TRISHA*'s number. She goes rigid.*

DEBBIE. Well, shall we . . .

DEBBIE, SHARON *and* DENISE *get up and move back to the first table, leaving* TRISHA. TRISHA *sits.*

DENISE. So then, what happened? To the check-out girl?

SHARON. Oh, yuh, well. So we waits until she comes off,

and just, you know, five or six of us, we jostles her. A bit.
Down this side alley. Pushes her about. An' pulls her hair for
her. Just, like, to caution her.

DEBBIE. Hey, Shar, remind me, wa'n't it that chair, over
there, one slag's sat in, wa'n't that where Karen Whitaker
was sitting, night we did her face in?

*SHARON quickly gets up, goes over to TRISHA's table. She
stands there. TRISHA had just picked up her coffee to take a sip
from it, and is stuck in terror.*

Uh – sugar?

*TRISHA, with her other hand, pushes the sugar bowl towards
SHARON. SHARON picks it up.*

Ta, slag.

*She turns back to return to the other table. TRISHA is taking a sip
of her coffee, as SHARON, suddenly, turns back and bangs the
sugar back down on the table. This causes TRISHA to spill her
coffee down herself.*

I'm on a diet, i'n I.

SHARON back to the other table.

'K, let's go. You coming, Denny?

DENISE. Sure.

DEBBIE and DENISE get up.

DEBBIE (*to DENISE, as they go*). Was just a little jostle, see,
Den, so as how she'd know.

*The GIRLS go out, DENISE trying hard not to look anywhere
near TRISHA. TRISHA is left there, coffee dripping down her,
crying. Music: The Shirelles: 'Will You Still Love Me
Tomorrow'.*

Scene Fifteen

FRANCES' *flat. The next day. It is in fact immediately before the
first scene of the play. The poster book lies on the table in front of the
sofa.*

No people on the set. As the record fades, the lights come up and
with them the sound of typing.
ROSIE and FRANCES call to each other from off, each side of the
stage.

ROSIE. Hey, Frankie!

FRANCES (*stops typing*). Yuh?

ROSIE. You ready?

FRANCES. In a *minute*.

ROSIE. What you doing?

FRANCES. Finishing some minutes.

Pause. Typing.

ROSIE. Frankie!

FRANCES (*stops typing*). Yuh?

ROSIE. These girls. You're sure they're competent?

FRANCES. Look, Rosie, do stop fussing 'bout those bloody
children.

ROSIE. OK.

Pause. Typing.

ROSIE. Hey, Frankie!

FRANCES (*stops typing*). Yuh?

Bell.

ROSIE. I'll go.

ROSIE crosses the stage.
Typing continues.
Then:

ROSIE. Hey, Frankie!

FRANCES. Yuh?

ROSIE. It's just the one! The other couldn't come!

FRANCES. OK!

Typing. TRISHA *comes in with* ROSIE.

ROSIE. So she couldn't come, then, your friend?

TRISHA *shakes her head.*

But you found the place all right?

TRISHA *nods.*

Well, good.

Slight pause.

Be with you in a minute, then.

ROSIE *goes out.* TRISHA *looks round. Then she sits on the sofa. The typing stops.*

FRANCES. Hey, Rosie?

ROSIE. Yuh?

FRANCES. What did it look like?

ROSIE. What did what what?

FRANCES. Did you think it looked like rain?

TRISHA *reaches for the book. Blackout and bring up Carole King. The record sticks, and swells.*

> It might as well rain
> It might as well rain
> It might as well rain
> It might as well rain

Scene Sixteen

The same. A couple of days later. It is earlier in the evening of Scene Two *of the play. The poster book is open on the table.* BREWER *stands there. He looks at the book.*

BREWER. Jesus Christ.

He shuts the book. FRANCES *enters, with a suitcase.*

FRANCES. Well, Mr Brewer.

BREWER. Ah. You off then?

FRANCES. Yes, I am off.

BREWER. On holiday.

FRANCES. Well, if you like.

BREWER. Abroad?

FRANCES. Why, should I?

Slight pause.
BREWER *smiles.*

BREWER. No.

FRANCES. No, not abroad. In fact my parents' place. They
have this house in Suffolk. And I'm going there.

Slight pause.

I'm going home to mother.

BREWER. Yes.

Pause.

FRANCES. I mean, she'll live. I mean, it's not like
manslaughter.

BREWER. I don't think anybody –

FRANCES. Don't they?

Pause.

BREWER. I think the HM thinks, it might be an idea, if you
popped in for a chat. I think he feels it might be the best,
before you go away. Not so much because of, um, Patricia,
as Denise.

Slight pause.

FRANCES. Oh, yes. The windows, in the science block.

BREWER. Indeed.

Pause.

The social worker feels that she – the messages that she
received – made her confused.

Pause.

Hence – Kristallnacht.

FRANCES. I see.

Slight pause.

Well, then. It's very kind of you.–

BREWER (*suddenly*). You know, Frances, I'm sure you'll find this hard to credit, but I did, once, long ago, believe that it was possible to change those kids. To make them different, how I thought they should be.

FRANCES. Well, bully for –

BREWER. And, just like you, I was appalled, disgusted with their lives, their tatty fantasies, obsession with domestic and cosmetic trivia, all that, and I tried to challenge them, disrupt them, force them to see the poverty of their own vision of themselves.

But then I changed my mind. And why I changed it, and you'll find this even harder to believe, the reason was my growing feeling that it was a little, just a little arrogant on my part, to think that I knew better what was good for them than they did.

And, you know, that what you've done, is you have taken from those girls their props, supports, the things that hold up their lives, and given nothing in return. You told them that they shouldn't be their kind of person, and the only choice they had was, on the one hand, for Denise, become a man, be what she thought you wanted her to be, take on the toughness and aggression, the machismo, be a thug, a bully-boy; and, on the other hand, Patricia, cut off from her femininity, despise it, left with nothing but despair. And I don't see, frankly, what else you could think that they could do.

Pause.
With a slight, almost apologetic little smile:

Well, that's –

FRANCES *turns on* BREWER.

FRANCES. Do you – really – think I haven't thought – about *exactly* –

The sound of the door stops FRANCES.
Enter ROSIE.

ROSIE (*not sure of the situation*). Well, hallo.

BREWER (*stands*). Hallo. I'm Nick. Nick Brewer. Frances' colleague.

ROSIE. Oh, I see.

BREWER. And, now, I think, perhaps I ought to –

FRANCES. Nick's been explaining, Rosie, how he views events.

ROSIE. Oh, has he?

FRANCES. Kindly popped round to put me right on human nature.

ROSIE. Nice of him.

FRANCES. And how to tamper with it's somehow to deform the natural.

Pause.
BREWER *decides to go.*

BREWER. All right, I suppose, that I can understand, why you . . .

FRANCES. Can understand?

BREWER (*at the exit*). That's what I said.

FRANCES. You patronising shit.

Pause. BREWER *turns back.*

BREWER. All right. I won't be patronising. I'll say what I mean.

FRANCES. You do that.

BREWER. And what I *do* mean, Frances, is that frankly I don't think, for you, this business has a thing to do with those two girls.

FRANCES. You what?

BREWER. They're just a sideshow, and the star is you. And, no, I'm not going to presume to even try and guess at why you see yourself as Joan of Arc, what kink that is, what went wrong when, but the result has been that you've transferred your agonies and insecurities and pain on to two schoolgirls, and what's happened is that you've destroyed them by your arrogant conviction that their choices, what they've chosen as their lives, their interests, their dreams, are worthy of contempt. And I hope all the other girls, the Debbies and the Jackies and the Jo's, I hope if they want nothing more than to be wives and mothers, if they've chosen that, they'll realise that what you and your twisted sisters offer is a great deal less, because its content, despite all the rhetoric, is bitterness, self-hatred and despair.

BREWER *sees that* FRANCES *is crying.*

Oh, my God.

Pause.
BREWER *doesn't know what to do.*

ROSIE (*quietly*). When I was 19, I was asked to this wedding. And at the reception afterwards, met Howard. We stood near each other, giggled at the speeches, drank the fizzy wine. And then he asked me to go out with him, and I said yes, so out we went, and then he asked, well, in a month or so, if I would be engaged to him, and I said yes, and so engaged we were, and then before I knew it I was being asked if I would love and honour and obey, and I said yes, and love and honour and obey I did, and shortly after that I must have stopped the pill, cos I had Damion and three years later I had Sophie, complications and my tubes tied up, and I do not recall, throughout that happy fairy tale, one single, solitary choice at all. I never chose to get engaged. Be married. Have my children. I was chosen.

BREWER. Yes, well –

ROSIE. Now, you will know the concept of the Deja Vu. The

feeling, I've done this, been here before. It's quite disturbing.
Even more disturbing is the feeling that I had, from time to
time, throughout my happy fairy life, a feeling in the night-
time, in the darkness, of Non Deja Vu, a sense of loss of
something that I should have been, but I hadn't, sense of
never really doing, never thinking, anything; a sense of being
thought and being done. Which you will doubtless find it
hard to understand. Because, although there's limits to your
choices, you can choose and map your life. Whereas, my life,
and Trisha's, and Denise's, aren't like yours, because they are
not mappable. They're mapped.

So don't you talk to me, to Frances or to them, about free
choice. Cos, on that score, dear Nick, you just don't know
you're born.

Pause.

BREWER. All I can say . . . is that a girl tried to kill herself.

ROSIE. Oh *Christ* –

BREWER. Another girl has gone berserk, and, there, your
friend is sitting on that sofa crying. They are all unhappy.
Look at her. They are all miserable, their misery was caused
by someone in this room, and I assure you that it wasn't me.
Goodbye.

He goes out.
Pause.

ROSIE. Well, what a shit.

FRANCES. You think so?

ROSIE. Yes, of course. Don't you?

FRANCES. Don't know.

Pause.

You see, I told her that life was waste. Oh, not exactly. Not
exactly in those words. What I said was, you can have a
better life, tara tara, let me take you up the mountain, away
from all of this, and I'll show you what it could be like. What
I didn't realise was that the route, away from her own life,

towards my gleaming fantasy, turned out to go through seven plateglass windows.

(*To* ROSIE.) Just don't know.

ROSIE. It wasn't wrong. It was right, to show her how it could be different. I mean, mean, surely, it was right to show her how her life could change.

(*Quite angry.*) I mean, for Christ's sake, Frankie, how can you say that it was wrong? How could you?

FRANCES *responds fast, with some aggression*:

FRANCES. You know, when *I* was 15, I remember, was the same as poor old Trisha. Yes, I used to think, like she did, when I met him at the candy store, and when he whispered sweet and secret nothings in my ear, and when we walked off hand in hand into the sunset, that in that very moment, suddenly my whole life changed.

But still, the thing was, I did know, p'raps unlike Trisha, deep down, that the whole shebang was so much shit. It wouldn't last. The blissful moment was, by definition, just momentary.

But when I was 19, and went to college, 1968, the dawn in which of course 'twas bliss to be alive, and when I met him at the demo and he whispered sweet and secret dialectics in my ear, and when we walked off hand in hand into the sit-in, and in *that* very moment, suddenly my whole life changed . . .

I thought it had.

And even more, I needed to believe *that* tatty teenage fantasy was going to be a blueprint for The Changing Of The World.

It's simple. Thought we could change people. We were wrong.

And so, friend Rosie, I am going home.

ROSIE. Frances. Don't go.

FRANCES *stands and goes to her suitcase*.

FRANCES. Back home. Where I'll be safe.

ROSIE. Stay here. At least a day or two.

FRANCES *picks up her case.*

FRANCES. Returning back, where I belong. Back to the past. Because I liked it there.

She remembers she's forgotten something. She snaps her fingers. Puts down her case, goes out.

ROSIE. Speak for yourself. Friend Frances.

A moment. FRANCES *re-enters. She has sunglasses.*

FRANCES. Sunglasses.

ROSIE. Look, Frankie.

FRANCES. Mm?

ROSIE. Look, Frankie, I just feel I ought to say . . .

FRANCES. Go on.

ROSIE. That I know why you believe the things you do.

Pause.

FRANCES. Well, I must own that, at times like these, that's more than I –

ROSIE. Because, when you were small, you told me. You could speak of little else. And I remember – how your eyes would blaze.

Pause.

FRANCES. Well, now. How does it go? When I was a child . . . I spoke as a child, but when . . . I can't remember how it ends. Something about growing up, and you can't be childish any more. St Paul. In One Corinthians.

She makes to go, then turns back.

You see, the *real* mistake, was thinking that that need, the need to think those things, was a rational decision. To convince oneself that one had woken up, one morning, had a glance in the mirror, and *decided, seen*, that all of history's the struggle of the classes, fancy that, that capital creates the means of its own overthrow, of course, that, well I never,

there appears to be this contradiction between the social
methods of production and the private ownership of capital,
well glory be, and all those rational cosmetics, smeared in
layers across that sad and lonely, desperate little face that I
had seen, that morning, in the mirror. Blueprint, change the
world. In fact, a blueprint to escape the world. And me. And
I've been on the run, from me, this seven years, and now at
last I'm going to turn me in.

I'm sorry we were wrong.

*She goes out. ROSIE left alone. Then, ROSIE takes a decision,
and follows FRANCES out.*

Scene Seventeen

*Music fades, and lights on a hospital ward. TRISHA sits on her bed.
ROSIE stands there, carrying a leatherbound book which she gives to
TRISHA.*
TRISHA looks at the book.

ROSIE. I brought you this.

TRISHA. Oh, yuh.

ROSIE. A book, by Charlotte Bronte.

TRISHA. Thanks.

Pause.

ROSIE How are you feeling, then?

TRISHA. Well.

Rubbing her tummy, ruefully.

Bit better.

ROSIE. Yuh. Have they been nice to you? The nurses and the
doctors?

TRISHA. Yuh. Been fine.

Pause.

The sister said it wasn't natural. Like what I did. A girl like
me. A pretty girl.

ROSIE. Well, you are very pretty.

TRISHA *a slight smile at* ROSIE.

TRISHA. Mm.

Pause.

S'true about Denise? Went mad, and smashing things?

ROSIE. I think that she felt guilty.

TRISHA. Oh. She would.

ROSIE. I'm sorry . . . ?

TRISHA. Oh just always . . . F'I'd been there . . .

ROSIE. Yes? What?

TRISHA. She wouldn't have. (*Pause.*) I'm pleased you came.

ROSIE. Well, I was glad to.

Pause.
TRISHA *nods.*

I know she'd want me to, send all her very best. Because she
cares so much, for both of you.

Pause. TRISHA *bites her lip.*

TRISHA. Mm. Well.

Pause. ROSIE, *decision*:

Look, Trisha.

TRISHA. Hm?

ROSIE. Just don't – forget it. Write it off. Just don't, pretend it
never happened. You might feel, must feel that everything
has stopped, but that's not true. What's happening is that
you're changing, and that isn't good or bad, but just – it's
true.

I mean, the feeling, carnage. Feeling smashed and broken.
That is what change feels like. You are feeling change.

You see?

Pause.

TRISHA. I s'pose so.

TRISHA troubled. She turns away from ROSIE. *She sees her mirror, picks it up.*

You know perhaps she's right? The nurse. It isn't natural. A girl like me.

TRISHA looks at ROSIE:

So what else can I do?

DENISE has entered. She has a big bottle of Pernod.

DENISE. Uh. Trish.

She gives a silly wave.

TRISHA. Oh, Den. Oh, Miss. Oh, this is Den.

Pause.

My friend.

ROSIE. I sort of gathered.

She smiles, stands and goes.
DENISE *goes to* TRISHA.

DENISE. Oh, Trish. You silly cow.

TRISHA. Oh, Den. You silly cow.

A moment. Then DENISE *affectionately mocking*:

DENISE. 'So what else can I do?'

Scene Eighteen

The music fades, as soft, warm lights fade up on the terrace of a big house in Suffolk. It is early evening on a beautiful September day, in 1975. The terrace furniture, including, perhaps a rocking chair, is old, good, bleached by the sun. Perhaps the odd old and well-used wooden toy. Certainly a rather battered ball.
  COLIN *stands on the terrace. He carries a rucksack. He puts it down. He takes off his jacket. He stands there, enjoying the sun.*
  FRANCES *enters, from the house, with two whiskies. She is dressed comfortably, in shorts and a tee-shirt. It is important that her*

clothes are sufficiently ageless that similar clothes could be worn by a teenager 14 years before.

FRANCES. Well, this is it.

She hands COLIN his drink.

COLIN. So, this is how the other half . . .

FRANCES. That's right.

Pause.

COLIN. So where are they? Your people.

FRANCES. They're in Crete.

She sits.

COLIN. It is, the view is really beautiful.

FRANCES. I love this place.

COLIN *sits*.

COLIN. So what you been doing with yourself, all summer long?

FRANCES. Oh, very little. Being waited on. And playing with my nephews and my nieces. Going walkies. Lying in the sweet and sticky, British middle-class embrace.

They are, in many ways, quite wonderful.

And seeing no one. From my other life. Reading no pamphlets. Engaging in no polemics or critiques.

Brightly:

And I haven't had a fuck for three months. You have no idea how comfortable the celibate existence can be.

How's, who is it, Sarah?

COLIN. I don't know

Slight pause.

It is quite, restful, as you say.

Slight pause.

Won't last.

FRANCES. Why not?

COLIN. I've got a job. Been offered, rather. Which will be, if I take it, quite the opposite of restful.

FRANCES. What is it?

COLIN. With Granada. Want to do a series, for the 50th anniversary next year.

Slight pause.

FRANCES. The anniversary of what?

COLIN. The General Strike.

FRANCES. Ah, yes. Researching?

COLIN. And presenting part of it.

FRANCES. Colin is giving up humble pedagogy to concentrate full-time on his mediastar career?

Pause.

COLIN. Yes, well. I think it's still important. For today.

FRANCES. Oh, yes, indeed.

Pause.

So raise the curtain. Lights and music. Yet another in our series of Great Moments that went wrong. Nine days that nearly shook the world. May Days that weren't.

COLIN. You what?

FRANCES. Oh, just a theory. That I have.

Pause.

COLIN. Do you think that I should take it?

FRANCES. There's a question?

COLIN. Yes. Of course there is.

Pause.

My contact, on the programme, is approximately thirty.

Works, in average, a 12-hour day. Commutes, by train or plane, from Golden Square to Manchester. Oh, he's a thrusting fellow, as they all are, thrusting and ambitious, eyes are never still, but darting round, to check who's up, who's down, who's out. And so they make their programmes, radical, progressive, calling for the overthrow of capital and for the building of a world of cooperation and solidarity, with a zeal, a lust for competition that would make the Soviet Olympic team look positively lackadaisical. And playing out a permanent audition. In the late night restaurants, and passing round the dry white wine, and dry white liberated ladies, from research, from hand to hand. Like relay batons.

So there has to be a question, if I want to join that Conga. Doesn't there.

Pause. End of confession. He stands.

Well. You want another?

FRANCES *looks at* COLIN.

FRANCES. Oh, deal Col. Dear Peter Pan.

COLIN. You what?

FRANCES. Oh, just. I'm sorry. What I called you, night I threw you out.

You have – this quite amazing innocence. This sense of, well, you always look surprised. At what is, let's be honest, pretty obvious.

Pause.

COLIN. I see.

With a slight smile.

Well, one could ask – If I am Peter Pan. Who have I come to visit, in her Wendy House.

Pause.

I'll get the drinks.

COLIN *goes into the house. Pause. Then* FRANCES *snaps her fingers.*

FRANCES. When I became a man, I put away childish things.

She laughs.

Oh, dear. Again. An axiom that seems not to apply.

Pause.

Dear Col. Dear me. With all these vipered bosoms. All these Wendy Houses, dreamy Suffolks, Golden Squares.

Why do we still . . .

Pause.
FRANCES *puts her feet up on the chair. She puts her arms round her knees. She looks, suddenly, very much younger.*
And we notice that the lights are changing. Instead of the warmth of the evening, it's a dazzling high summer afternoon.
And ROSIE *tiptoes in behind* FRANCES. ROSIE *is dressed in shorts and a T-shirt. She – and* FRANCES *– are 13 years old. It is the summer of 1961.* ROSIE *puts her hands over* FRANCES' *eyes. A little struggle and quite a lot of giggling follows.*

ROSIE. They're gone.

FRANCES. All day. To Lowestoft.

ROSIE. To see your rich aunt. Your very very rich relations.

FRANCES. Stop it. Where have you been?

ROSIE. I went swimming. In your very very nice expensive swimming pool.

Pause.

FRANCES. I didn't know you could swim.

ROSIE. Hidden depths.

She 'swims'.

I didn't like to with your family.

Pause.

D'you think they like me?

FRANCES. Yes of course.

ROSIE. Don't think your dad does much.

FRANCES. Well I don't like him much.

ROSIE (*imitation; plummy voice*). 'Now shake a leg there Rosie.'

FRANCES (*imitation*). 'Top of the morning then old girl.'

ROSIE (*imitation*). 'Well if it isn't Frankie's little friend.'

They roll about.

FRANKIE (*imitation*). 'So what's your poison, Rosie?'

ROSIE (*imitation*). 'Well, I'll drink to that.'

FRANKIE *picks up the ball and tosses it.* ROSIE *catches it. They play with the ball. Finally,* ROSIE *stuffs the ball up her T-shirt. They giggle. The laughter subsides.*

FRANKIE. Are . . . you . . . going to have a baby?

ROSIE. I should think so. Yes.

FRANKIE. How many?

ROSIE. I told my mum I was going to have eight.

FRANKIE. That's quite a lot.

ROSIE. She said that I'd soon change my tune.

FRANKIE. Sometimes I'm not sure if we should.

Pause. ROSIE *is rolling the ball under her hand.*

ROSIE. Mm?

FRANKIE. With you know. If they're going to blow the world up anyway.

ROSIE *rolls the ball under her hand and lifts it high. She turns it.*

ROSIE. I turn ze vorld.

Pause.

I run ze vorld.

FRANKIE. Just for a day.

ROSIE *throws the ball to* FRANKIE. *They play with the ball.* FRANKIE *find the ball in front of her crutch. She holds it there and giggles.* ROSIE *giggles.*

Do you wish you'd been a boy?

ROSIE. I think my dad does.

FRANKIE. But do you?

ROSIE. Nar.

A game developing.

Hey can you do backstroke?

FRANKIE. Backstroke? Yes of course.

ROSIE. And breast-stroke?

FRANKIE *and* ROSIE *doing the breast-stroke on the bench.*

FRANKIE. Sure. (*She 'swims'.*) I'm going to be sick . . .

ROSIE. And butterfly?

It becomes very energetic. In the midst of it all:

FRANKIE. I must I must.

ROSIE. – improve my . . .

They fall back exhausted in the backstroke position. Their heads are upside down.

FRANCES. Hey. Do you think about the future?

She's pronounced it 'foocher'.

ROSIE. What, the flowers?

FRANCES (*silly*). No, the fu-ture. What will Chance to Come To Pass.

ROSIE. Not much. I mean, I don't think about it much. Not very very much.

FRANCES. I do.

Pause.

I wonder. What d'you think we'll be like in ten years time.

ROSIE. Dunno.

They change position.

ROSIE. I think we'll still be friends.

FRANKIE. Do you?

ROSIE. Oh yes, I'm sure.

Pause.

FRANKIE. Is that a promise?

ROSIE. Yuh. A promise.

FRANKIE. Cross your heart and hope to die?

Pause.

ROSIE. 'I'll drink to that.'

Pause. A questioning look.

Hey. Can we?

Pause.

FRANKIE. Yes. Why not. Go on.

ROSIE goes out to raid the drinks cupboard. COLIN enters with drinks. The lights are changing back to the September evening.

COLIN. Well, I must say, your dad's well stocked.

FRANCES (*takes her drink*). Oh, yes. He is.

As the lights have changed fully.

He's excellently stocked.

COLIN sits.

FRANCES. You know, I think I'm going back.

COLIN. Back where?

FRANCES. Back home.

COLIN. Is this not home?

FRANCES. Oh, no.

Pause.

I've passed the point, of no return. The Wendy House was smashed, oh, long ago.

Pause.

She jumps up, quite brightly, going towards the house, and turning back to COLIN.

So. Back. To all the mess and muck and guilt and failure and missed opportunity. Remembering, perhaps, occasionally, what all that pain is for.

So what else can I do?

COLIN *and* FRANCES *look at each other.*

Bring in Vivaldi's 'Winter'.

Scene Nineteen

FRANCES *stays there.* COLIN *goes. Enter* TRISHA *and* DENISE. *They are grown-ups now. And* ROSIE *enters, in adult clothes, with a wrap for* FRANCES, *as the music fades.*

TRISHA. She'd always been the dreamy one, forever longing for the one true love that would transport her into endless bliss.

FRANCES. So perhaps it was predictable that she'd get married to an up-and-coming chap in chips, and settle down.

ROSIE. And as soon as she clocked that his eye was wandering, she saw to it that she got pregnant pronto, and now she and Emma live on alimony and are blissfully content.

DENISE. She'd always been the do-or-die type, full of madcap notions, wild ideas and harebrained schemes.

FRANCES. And so maybe it wasn't much of a surprise when having quite dramatically failed a tranche of O levels, she was picked up by this bloke who took her first to London, then New York –

ROSIE. Where, via a number of adventures, she became an action painter with an arts and crafts collective off Canal St called Gynocracy.

RUTH *has entered.*

FRANCES. And *she* had always liked the writing.

RUTH. And so those who'd known her weren't too shocked to learn that she had penned a 'witty, bitter and astringent' –

ROSIE. But essentially romantic novel.

FRANCES. Well, essentially of the *genre* –

ROSIE. Which had been eagerly received by the public and the critics.

RUTH. Even though some feminist reviewers weren't quite sure how to read its tone.

FRANCES. But most importantly, for her, the book provoked a shoal of letters, from the past.

TRISHA. Dear Miss, we never knew you were an *author*.

DENISE. Miss, you never let on you wrote books.

RUTH. Dear Frances, I'm not sure if you'll recall –

FRANCES. All of which were full of quite the most surprising if not downright shocking news.

TRISHA. In fact, miss, I got work, with an employment agency. I give advice, like to young people, on pursuing a career.

DENISE. In fact, miss, I got pregnant. By an accident. And me and Josephine, we jumped the list, and got this flat.

TRISHA. And I like it cos of what they say. The ideas that they come up with, about what they want to do. I mean, they call 'em stupid, and fantastical. But I say, well, you may be right, but it's as good a place as any to begin.

DENISE. And I like it cos we got self-management, and it's muggins who gets sent down to the council – as the loudmouth one sez *they* – about things like the rubbish and the lifts and how this patch of land we got behind the flats we could use for allotments, place for things to grow.

RUTH. And in fact, I dropped out of sociology. And dropped the squatting too. And my lover got this offer, a sabbatical in Oregon. But I decided not to go, but to stay and drop back in.

And took a course. Of all things, in accountancy.

And now it's mainly mainstream stuff. But there's still some clients, co-ops, and collectives, a partnership of women plumbers, still a magazine or two. All in a state of utter shambles. All in most urgent need of auditorial first aid.

But I won't let my partners touch 'em. 'Cos they're mine.

ROSIE. And despite the fact that alimony has its limits . . .

TRISHA. And although Patricia became bitterly aware of market factors beyond anyone's control . . .

DENISE. And notwithstanding that Denise was personally blamed for everything from falling reading standards to the rise in crime . . .

RUTH. Still they had dreams.

FRANCES. And Frances wrote them down.

Pause. We begin to hear the Vivaldi again.

DENISE. And little did they think.

TRISHA. And who'd have thought,

ROSIE. And how could they have known . . .

FRANCES. That those dreams would stand them all in such good stead in the times that were to come.

The WOMEN *look at each other. A moment. The Music swells, and the lights fade.*

Maydays

Maydays was first presented by the Royal Shakespeare
Company at the Barbican Theatre, London, on 13 October
1983, with the following cast:

JEREMY CROWTHER	John Shrapnel
PAVEL LERMONTOV	Bob Peck
MIKLOS PALOCZI	Ken Bones
CLARA IVANOVNA	Stephanie Fayerman
OLD WOMAN	Brenda Peters
FORGACH	Raymond Bowers
SOVIET SOLDIERS	Richard Clifford, William Haden, Robert Clare, Robin Meredith, John Tramper
HUNGARIAN PRISONERS	Simon Clark, Floyd Bevan, Alexandra Brook
MARTIN GLASS	Antony Sher
CLARK SULLIVAN	David Troughton
CATHY WEINER	Lesley Sharp
JAMES GRAIN	Malcolm Storry
AMANDA	Alison Steadman
PHIL MANDRELL	Brian Parr
BRIAN	Phillip Walsh
JUDY	Sara Mair-Thomas
PUGACHEV	Geoffrey Freshwater
STUDENT	Floyd Bevan
POLICEMAN	Raymond Bowers
TEDDY WEINER	Don Fellows
OFFICIAL (MVD)	Robin Meredith
DETECTIVE	Geoffrey Freshwater
KOROLENKO	David Troughton
PRISONER	Simon Clark
OFFICER	William Haden
DOCTOR	Anna Fox
CHIEF OFFICER	Robin Meredith

PAPERSELLERS	William Haden, Richard Clifford, Simon Clark, Floyd Bevan, Anna Fox, John Tramper
RON	Robert Clare
LIBERTARIANS	Floyd Bevan, Alexandra Brook, Lesley Sharp
MRS GLASS	Brenda Peters
SMOKING PARTYGOER	William Haden
MOLLY	Stephanie Fayerman
OFFICIAL (FRANKFURT)	Raymond Bowers
YOUNG MAN	Brian Parr
HUGH TRELAWNEY	Tony Church
TANIA	Jayne Tottman
WOMEN	Anna Fox, Alexandra Brook, Lesley Sharp

Directed by Ron Daniels
Set designed by John Gunter
Costumes designed by Di Seymour
Music by Stephen Oliver
Lighting by Chris Ellis
Sound by John Leonard

The play takes places in England, Hungary, the United States and the Soviet Union. It begins in 1945 and ends in the early 1980s.

The play was written to use doubling extensively. It may be performed comfortably by a company of 14 men and 5 women.

Act One

It has always been an intellectual axiom that Britain is half-dead, and if there is no rallying-point abroad, some people are going to do no rallying at all. It would not occur to them that the Welfare State is worth rallying to. At home, indeed, very few causes offer themselves to the cruising rebel. No more millions out of work, no more hunger-marches, no more strikes; none at least that the rebel can take an interest in, when the strike pay-packet is likely to be as much as he gets himself for a review of Evelyn Waugh or a talk about basset-horns on the Third Programme . . .

Kingsley Amis, *Socialism and the Intellectuals*, **1956**

A number of Western commentators have stressed the role of a 'generation gap' in the rise of Soviet dissent. According to this theory, dissent is largely the work of the post-war generation. This younger generation was shocked and repelled by the revelations of its parents' complicity, whether active or passive, in Stalin's repressions; having grown up in relative security and prosperity, it is more willing to assume the risks of outspoken criticism than its elders, who cherish the peace and stability they have at last achieved. From this perspective, Soviet dissent may appear to be a local branch of the world-wide youth rebellion of the late sixties and early seventies, rejecting, like its foreign counterparts, 'bourgeois' materialism, social conformity and political hypocrisy . . .

Marshall S Shatz, *Soviet Dissent: Historical Perspectives*, **1969**

In the advanced capitalist countries, the radicalization of the working class is counteracted by a socially-engineered arrest of consciousness, and by the development and satisfaction of needs which perpetuate the servitude of the exploited . . . No economic or political changes will bring this historical continuum to a stop unless they are carried through by men who are physiologically able to experience things, and each other, outside the context of violence and exploitation.

Herbert Marcuse, *An Essay on Liberation*, **1969**

ACT ONE

Scene One

May Day, 1945. England.

Red flags fly, red banners swirl, red streamers billow. 'The Internationale' plays.

Through the hangings marches a young man, JEREMY CROWTHER, *at the age of 17. In his northern voice, nervously at first, but growing in strength, he addresses a large, enthusiastic — even triumphant — crowd.*

JEREMY CROWTHER. Comrades. This May Day of all May Days it is a privilege to deliver the fraternal greetings of the Young Communist League.

Comrades, it was the great V.I. Lenin who once said, revolutions are festivals of the oppressed and the exploited. Today of all days, the working-class has cause for festive celebration. The Great Anti-Fascist war is won. All over Europe, warmongers and capitalists are shaking in their shoes.

Comrades, we have been asked a thousand times what we mean by socialism. As throughout the continent the toiling masses rise to liberate themselves from tyranny, to fashion with their own hands their own New Jerusalem, we can at last say: *this* is what we meant.

'The Internationale' cuts out. The hangings fly away.

Scene Two

A military barracks in Budapest, 5 November 1956. Upstage, a bench, one Soviet SOLDIER *by the exit, a* 2ND SOLDIER *and a* SERGEANT *by the bench. A Hungarian civilian* PRISONER *sitting on the bench, hands on head. In addition to the scripted events in the upstage area, there is a constant bustle going on, busy people marching to and fro with papers and documents. Downstage, a little office area, with a table and three chairs, on one of which a Soviet Army* STENOGRAPHER *sits typing. On her table are a pile of files, a cardboard box, and a radio, from which an operetta tune is emanating. Two* PRISONERS *are marched in by a* 3RD SOLDIER.

3RD SOLDIER. At the double move move move.

SERGEANT. Name.

2ND PRISONER. Szilagyi, Bela.

SERGEANT. Name.

The 3RD PRISONER *does not reply.*

Name!

3RD PRISONER. Paloczi, Miklos.

SERGEANT. Sit. Hands on head.

They do so, as a Soviet lieutenant, PAVEL LERMONTOV, *comes into the office, from a side entrance. He is twenty-seven. The* STENOGRAPHER *stands quickly; after a moment, she switches off the radio.*

LERMONTOV. You like operetta, comrade?

STENOGRAPHER (*after a second*). Oh yes, comrade lieutenant, very much. Do you?

LERMONTOV. Well, yes, yes.

He looks in the cardboard box. It is full of the paraphernalia of urban guerilla war: broken milk bottles, oily rags, a piece of chain, a flick-knife, a hammer, a couple of hand-grenades. As he does so, a 4TH SOLDIER *marches a* 4TH PRISONER *into the upstage area, and the* 2ND SOLDIER *brings files into the office, puts them on the desk, and goes upstage.*

SERGEANT. Name.

4TH PRISONER. Erica Molnar.

SERGEANT. Molnar, Erica. Sit down.

She sits down as the STENOGRAPHER *reaches out to put the radio on.*

LERMONTOV. But perhaps, not now.

He picks up a file and looks through it.

STENOGRAPHER. It's a very beautiful city. Perhaps that's why they produce such beautiful music.

LERMONTOV. Yes, I think, in fact . . . Where do you come from, comrade?

STENOGRAPHER. Oh, just a small village, Comrade Lermontov.

LERMONTOV. And have you ever been to Moscow? Leningrad?

The STENOGRAPHER *shakes her head, smiling. A* 5TH PRISONER *is brought in by the* 3RD SOLDIER, *who shakes his head at the* SERGEANT.

Well, they are beautiful cities, too. And they have their music.

He's making to go upstage, as the 5TH PRISONER *sits. A thought strikes him.*

What's your name?

STENOGRAPHER. Clara Ivanovna.

LERMONTOV. No, I meant — no, that will do. Clara Ivanovna, summon for me, if you will, M. Paloczi.

The STENOGRAPHER *goes to the upper area and calls.*

STENOGRAPHER. M. Paloczi!

The SERGEANT *nods to the* 3RD PRISONER. *The* 2ND *and* 3RD SOLDIERS *pull him to his feet and push him into the office. He is* MIKLOS PALOCZI, *twenty-one years old, wearing a long grey overcoat and a slouch hat. He looks a bit like a gangster. His face is bruised and there are traces of blood. The* STENOGRAPHER *comes back to her table. The* SERGEANT *goes out.*

LERMONTOV. Sit.

> PALOCZI *sits. The* SOLDIERS *withdraw. The*
> STENOGRAPHER *picks up a notepad and pencil.*
> LERMONTOV *is consulting the file as he speaks.*

> My name is Lt Lermontov. Your name is Miklos Paloczi. You
> are twenty-one years old, and a student. You were arrested at
> three o'clock this morning, in charge of a radio transmitter
> broadcasting illegally from a lodging in the Corvin Alley
> district.

> PALOCZI *says nothing.*

> Yesterday afternoon, you made a broadcast of an apparently
> slanderous character. Your broadcast was as follows:

> *He reads:*

> 'Comrades, take care! Counter-revolutionaries are everywhere.
> No less than ten million landowners and capitalists and —
> bishops roam the country, laying waste to all that they
> survey. Even the strongholds of the proletariat have not
> escaped infection. Forty thousand aristocrats and fascists are
> on strike in Csepel, aided and abetted by the forces of
> imperialism. Comrades, vigilance! The revolution is in danger.'
> Could you explain this to me, please?

> PALOCZI *says nothing.*

> I'm afraid I don't speak Hungarian. Do you speak Russian?

> *Slight pause.*

> I speak German just a little.

> *Slight pause.*

> English?

PALOCZI. I can speak Russian. We can all speak Russian.

LERMONTOV. Good.

PALOCZI. 'Csepel' is pronounced 'Shaypell'. It is a large
industrial district to the south of Budapest. It's where a
general strike is going on. You may have heard about it.
Budapest is the city you have just invaded. It is the capital of

Hungary, an independent Republic of ten million people —

LERMONTOV. You're saying that the working-class of — Csepel, are all fascists?

Pause. PALOCZI *shakes his head.*

PALOCZI. I was being — irony. Ironical.

LERMONTOV. Comrade, I would seriously advise you not to be too clever. It was, after all, your government who invited us to aid you, in your struggle against the White Terror and reaction.

There is a commotion developing upstage. An OLD WOMAN, *dressed in black, and carrying a string bag, is forcing her way in from the street, past the* 1ST SOLDIER.

OLD WOMAN. Where are my sausages?

1ST SOLDIER. Hey, you can't go in there —

LERMONTOV. We are all well aware of where we are, and why we're here.

OLD WOMAN (*to a* 2ND SOLDIER). Hey, you! I want my sausages.

LERMONTOV *aware of the commotion.*

2ND SOLDIER. What's this?

1ST SOLDIER. I don't know, it's some old —

LERMONTOV (*to* PALOCZI). Please excuse me.

LERMONTOV *and the* STENOGRAPHER *to the doorway between the office and the upstage area.*

2ND SOLDIER (*taking the* OLD WOMAN's *arm*). Now, granny, you can't come in here.

1ST SOLDIER. She's crazy.

OLD WOMAN. Come on, where are they? Hey?

LERMONTOV (*to the* STENOGRAPHER). Find out what's going on.

STENOGRAPHER. She wants something I think.

LERMONTOV. That much is clear. Please find out what, and
why.

The STENOGRAPHER *to upstage area.*

OLD WOMAN. You said that there'd be sausages on Monday.
And some beetroot. I demand my sausages!

She breaks free.

PALOCZI. I can tell you what she wants.

STENOGRAPHER (*to* 1ST SOLDIER). What's going on?

1ST SOLDIER. Oh, some old crazy Magyar thinks we're s'posed
to feed her.

The OLD WOMAN *is trying to find her sausages. The first*
TWO SOLDIERS *in chase. The* 3RD SOLDIER *nervously*
keeping the PRISONERS *covered.*

OLD WOMAN. Where are you hiding them?

1ST SOLDIER. Now, come on, granny, off we go —

PALOCZI (*to* LERMONTOV). Till yesterday, this barracks was
a distribution centre. For the free food that the peasants
brought us from the villages.

2ND SOLDIER (*grabbing the* OLD WOMAN). There — is — no
— food. Here — is — the — army. There — is — no — entry —
here.

The OLD WOMAN *is at the exit.*

OLD WOMAN. Huh. All the same. You take the food and fuck
the peasants, eh? This time, 'the real revolution'?

The FEMALE PRISONER *laughs. The* 3RD SOLDIER
threatens her. The OLD WOMAN *spits.*

Tchah. Budapesti.

The 1ST SOLDIER *manhandles her out.* LERMONTOV
suddenly, to PALOCZI:

LERMONTOV. Free food?

PALOCZI. That's right.

LERMONTOV. The peasants bring the cities food, for nothing?

PALOCZI. You know, it's no wonder you're all told to stay inside your tanks. Or else you might find out what's happening here.

The STENOGRAPHER *returning.*

LERMONTOV. So why not tell me.

STENOGRAPHER. It was some mistake. It's sorted out, now, though. She's gone.

The STENOGRAPHER *sits and opens her notebook.*

LERMONTOV (*to* PALOCZI). So why not — *tell me*?

PALOCZI *is silent. Then a slight nod of his head towards the* STENOGRAPHER, *sitting with her pencil.*

Please leave us.

STENOGRAPHER. Beg pardon?

LERMONTOV. I said, please leave us for a moment.

STENOGRAPHER. But I was told —

LERMONTOV. Can't you hear what I am saying? Do I have to spell it out in semaphore? Please go away.

The STENOGRAPHER *goes. But on her way out, she overhears:*

They're some of them so slow and *stupid.* Villagers. They've never seen a city. So. Tell me. Why the peasants give away their food for free.

PALOCZI. You really want to know?

Slight pause.

LERMONTOV. It's my job to find out what is happening here.

Pause.

PALOCZI. Oh, well. Why not. What else have I to lose?

He takes off his hat, tosses it on the table, puts his feet up.

A dialectic, Comrade Lermontov. Thesis: 1947. I remember May Day. I was fourteen. Our liberation, from the landowners and counts. A real revolution, bubbling from below. Oh, very rushed and slapdash, but — still, real. And ours.

And then, antithesis, we found it wasn't ours, but yours. Sold to you cheap, bought from you dear. Your language and your culture papered over ours. And, if I may say so, your techniques of popular administration. And people felt betrayed. We felt betrayed .

LERMONTOV. And, synthesis?

PALOCZI. OK. A meeting. In a country town. All talk, and shouting, bickering and chaos; someone trying to organise a march on Budapest, they stopped that, someone else attempting to brew up tea on the bars of an electric fire. And a group of stolid peasants in some corner, furrowed brows, attempting to elect something or other; and they apologised, to me, I can't think why, that it was all taking such a time. You see, they hadn't actually elected anything before. They had to work out how to do it as they went along. And it was 1947 once again. And I thought, glory be. This time, it's actually real.

LERMONTOV. But communists were murdered.

PALOCZI. Were they?

LERMONTOV. Criminals and killers were set loose. Ordinary communists, good communists were lynched. Their hearts cut out.

PALOCZI. Maybe.

LERMONTOV. These things occurred.

Pause. PALOCZI *put his feet down.*

PALOCZI. Look. A revolution is a festival. Lenin said that, I was surprised to learn. And the thing about a festival is that it's very tricky to control. We have been drunk this last few weeks. For most of us, exhilaration. But for some, revenge. Mistakes get made. But the point is, that some crazy drunk stopped the collectivisation of the farms. And compulsory deliveries of food. And so the peasants loaded up their carts with everything that they could spare, and brought it here,

and gave it to the people. Because, at last, they trusted them.
You know, I imagine, comrade, 1917 was very much a
festival.

LERMONTOV. You know, you're right. I think there's been an
error.

PALOCZI. Well —

LERMONTOV. I think you're the wrong man. You are not
Miklos Paloczi.

PALOCZI. Eh?

LERMONTOV. I think it's a mistake, and you should go.

He's marking the file. Quickly:

Go now. Go anywhere. You can still get to the border. Now!

PALOCZI *stands, his face is white.*

PALOCZI. Why, Comrade Lermontov?

LERMONTOV (*deliberately*). Because — I am of the view —
that revolutions should correct mistakes. If they are not to
lose the people's trust. And so — I'm trusting you.

Slight pause.

The border! Now!

PALOCZI (*blurted*). Will I get five yards beyond that door?

LERMONTOV. Maybe. Who knows?

PALOCZI. Give me your revolver.

LERMONTOV. You know I can't do that.

PALOCZI. I won't get far without it.

LERMONTOV. I can't go that far.

Slight pause. LERMONTOV *goes to the box of confiscated
weapons, and finds the grenade. He hands it to* PALOCZI.

Take that. It is — a sort of hand grenade.

PALOCZI *grins, puts his hat on, turns to go.*

How long?

PALOCZI. How — what?

LERMONTOV. For how long, do you think, will peasants give their food away? A month? A year? For ever?

Pause.

PALOCZI. Maybe. Who knows.

He looks at the grenade and smiles.

It's one of ours.

LERMONTOV *nods to the side door, and* PALOCZI *slips out.* LERMONTOV *makes another note on* PALOCZI's *file. There is a burst of gunfire from offstage.* LERMONTOV *looks towards it. Then, quickly, to the upstage area:*

LERMONTOV. Next!

TWO SOLDIERS *jab and shove the* 5TH PRISONER *into the office. He is extremely elegant, in his good overcoat and jewellery. He is* COUNT ISTVAN FORGACH. *The* SOLDIERS *go out.*

Russian?

Pause.

English?

Pause.

German?

FORGACH. Fluently.

LERMONTOV *looks at* FORGACH. *Then he looks through the files.*

LERMONTOV. Name.

FORGACH. I am Count Istvan Forgach.

LERMONTOV. Address?

FORGACH. Up until the 27th of October, the labour mines at Piliszentivan.

LERMONTOV. Since then?

FORGACH. The Gellert Hotel.

LERMONTOV. Occupation?

LERMONTOV *turns to* FORGACH, *having found the file.*
FORGACH *smiles.*

I mean, before.

FORGACH. Oh, I'd say . . . class enemy.

LERMONTOV. Are you a fascist?

FORGACH. Well . . .

A shruggy smile.

You know, before the war, we had a saying that seems to me
appropriate. Anti-semitism, it was said, is hating the Jews
more than is absolutely necessary.

LERMONTOV. What?

FORGACH. I'm a Hungarian.

A shout from outside.

VOICE: Help! Help me, please . . .

LERMONTOV. What's that?

A YOUNG SOLDIER *rushes into the upper area. He is badly
burnt. His hands in front of his face, his uniform ripped and
charred. He is followed by the* 1ST SOLDIER. *The* OTHER
SOLDIERS *rush to his aid, one turning back to cover the*
PRISONERS. *The* STENOGRAPHER *appears.*

YOUNG SOLDIER. Oh, Holy Mother help me.

LERMONTOV *towards the upper area, drawing a revolver.*

FORGACH. It appears to be some class of commotion.

1ST SOLDIER (*to* 2ND SOLDIER). A doctor, get a doctor,
quick.

The STENOGRAPHER *to the* YOUNG SOLDIER *as the*
2ND SOLDIER *runs out.*

YOUNG SOLDIER. Oh, no. God have mercy on me. Help me.
Please.

The STENOGRAPHER *and the* 1ST SOLDIER *help out the*
YOUNG SOLDIER. *We still hear him crying.* FORGACH
takes out a thin black cigar and lights it.

The STENOGRAPHER *re-enters to* LERMONTOV.

STENOGRAPHER. It's terrible. A barricade. And no one there. He stopped and opened up his tank, to take a look . . . They think, it was a young man with a hand-grenade . . .

LERMONTOV *turns, back into the office.*

FORGACH (*smiling, with a little wave*). Quite simple. God save Hungary.

LERMONTOV *shoots* FORGACH *twice.* FORGACH *slumps to the floor.* STENOGRAPHER *enters the office.*

STENOGRAPHER. What — happened?

LERMONTOV. Shot, while trying to escape.

Pause. The STENOGRAPHER *looks round.*

STENOGRAPHER. Where is — Where's the other one?

LERMONTOV. He wasn't who we thought he was. It was a mix-up. Such things happen. All the time.

STENOGRAPHER. There was some shooting, out there. Just before . . .

LERMONTOV. Apparently, they missed.

He strides out quickly. The STENOGRAPHER *looks at* FORGACH. *She realises he's still alive.*

FORGACH. Please. Help me.

Scene Three

Spring, 1962.
The stage is empty. A seventeen-year old schoolboy, MARTIN GLASS, *stands alone in the middle of the parade ground of a minor public school. He wears army uniform, on which is prominently pinned the badge of the Campaign for Nuclear Disarmament. It is pouring with rain.* MARTIN *is dripping wet. He's been out here for some considerable time.*

A SCHOOLMASTER *cycles on to the stage. He is* JEREMY CROWTHER. *He is thirty-three, he wears a black plastic mac and a black sou'wester. He cycles round, then cycles to*

MARTIN, *stops, and dismounts.*
   MARTIN *comes to attention.*

JEREMY. Uh — Glass, isn't it?

MARTIN. Glass, Martin B., yes, sir.

   Slight pause.

JEREMY. It's — pretty wet out here, Glass.

MARTIN. Yes, it is that, sir.

   Slight pause.

JEREMY. Now, you're in St Augustine, am I right?

MARTIN. No, sir. Sir Thomas More.

JEREMY. I see.

   Slight pause.

   Well, um, whatever, shouldn't you be there? I mean, parade
   fell out, what, best part of two hours ago.

   Slight pause.

   Glass, what are you doing here?

MARTIN. I was ordered to stay here, sir. After fall-out, sir. By
   Mr Sands. The adjutant.

JEREMY. Yes. Why?

MARTIN. Gross disrespect for the queen's uniform, sir.

   JEREMY *is forced to acknowledge* MARTIN's *badge.*

JEREMY. Oh, yes. Of course. Did Mr Sands give any indication
   of how long . . .

MARTIN. Till further notice, sir.

JEREMY. I see.

   Pause. JEREMY *looks up to the sky.*

   You know, it's quite interesting . . . The shape, I mean the
   actual construction of the symbol . . .

MARTIN. Is it, sir?

JEREMY. Yes. It's very clever, the, uh, two arms at the bottom,

are the semaphore for N, nuclear, the top bit is the
semaphore for D, disarmament, the middle as a whole's the
broken cross, symbolic of the death of man, while the circle,
you see, represents the unborn child . . . look, this is
madness, you'll catch your death, I think you must come in.

MARTIN. Is that an order, sir?

JEREMY. Well, if you like.

MARTIN. It's not really a question of what I like.

JEREMY. All right, then. It's an order.

MARTIN (*to attention*). Sir!

Then MARTIN *breaks attention and makes to go.*

JEREMY. Look, Glass . . . Sir Thomas More is miles away. My
cottage is just over there. I think you ought to get something
hot inside you.

MARTIN *turns back to him.*

MARTIN. Yes, sir. Fucking right.

A transfer. MARTIN *leaves with the bicycle,* JEREMY *comes
downstage and starts to take off his waterproofs, as a table
and three chairs — on one of which hangs* MARTIN's *sodden
uniform — are set up behind him.* JEREMY *calls offstage.*

JEREMY. So what did he say then?

MARTIN (*off*). Who, sir?

JEREMY. Mr Sands.

MARTIN (*off*). Oh, it wasn't so much 'say', sir, as 'harangue'.
The matter of my class seemed to figure large. Apparently,
my attitude to the H-bomb is a consequence of my people's
income.

Enter MARTIN, *rubbing his hair with a towel.*

JEREMY. Why, are they very rich?

MARTIN. No, sir. My pa's a vicar. He's got a bit of private
income, but it's been considerably eroded over recent years.

JEREMY. I'm sorry.

MARTIN. Well — his own fault, as it happens.

JEREMY. Oh. How so?

MARTIN. After the Sharpeville massacre, he insisted that we sell our shares in anything that had connections with South Africa. He didn't re-invest too wisely. Pretty tough to make ends meet.

JEREMY. Do you want some Horlicks?

MARTIN. You bet. Thanks.

He sits and sips a mug of Horlicks at the table.

JEREMY. Why do they keep you here, then?

MARTIN. Oh, I think . . . some sad, pathetic concept of propriety. My mother's concept, that is. She's a very proper woman. You know, the type who thinks the *dolce vita's* something you look up in Baedeker.

JEREMY laughs.

I mean, like the vicarage is next door to a US Air Force base, bang in the fucking firing line, so she supports the annihilation of the species as a simple point of social etiquette. You know.

JEREMY laughs again.

I mean they've got a 1957 Morris Oxford. And when they come to Speech Day, she insists they park it half a mile away and walk. So as not to Show Me Up, As if I cared.

JEREMY. You sound as if you care.

MARTIN. Well, it makes me angry. My mother, trying to ape those people who could buy us up, and all we've got, and not bother with the change.

JEREMY (*with a gesture to the badge on* MARTIN's *tunic*). And that? That makes you angry too?

MARTIN. Not in the same way, no, sir. That is because it's right. As I imagine you think too.

JEREMY. Well, as it happens, I have sat down in my time.

MARTIN. Gosh, have you, sir? And been arrested?

JEREMY. Nearly. Twice.

During this speech, MARTIN takes out ten cigarettes, and a box of matches. He takes out a cigarette and opens the matches. They are sodden. JEREMY looking on in some panic.

MARTIN. Then I imagine you'd resent as much as I do the idea you want to ban the bomb because you want to kill your mother. Kind of, kindergarten Freud, I imagine you'd regard it, sir.

JEREMY. Well, yes.

MARTIN. Look, sir. I'm sorry, but it has been quite a day. Do you have a light?

JEREMY. A light?

MARTIN rattles the damp matches.

Look, strictly speaking . . .

As he finds a box of matches and gives them to MARTIN, lamely:

They're terribly bad for you.

MARTIN (*lighting up*). I'm always keen to see, sir, how far people are prepared to go.

JEREMY. Well, are you now.

MARTIN. And in your case, sir, it's particularly interesting to me, how you end up here at all.

JEREMY. Why's that?

MARTIN. Being a communist, and so on.

Pause.

JEREMY. Um . . .

MARTIN. Bit of a turn up for the books, I'd say.

JEREMY. What makes you —

MARTIN. Wavish, Roger P., in Kant, has this pa who was a red at Trinity. For a birthday present, he gave me a copy of the *Daily Worker* for the day that I was born. May the second, 1945.

Slight pause.

I assume that you're the same J.H. Crowther, sir?
'Throughout the continent, the toiling masses rise'?

Pause.

JEREMY. Well —

MARTIN. I mean, a ban-the-bomber, you could be a Methodist
or a vegetarian or something. But actually in The Party.
Wavish and I view that as really cool.

Pause.

JEREMY. Well, I'm afraid I'm not in it any more.

MARTIN. Why not, sir?

JEREMY. Because I left it over Hungary.

Slight pause.

Well, more accurately, I left it at the time of Hungary. It was
actually 'over' what were called my 'obstinately opportunist
tendencies'. Or, put another way . . . Look, is this of any
interest at all?

MARTIN (*sweetly*). Oh, very much so, sir.

Slight pause.

JEREMY. Well, it was really very simple. They sent this
apparatchik up, to explain the line. Those brave, wild
revolutionaries in the streets of Budapest, 'objectively' the
agents of imperialism. And I thought then — oh, come on, do
you really want this man to run the country? And I left. And
it was — just like that.

MARTIN. And you ended up —

JEREMY (*sharply*). I picked this place out with a pin. It seemed
a reasonable alternative to busking in the Underground,
that's all.

MARTIN. But, really? Just Like That?

Pause.

JEREMY. All right, then. Look. I didn't go to Trinity. In fact,

I was born in Halifax. And although my family would not
have known an opportunist tendency had one leant over and
bit them — in fact they thought that reading stunted growth
— we all knew people who had elder brothers, fathers,
friends, who were either near or in the Party. And some of
them, the best of them, went off to Spain. And the very best
of those did not come back.

And so when *we* came of age, when it was all over, the
thirties, and the war, we had this feeling we were fifteen
years too young. And I tell you, there's no stranger feeling
than the feeling that instead of being past it, it's past you.

And what we'd missed, of course, was all the glory. All
that certainty, that once you'd cracked the shackles of the
system, every man indeed would be an Aristotle or a
Michelangelo. Because in a way, it had already happened.
And it hadn't turned out how we thought it would at all. Oh,
it was decent, sure, and reasonably caring, in its bureaucratic
way . . . And indeed there was full employment and high
wages and although there was still some miserable poverty,
there was less of it than there'd ever been before . . . And, for
us, of course, we did particularly well, there were
scholarships, and places at the less pretentious redbrick
universities, and some of us wrote poetry, and others novels,
and some were published, and some not . . . And we worked
on literary magazines, or the Third Programme, or we
didn't . . .

But you realise there's something missing. The working
class is freer than it's ever been. But somewhere, in the
no-man's-land between private affluence and public squalor,
somewhere inside the Hoover Automatic or the Mini-Cooper,
behind the television or underneath the gramophone, those
wonderful possessions . . . You hear a kind of scream. The
scream of the possessed.

And you realise there's all the difference in the world,
between liberty and liberation.

MARTIN *has taken a manuscript from his pocket.*

JEREMY (*a glance at his watch*). Now look, old boy —

MARTIN *suddenly jumps on a chair and reads his manuscript:*

MARTIN. And like a peace bomb a still gentle bomb a shalom bomb a non-bomb a still small voice on the switchback a still sane whisper on the wheel

Written on walls of houses fallen written amid bomb site rubble in the spaces in the skyline

Tattooed on the translucent flesh of the children of the ashes the daughters of the dustbowl the class of August 1945

Carved in the gravestones of the nations of the dead and etched like acid on the frontal lobes of the poisoned gnomes who live beneath the earth the Kremlin gremlins and the Penta-megamen

Etcetera, etcetera . . .

The single word — Resist.

He gets down.

It's called *Beyond.* I'm aware that it's derivative. But I imagine I'll grow out of that. The title's after Sartre. He said that he was only interested, now, in what lies beyond despair.

He looks at JEREMY.

Not bang in the middle of it, Mr Crowther.

JEREMY. Well. I suppose — touché.

MARTIN *takes off the dressing-gown and gets dressed.*

MARTIN. You see, I think —

JEREMY. Yes, what?

MARTIN. For you, sir, the mass of people seem to be, just victims. Passive and inert. To be pitied, yes, to be the object of your agonised compassion . . . But basically, a lump of stodge. Whereas, in my view, there will come a time, when you'll hear that scream in unison. And when you do, when they've really cracked the shackles of the system for themselves — who knows how many Michelangelos could bloom?

He makes to go.

JEREMY. You're right. Of course.

MARTIN. I'm sorry, sir?

JEREMY. Oh, yes. But perhaps, who knows, there'll come a time we'll find some brave wild kids on *our* side of the wire, who'll do it, really get it right. *This* time.

You see, it wasn't 'just like that'. In fact, it smashed my life.

Pause.

MARTIN. Sir, I do think I understand. I'm sure that, if I was you, I'd wish I'd been a red — at Trinity or anywhere — who'd been to Spain.

He turns and goes. JEREMY *looks at the poem, which* MARTIN *left on the table.*

JEREMY. 'And even to be glimpsed behind the tired and chicken-wired eyes of those who cannot quite remember what it was to feel alive . . .'

He looks up. To himself:

Not 'just like that', remotely.

Scene Four

A railway track in Northern California. Summer, 1967. The track runs upstage/downstage. A young man with a bullhorn, CLARK SULLIVAN. *He shouts at a group of anti-draft* PROTESTERS:

CLARK. Let's go let's go let's go let's go let's go.

The PROTESTERS *run and sit on the track, downstage.* MARTIN *at the side.* CLARK *to the stragglers, including* MARTIN:

Let's *go.*

MARTIN *runs to join the* PROTESTERS *sitting on the track as the train enters from upstage centre. It judders to a halt a few feet from the* PROTESTERS.

Now we don't have too much time here, people. Everyone link arms. If you don't know the person next to you, say hi.

To two MALE PROTESTERS:

Hey, give us a hand up here.

As CLARK *is hoisted on to the two* PROTESTER's *shoulders,* MARTIN *speaks to the* YOUNG WOMAN *next to him.*

MARTIN. Hallo. I'm Martin Glass.

CATHY. Hi there. I'm Cathy Weiner.

MARTIN. I'm from Britain.

CATHY. You don't say.

CLARK *speaking upstage, towards the train, through the bullhorn:*

CLARK. Good morning, fellow Americans. I am speaking to you on behalf of the Butch Cassidy Division of the Bay Area Brigade of the Draft Resisters International.

MARTIN. Who is this guy?

CATHY. His name's Clark Sullivan. He's big in the Movement round these parts.

MARTIN. Well, so it would appear.

CLARK. We have stopped your train in order to tell you why we think you should quit the army now and refuse to fight their scabby, skunky little war.

CATHY. His father's the President of Petroleum Incorporated of Connecticut. His mother's in the DAR. He's into smashing American Imperialism.

MARTIN. Yes.

CLARK. You been told by the Man that you're going out there to kill a lot of little yellow people dressed in black pyjamas who could not eat shit. Well, we're here to tell you that those ginks out there are winning. And the only ass that's going to get kicked is yours.

CATHY. Oh-oh.

NATIONAL GUARDSMEN, *wearing gasmasks, running in and forming a line either side of the track.* CLARK *turns to the* PROTESTERS.

CLARK. 'There does come a time.'

PROTESTERS. There comes a time.

CLARK. When the operation of the machine —

PROTESTERS. When the operation of the machine —

CLARK. Becomes so odious —

PROTESTERS. So odious —

CLARK. Makes you sick at heart —

PROTESTERS. So sick at heart —

CLARK. That you can't take part, and you've got to put your bodies on the gears —

PROTESTERS. The gears!

CLARK. And on the wheels —

PROTESTERS. The wheels!

CLARK. On the levers, on all the apparatus —

PROTESTERS. All the apparatus!

CLARK. And you've got to make it stop.

The NATIONAL GUARDSMEN *are in place. Silence.*

OK now, boys and girls. For the next five minutes, we have got to be like the Panthers. Be like the freedom fighters of the world. We must be the Vietnamese.

Pause. The clink and clunk of tear gas cannisters being loaded into launchers. MARTIN *whispers.*

MARTIN. What happens now?

CATHY. Well, I guess there'll be some tear-gas. And they'll move in, I'd imagine, with their night-sticks. And it's ten to one we'll all get busted, and we'll all get hurt.

MARTIN. And then?

CATHY. I guess — we stop the war.

Slight pause.

Have you seen *The Battle of Algiers?*

OFFICER. Fire!

Launchers fired. The stage fills with smoke. The
GUARDSMEN move in. Then, darkness.

Scene Five

In the darkness, the voice of JAMES GRAIN, *through a*
microphone.

JAMES. Comrades, my name is Grain, and I'm on the Central
Committee of an organisation called Socialist Vanguard.

Lights on.
   A meeting hall in a students union in the Midlands, May
1968. JAMES GRAIN *is thirty-five.*

Comrades, this is an extraordinary meeting, and it is a
measure of the extraordinary epoch through which we are
moving. As countless speakers have stated here today, we
have witnessed, over the last five months, events that would
have seemed unthinkable even a year ago. The Tet offensive
of the National Liberation Front in Vietnam. The *de facto*
resignation of the President of the United States. Most of all,
today, in France, not just ten thousand students but ten
million workers pose a challenge, not only to this policy or
that, or even to this government or that, but to the power
and legitimacy of the state itself. And we can see it even
here.

   But, comrades, forgive me for one note of caution.
Comrades, read the writing on the wall.

He gestures to the banners that we imagine are hung around
the hall.

'Don't demand: occupy.' Yes, that's fine. And 'Victory to
the NLF.' That's good as well, that's right, we don't want
peace in Vietnam, but victory.

   'The Revolution is the Festival of the Oppressed.' That's
very good indeed. But in fact, it's only half the story.

   It's a quote from Lenin. Yes, I'm afraid so, Lenin. Let me

read the whole of it to you.

He reads:

'Revolutions are festivals of the oppressed and exploited . . .
At such times the people are capable of performing miracles.
But we shall be traitors and betrayers of the revolution, if
we do not use the festive energy of the masses to wage a
ruthless and self-sacrificing struggle for the direct and
decisive path . . .'

What is that path? Where should we go? To coin another
slogan: What Is To Be Done?

Pause. He looks round.

Let me explain.

Scene Six

*And old house in the Midlands, May 1968. Mid-evening. Upstage
is a sitting-room area, with old furniture, a black and white TV
set, sleeping bags. Downstage is the eating part of the kitchen: a
table, chairs, a washing line with nappies, a plastic clothes
basket.*

Between the two areas, an old duplicator on which PHIL *is
running off a leaflet. He's twenty, from Birmingham. The
duplicator run finishes.* PHIL *removes the stencil as* CLARK
SULLIVAN *enters with a rucksack. He puts it down.* PHIL *is
standing with the inky stencil and its backing sheet, not
knowing what to do.* CLARK *goes to the clothes line, takes
down a nappy, tosses it in the plastic basket, and clips the
stencil on to the clothes line.*

PHIL. Ah. Smart thinking.

CLARK. Don't mention it. How many pages?

PHIL. Eight or nine.

CLARK *takes all the nappies down, and puts them in the
basket.*

Even smarter.

PHIL *sees the rucksack.*

Where are you off to?

CLARK. California.

PHIL (*not really listening*). Oh, ar?

PHIL putting a new stencil on. CLARK takes an envelope from his pocket, and clips that, too, on to the clothes line. Then he picks up the rucksack and goes out. PHIL tries to start the machine.

Oh, come on. Just for mother, eh?

He kicks the machine. It starts.

I love you.

As PHIL takes the already duplicated pages from the basket, kneels on the floor and lays them out to collate, AMANDA enters from another part of the house, with a tray of dirty mugs. She notes the duplicator, the stencil on the line, but not, as he is obscured, PHIL. AMANDA is twenty-one.

AMANDA. I don't believe this.

PHIL pops his head up.

PHIL. So then, what d'you think?

AMANDA. Of what?

PHIL. The Roneo. I got it, knock down, from the Catholic Association. I wasn't sure they'd take to selling off their surplus to the Socialist Society, so I told 'em I was from the Hockey Club. Apparently, they needed cash for a trip to Lourdes.

The machine stops.

They could have taken this along as well.

He hits the machine. It goes.

Ave Maria.

Enter MARTIN from the street. He now wears a moustache.

AMANDA. Martin.

MARTIN. Amanda.

AMANDA (*taking the tray into the kitchen*). How was the conference?

MARTIN. Weren't you there?

AMANDA (*off*). Of course I wasn't there. I was dragging Tania all round fucking Lipton's, wasn't I?

MARTIN. Par for the course. Maoists all morning, Trots all afternoon.

AMANDA (*off*). Which Trots?

MARTIN. SV.

AMANDA *reappears*. PHIL *changing the stencil*.

AMANDA. Take care, sir. You speak of the Party I love.

MARTIN. I know.

CATHY *appears from elsewhere in the house. She wears a jacket over a nightie, and woolly socks. She goes through to the kitchen, singing.*

CATHY. 'All the leaves are brown, all the leaves are brown, and the sky is grey . . .'

She has gone.

AMANDA. Now, where are the Leeds Two, I wonder?

Doorbell.

Ah. They've lost another key.

She goes to answer the door. During the following, CATHY appears with a plate of raw vegetables, goes to the upstage area, sits, and reads a book as she eats.

PHIL. Red Barcelona. Spanish Civil War.

MARTIN. Beg pardon?

PHIL. Cautionary tale. In 1937, Catalonia. The anarchists collectivised the factories, the farms, the trains, the cinemas, the stores. Even the greyhound tracks. But then the communists decided that the Revolution had to wait, in the interests of defeating Franco, and the anarchists were smashed. By the communists, that is. Five Days in May. Five hundred dead.

MARTIN. Point, Phil.

PHIL. The CP, 1937. The SV, 1968. In my view, anyway. Same glint. Same steely eye. Same cast of mind.

MARTIN (*helping* PHIL *with his duplicating*). Well, my basic problem with the Socialist Vanguard is more prosaic. It's that, if you want to be a member, they tell you the ten funniest jokes in the history of the world —

PHIL. And if you don't smile once —

PHIL. } You're in.
MARTIN.

AMANDA *has brought in* JAMES GRAIN.

JAMES. Good evening. I'm James Grain.

MARTIN. Oh, yes. Hallo.

JAMES. And I assure you, I'm a laugh a minute.

AMANDA. Sit down, James.

JAMES. Thank you.

JAMES *sits at the table.* PHIL *returns to his work.*

And you are Martin Glass.

A bang at the door. Enter BRIAN *and* JUDY. *They are students from Leeds.*

BRIAN. Hi, Mand.

JUDY. Hi, Mand.

AMANDA, Hi, Bri. Hi, Jude.

JUDY. Hi, Mart.

MARTIN. Hi, Jude. Hi, Bri.

BRIAN. Hi, Phil.

PHIL. Hi, Bri.

JUDY. Hey, news.

BRIAN. Yur, right.

JUDY. Hi, Cath.

CATHY (*waving*). Hi, hi.

BRIAN puts on the television.

JAMES. I'm finding this a bit hard to work out.

We see the flicker of the television on the faces of BRIAN and JUDY, who are watching the Nine O'Clock News.

AMANDA. Brian and Judy are from Leeds, for the conference. Martin and Phil are my permanent lodgers. Cathy and Clark are my temporary lodgers. Clark is evading conscription, and so Martin sweetly told him he could crash. Martin met them in America. He spent a summer out there. Way out.

JAMES. Yes, I know. I read his pieces in — what was it? *Insurrection?*

MARTIN. *Stick Up.*

JAMES. Yes. Led me to think, in fact, it might be time you joined.

MARTIN. I'm not exactly what you'd call a joiner.

JAMES. Then perhaps you're not exactly what I'd call a revolutionary.

Pause.

MARTIN. Which party would you recommend?

JAMES. Socialist Vanguard is a revolutionary grouping of militant youth, students, intellectuals and above all, workers. We are not to be confused with the Socialist Alliance, from whom we split, or the Left Opposition, who split from us, or Workers' Struggle, who split from them, or with the League for Revolutionary Socialism, who never split at all, they just burn people out, hence the ten funniest jokes joke, which was first used about them when you were still in nappies. We should also be distinguished, in passing, from the Revolutionary Marxist Fraction, the International Communist Current, and the Marxist Workers' Tendency. All clear so far?

MARTIN. Yes. Absolutely. What's the difference?

JAMES. They're wrong and we're right.

MARTIN. Right about what?

JAMES. Well, where to start.

Pause. JAMES gives a slight nod to AMANDA, who goes upstage. She watches television, but with half an ear on MARTIN and JAMES' conversation.

I'd say — primarily — we're right in being internationalists. In ascribing the failure of the Soviet Revolution — and indeed of the other revolutions made in its image — to the Stalinist betrayal, the attempt to build socialism in one country. And we're right too to believe that what is going on today in almost every Western country — what you describe so elegantly in your articles about America — is in many ways a genuinely revolutionary phenomenon.

MARTIN. Well, good.

JAMES. The rejection of the centralised rigidities of old left politics.

MARTIN. I'd go along with that.

JAMES. The creation in their stead of a new left politics in which the means and ends of revolution are the same.

MARTIN. Well, I couldn't put it better my —

JAMES. A politics defined primarily by the belief that it is possible to build the New Jerusalem within the very belly of the monster, not in the future, but in the here-and-now.

MARTIN. I think, in fact, that's how I put it. Glad that you agree.

JAMES. I think, in fact, about your articles, the word I used was 'elegant'.

Pause.

MARTIN. Go on.

JAMES. Well, the fact is, for a start, that in your articles, you used the word 'working', as an adjective preceding 'class', precisely once. In a sentence full, as I recall, of dismissive references to motor-cars and Hoover Automatics.

Slight pause.

MARTIN. Yes, I see.

JAMES. Not sure you do. Look. For twenty years or so, the
myth's been growing that the Western working class has been
bought off, sucked in, and that the future for the Revolution
lay with peasants in Bolivia, or blacks in the cities of America,
or students, or communards in San Francisco or Vermont,
or with anyone, except the working class. In many learned
volumes, in many different ways. But do you know what's
happening? Catastrophe. The workers haven't got round to
reading all these worthy tomes. They haven't heard they've
been sucked in. Someone forgot to tell them, obviously, and
so ten million of them, silly fools, are out on strike in France
today.

MARTIN. Sparked off by whom?

JAMES. Oh, the students. Absolutely. The disaffected young.
The freaks, the anarchists. But it didn't end there, and it
couldn't end there. Which is why we're in the business of
turning freaks and anarchists and hippies into revolutionary
socialists, and not the other way round.

MARTIN. You mean, turn.

He makes the peace sign — Churchill's Victory-V

to

He makes the clenched-fist sign.

JAMES. Well, if you like.

MARTIN. Not sure I do.

JAMES. Then do ask yourself the question, if we don't, where
they will be in five years time, when the carnival is over, and
it's back to the long haul? Where will *you* be?

MARTIN. I'm sorry, I don't understand.

JAMES. They will find that in the long-term it just doesn't
work. That, ultimately, all the communes and collectives and
co-operatives do not confront the basic issue of the
ownership of capital. And when they realise that violence

and greed and xenophobia are not the products of men's minds but of their circumstances, they will either drift away, so slowly they don't notice, or they'll take revenge upon the inadequacies of the world by turning to the bullet and the bomb, the weapons of despair.

So it is legitimate to ask of them, of you, of everyone who claims to be a revolutionary: what sacrifices are *you* prepared to make, to prove that you're a real traitor to your class, that you're not just — on holiday?

Pause. MARTIN suddenly turns, goes upstage and out. AMANDA stands there.

AMANDA. Well, I suppose — it's only rock and roll.

JAMES comes upstage.

JAMES. What's going on?

BRIAN. Troop movements outside Paris. And they've stopped Cohn-Bendit coming back to France.

JUDY. And the CGT have prevented students talking to the Citroen workers.

BRIAN. Renault.

JUDY. Sorry.

BRIAN. Renault-Billancourt.

AMANDA. And the CP says the situation isn't revolutionary.

BRIAN. Well, that's it, back to Ronan Point.

AMANDA switches off the television.

PHIL. Just watch it all come down.

PHIL goes back to his duplicator.

CATHY (*suddenly*). Hey, has anyone seen Clark?

Head-shaking. PHIL doesn't hear until during:

You know, big guy, with the moustache and the long hair and the funny accent? Must have noticed him around —

PHIL. Here, earlier. Said, going out.

CATHY. Out where?

PHIL. Um . . .

CATHY. Jesus.

PHIL. Colchester.

CATHY. Where's Colchester?

PHIL. Or Canterbury? Something. Ca. I'm sorry. Somewhere, sounds like 'California'.

JAMES (*to* AMANDA). I ought to go.

CATHY. Like *California?*

> JAMES *goes to pick up his file.* CATHY *rapidly goes out, bumping into the re-entering* MARTIN. MARTIN *has some documents.*

Excuse *me.*

> *She is gone.* MARTIN *quickly to* JAMES *at the table.*

MARTIN. My father is a clergyman. He doles out opiate to the masses three times every Sunday. And his father had a little money, and when I was twenty-one, a portion of it came to me.

> *He takes out a lighter and sets fire to the documents, which are share certificates.*

Phoenix Assurance, ordinary, 50, British Petroleum, ordinary, 25 —

> *The* OTHERS *reacting.*

AMANDA. Hey, Martin —

MARTIN. Unigate Dairies, preferential, 60, Beechams —

> AMANDA *runs into the kitchen.*

PHIL. Jesus Christ.

MARTIN. Ordinary, 70 —

JUDY. What's going on?

MARTIN. The estimated value of the whole portfolio —

> AMANDA *rushes back in with a saucepan of water.*

AMANDA. For God's sake, put that lot in here —

MARTIN. Two thousand, seven hundred —

AMANDA grabs the flaming certificates and throws them in the saucepan.

AMANDA. There.

Pause.

PHIL. Hey, wow.

Pause.

JAMES. You idiot. If you hadn't wanted them, you should have given them to us.

Pause. PHIL, BRIAN and JUDY return upstage.

MARTIN. I'm sorry. That was quite ridiculous.

JAMES. In fact, you can write off, and they'll send you duplicates.

Slight pause.

I'm just sorry that you missed the point, that's all.

MARTIN. What do you mean?

CATHY re-enters hurriedly. Her brow furrowed, she looks round the room. Then she sees the note on the washing line. She goes over, opens it and reads, as:

JAMES. I mean that I frankly couldn't give a toss about your guilty conscience, I don't even care if you're repressing latent homosexuality, or if you really want to kill your mother. All that bothers me, and the point that I was trying to make, is that until you purge that guilt, until you sacrifice your individual conscience, then you will be frankly useless to the business which now faces us.

MARTIN. Which is?

JAMES. The building of a party strong and hard and disciplined enough to provide at least the means whereby the masses can seize human history. That's all.

MARTIN (*suddenly, to* AMANDA). Do you agree with this?

AMANDA. Yes. Yes, of course I do.

Pause. CATHY has read the note. In it, a pendant on a chain.

CATHY. You shit.

(*To* PHIL). You shit. You . . . Fucking Canterbury.

She runs into the kitchen.

PHIL. Obviously wrong.

Pause.

AMANDA. Martin. It would be wonderful if it could all be nice. Make love not war. CND marchers, singing 'We Shall Overcome', as they shuffle through a dripping English Easter afternoon. But there comes a point, there really does, when you have to think about the other side.

JAMES. Hear hear.

AMANDA. Like, my father-in-law is in the building trade. Employs three men. And treats them better than he treats himself. How could it possibly be moral, right or good, to take that firm away from him? But the point is that that little firm is just the bottom of a pyramid. And at the top sit General Motors, Boeing, Standard Oil and Chase Manhattan. And he understands that if they go, he goes. And there are millions like him. Who come the crunch will take up arms, will fight and maim and kill, to keep that pyramid in place.

JAMES. Yes. There is that phrase of Trotsky's.

MARTIN. What's that?

JAMES. Human dust.

Pause.

PHIL. Red Barcelona.

Pause.

MARTIN. Yes.

He turns to BRIAN *and* JUDY.

Now, look, it's ten to ten, does anybody fancy one before they close?

CATHY *has reappeared. She's still very angry. She has the note in one hand, the pendant in the other.*

CATHY. Now I have, before you guys depart. To raise a certain matter.

Slight pause.

It's about my grapefruit. Now to you, it may be just a yellow, spherical . . . But it's kind of vital to my dietary requirements. Do you dig? I mean, I have to eat a half a grapefruit every half a day.

Slight pause.

Now, you people mustn't get me wrong here. The communal life. Right on. But I'll thank you, nonetheless . . . I'll thank you all . . . to leave my food alone.

Pause.

AMANDA. We're talking about grapefruit?

CATHY. Yes.

Pause. She crumples the note in her hand.

He wants to be the fucking Vietcong. Petroleum Incorporated. Joining up. To be the fucking Santa Barbara division of the Vietcong.

Pause. She plays the pendant through her fingers.

Burn baby burn.
To Bring The War On Home.

Pause. She bangs her temple with the flat of her hand.

Please excuse me.

She goes out.

JUDY. Bri, you go.

BRIAN. Beg pardon?

JUDY. Shan't be long. You go.

JUDY goes out after CATHY. Pause.

PHIL. Her dad was in the Party in the thirties. Lot of guilt there. Lot of mess. Hard to snap your fingers, will it all away.

He goes out with MARTIN, to the street. BRIAN follows. JAMES and AMANDA left alone.

JAMES. I think I must go now.

AMANDA. Oh, must you?

JAMES. Catch the last train. I've a meeting, early in the morning.

AMANDA. Well, of course.

Pause.

I've got some scotch, I think, in case you'd like one for the road.

JAMES. Well, that might be very nice.

AMANDA *goes into the kitchen, returning with half a bottle of scotch and two glasses. She pours.*

AMANDA. And in fact . . . In fact, there is a train at 7.30 in the morning. Gets you into London, oh, by half past nine.

Slight pause.

If you should care to . . .

JAMES. Well, that might be even nicer.

AMANDA *gives* JAMES *his scotch.*

Father-in-law?

AMANDA. We separated. Shortly after Tania —

JAMES. Yes.

Pause.

AMANDA. Let's go and fuck, OK?

She walks upstage, JAMES *following, as* MARTIN *burst back in.*

MARTIN. Look —

AMANDA *and* JAMES *stop.*

Look, the point is, that I didn't mean . . .

He clocks some of the situation.

But I have decided. No.

Slight pause.

JAMES. Well, history will have to muddle on without you, Martin.

He looks to AMANDA, *who gestures the direction of the stairs.* JAMES *goes out.* AMANDA *follows.* MARTIN *left alone.*

Scene Seven

Red Square, Moscow. August 1968.

   A couple of POLICEMEN. *Two men downstage. One is a rather dusty-looking man of thirty-five or so, a cigarette hanging from his mouth. His name is* PUGACHEV. *The other man is* LERMONTOV, *now thirty-nine.*

LERMONTOV. Comrade Pugachev.

PUGACHEV. Comrade Lermontov.

LERMONTOV. Leonid Sergeyevich, doctor of philology, candidate member, the Academy of Sciences.

PUGACHEV (*not sure of the point*). Pavel Mikhailovich, translator, the Institute of African and Asian Peoples. What is going on?

LERMONTOV (*striding off*). We are going on a scientific expedition.

PUGACHEV (*following, unhappily*). In Red Square?

LERMONTOV. That's right. Because this is where it happened.

PUGACHEV. Speaking in English?

LERMONTOV. They will think it is some obscure Islamic dialect. They will think we are tourists from Tadzhikistan.

PUGACHEV. Tourists don't do this.

LERMONTOV. This is the first place.

PUGACHEV. I have never seen a tourist doing this.

LERMONTOV. This is the position of the pram, wheeled by the poetess. Who meets the other six, who have converged on the square from different directions, choosing this spot because it's nowhere near a traffic lane.

   Pause.

PUGACHEV. I see.

LERMONTOV. The poetess reaches under the mattress of the pram — under her baby — and produces banners. One bears the ancient Polish slogan: 'For your freedom — and for ours'.

PUGACHEV (*making to go*). Yes, fine, Pavel —

LERMONTOV. And if you take another step, I will shout out what the other banner said, in Russian.

PUGACHEV *stops*.

PUGACHEV. All right. Just make it quick.

LERMONTOV. They sit here, on the ground. A whistle blows. KGB men, in civilian clothes, rush from all sides.

PUGACHEV (*looking round warily*). Yes, they have a tendency to do that.

LERMONTOV. As they run, they shout: 'Look at those Jews and traitors!'

PUGACHEV. And that too.

LERMONTOV. The art historian is here, when they hit him in the face and break his teeth. The physicist is here, when they hit him with a heavy suitcase. The cars arrive there, there and there, and take the six away. The mother and her baby sit here for ten minutes, till they come and take her too. They beat her in the car. The other slogan reads: 'Hands off Czechoslovakia'.

Pause.

PUGACHEV. Yes, of course I heard about it. There was a meeting at the Institute, to condemn the hooligans.

LERMONTOV. I am assembling a petition.

PUGACHEV. Comparisons were drawn with those student anarchists who used to read out dirty poetry in Mayakovsky Square. Schoolboys, attention seekers, juvenile delinquents.

LERMONTOV. The petition quotes the Soviet Constitution, Article one hundred twenty-five —

PUGACHEV. Look, Pavel, I'm sure it's all a terrible mistake —

LERMONTOV. I was in Hungary. I was sure that was a terrible mistake. Till I saw it happening again.

Pause.

PUGACHEV. I don't think I've ever seen you quite this angry.

LERMONTOV. I have been quite this angry only twice before. Once was in Hungary. The other was when I learnt about my father.

Slight pause. PUGACHEV *looks miserable.*

He'd joined the Komsomol in 1923. In 1931, he volunteered to help collectivise the peasantry. And when he realised that what that actually meant was helping to annihilate the peasantry, he was arrested, charged and tried for 'insufficient revolutionary vigilance'.

PUGACHEV. Uh — was he — ?

LERMONTOV. No, as it happens, he was rehabilitated, just in time to die defending Leningrad. It had all been 'a terrible mistake'.

Slight pause.

PUGACHEV. Look, can we go now, please, Pavel?

LERMONTOV. My petition reads —

PUGACHEV. I'm afraid my memories are less, dramatic.

LERMONTOV. To the Procurator General, the Union —

PUGACHEV. I just remember living with three other families in a freezing room divided by old sheets hung from the ceiling.
And being hungry from the age of eight to the age of seventeen.
Look, of course I'm on their side.
But a demonstration, seen by no one. Lasting 20 seconds.
Now, that is just — ridiculous.
I'm so sorry, Pavel Mikhailovich.

He goes. The POLICEMEN *look at* LERMONTOV.
LERMONTOV *takes a paper from his pocket. He unfolds it.
It's a map.*

LERMONTOV (*to the* POLICEMEN). I think — I'm lost.

Scene Eight

A corridor in a building in Leeds University. October, 1969. A sprayed slogan: THE UNIVERSITY OF LIFE. *Off the corridor, an office, with a desk. On it, a telephone, and a certain amount of mess, paper cups, beer cans, etc.* JEREMY *is in the corridor, looking at the slogan. He wears an overcoat, and carries a briefcase and a copy of 'The Times'. A knot of* STUDENTS, *a little way away, in animated discussion.*

JEREMY. Sadly, in fact, the University of Leeds.

JEREMY *turns to go into the office. One of the* STUDENTS *notices* JEREMY. *It's* JUDY.

JUDY. What the hell — (*Coming over to* JEREMY.) Excuse me, 'scuse me —

JEREMY. Yes?

JUDY. Who are you?

JEREMY. My name is Crowther. I teach English Studies. This is my office. Who are you?

JUDY. Can I ask you, how you got in here?

JEREMY. I walked in.

JUDY. Through the lobby?

JEREMY. No, the mezzanine. It's easier, from where I park my car. Why d'you ask?

JUDY (*calls to the other* STUDENTS). The mezzanine!

A couple of STUDENTS *rush out. Another* STUDENT — *it's* BRIAN — *comes over to* JEREMY *and* JUDY.

JUDY. I'm sorry, but you shouldn't have got in. The building's occupied.

JEREMY. I see. By whom?

JUDY. By us.

JEREMY. Who's us?

JUDY. The student's union.

JEREMY. I thought you had a building of your own.

Very slight pause.

I'm sorry, what I mean is —

BRIAN. Hi. The reason for this occupation is that the University is allowing military recruitment on campus. Specifically, the TA has a stall here, for the freshers, in the lobby of this building. Please — do have a leaflet.

JEREMY. Thank you.

BRIAN. Not at all.

JEREMY. Well, now, look, I'm sure it's most objectionable —

JEREMY *looking at the leaflet, as he speaks.*

BRIAN. Then why don't you object?

JEREMY. But I have got three months mail . . . And a class to give, as well . . .

BRIAN. I rather doubt if they'll turn up.

JEREMY. And actually —

JUDY. Oh, go on, teacher. Be a traitor to your class.

JEREMY (*snaps*). Are you aware . . . that, in this document, you have, at a cursory glance, split four infinitives?

JUDY *and* BRIAN *look at each other.*

And are you, I just ask for information, actually serious in claiming that this — seat of learning is 'a velvet glove, wrapped round the fist of neo-fascism'?

Slight pause.

That's f-a-s-*h*-i-s-m?

JUDY. Look, it's very simple. Military recruitment —

JEREMY (*moving to the door at his office*). Yes, I fully understand the *casus belli,* but I must insist —

JUDY (*blocking* JEREMY). Beg pardon? *Casus* what?

JUDY *and* JEREMY *glare at each other.*

JEREMY. It's an expression, taken from the Latin. Latin is a language, spoken many years ago in Italy —

JUDY. My pa was in the war. Conscripted, from a back-to-back in Huddersfield. He didn't see an inside tap till he was seventeen. At 19 half his face was blown away, on a beach in Normandy called Gold.
   You take one step, I'll kick your balls in, sir.

Pause.

JEREMY. I fought for this. I fought for you. Wrote articles. Gave evidence to commissions. To cut a clearing in the groves of academe, for People Just Like You.

BRIAN. Well, thanks a bunch.

JEREMY. But a demonstration, in a corridor. Now that is just — ridiculous.

JUDY. I'm sorry, Mr Crowther.

A STUDENT runs in.

STUDENT. Hey. Pigs, swarming through the fucking mezzanine.

BRIAN. Let's go.

JEREMY. I am — if you'd just listen — on your bloody side.

He realises he's alone. He takes out his keys, goes to the office. Realises the door is ajar. Pushes it open. He goes in. Drinks in the scene. He sits. In a sudden gesture, he sweeps the paper cups and debris off the desk. Then he unfolds 'The Times', which is open at the letters page. He circles a letter with a pen.

'Dear Sir, I would like to bring to your attention . . . the case of P.M. Lermontov . . .'

He picks up the telephone, dials 0:

Hallo, could you get me Directory —
I'm sorry?
The revolution is the festival of *what?*

He puts the phone down. A moment. Then he stands, goes into the corridor as two POLICEMEN run in.

POLICEMAN. Ah, professor. Have you seen — ?

JEREMY. Now, chance'd be a fine thing.

Pointing:

Thataway.

Scene Nine

The voice of RICHARD NIXON, *speaking on 30th April, 1970.*

RICHARD NIXON. Tonight, American and South Vietnamese units will attack the headquarters of the entire communist military operation in South Vietnam. This key control centre has been occupied by the North Vietnamese and Vietcong for five years, in blatant violation of Cambodia's neutrality. This is not an invasion of Cambodia.

AMANDA's *house. 1st May, 1970.* CATHY *sits cross-legged on the floor, downstage, wearing stereo headphones, connected to a record player, playing a pile of singles. We cannot hear the music.*

Upstage, AMANDA *and* TEDDY WEINER, CATHY's *father. He wears a light overcoat and carries a briefcase. He is fifty-two years old.* NIXON's *voice comes from the TV news.* AMANDA *switches it off.*

AMANDA. The first of May 1970. First May Day of the new decade. And your president goes mad.

WEINER *puts down his case, lays his overcoat over it.*

How did you hear?

WEINER. They have a telex at the conference. It's quite a story, after all. His father's a big wheel in oil.

AMANDA. I know.

WEINER *looks at* AMANDA.
WEINER. 'The second time as farce.'

WEINER *goes downstage to* CATHY. *He pulls up a chair, sits.*
Hi there.

CATHY *pulls off the earphones, looks at him.*

CATHY. Oh, Dad. What are you doing here?

WEINER. I've come to share my daughter's grief.

CATHY. You've come to 'share'?

Pause.

WEINER. What can I say?

CATHY *looks away.*

AMANDA. You could — you could explain, to both of us — 'the second time as farce'.

MARTIN *and* PHIL *come in. They are dressed in vaguely paramilitary gear —* MARTIN *in bits and pieces of his old school army uniform — a little bruised and battered, but in high good spirits.*

MARTIN. Well, have we not had the very merriest of May Days.

PHIL. Have we not indeed.

MARTIN. I should make it clear from the outset that I am
actually a member of the Warwickshire County Cricket Club,
and thus am entirely within my rights to use club premises,
although the rules are mute about doing so at three a.m. in
possession of eight cans of weedkiller. And, indeed, all would
have been quite cool had not the authorities decided to
floodlight the wicket and surround the bloody thing with ten
feet of barbed wire.

He picks up some of the atmosphere.

Good afternoon. I'm sorry, my name's Glass, this is my best
pal Phil, we live here, we have been arrested, beaten up,
we've spent the day in jail, it's not a matter of cosmic
significance, of course, but —

PHIL. Mart.

MARTIN. Um — yes? Hallo? Who is this person, please?

AMANDA. Clark Sullivan was blown up by his own bomb at a
US Air Force Base in Southern California early yesterday.

Slight pause.

And this is Cathy's father.

PHIL. Wow.

WEINER. It's a quotation from Karl Marx. It used to mean a lot
to me. It's a passage about history repeating. Events
occurring, as one might say, twice. First time as tragedy —

AMANDA. The second time as farce. Yes, sure. I know the
reference. That doesn't quite answer my question.

WEINER. OK. You want an answer, you can have one. Of a sort.

Slight pause.

Imagine, if you will, a people. As it happens, mine. Who were
suffering the most terrible and brutal persecutions, and who
one day slipped away. In the early years of this, what was
bound to be the most glorious of all the centuries. And who
came, in dribs and drabs, to the greatest city in the greatest
country in the world, a place where even then the buildings

scraped the sky, and set to work, to earn a future for
themselves and for their children.

But, then, quite suddenly, for reasons that at first seemed
quite obscure and even arbitrary, their world crashed down
around them. And they watched the little they'd created
lessen, and then crumble to an ash between their fingers. And
perhaps they felt it was their fault, their punishment, for
having had such dreams about themselves.

But we, their children, who'd been born in the great city,
we didn't feel we were to blame. And some of us, who
travelled through the city to its seats of learning, we met
older men, who *proved* to us we weren't to blame, and, even
more who proved to us who was to blame, and even more
who explained to us the reason for the whole of human
history, the way it was, the way it is, and how, by the
application of man's reason, all of it could change. And if all
of that wasn't marvellous enough, they told us, we would be
the ones to change it. And we looked before us to the City
of the Future, to a light so dazzling and sharp that nothing
was distinct but everything was glorious.

But of course there was a price to pay, for the privilege of
this exclusive vision, and we were told we'd have to sacrifice
our own opinions, our own thoughts, and submit ourselves to
orders from above that often seemed odd, confused, and
contradictory; and even, sometimes, just plain evil. But we
willed ourselves to do it, and indeed there was a pleasure in
that exercise of will, there was a passion in the sacrifice, just
like the scoring pain of staring into light, which by the very
sharpness of its blinding celebrates the fact that if you
wanted to, you'd see.

But then, there came a war. And in countries far away
from us, but still quite near for our mothers and our fathers,
a real sacrifice was being made, whose victims had not chosen
it themselves, but had been chosen. And it was cruel and
terrible beyond all reason, and our mothers and our fathers,
who'd escaped it all those years ago, closed up their eyes,
tight shut, and tried not to admit to anybody, least of all
themselves, the guilt they felt that they weren't there.

But their children's eyes were open. And we looked back

to the future, to another country, which, if any country was the future, we had always seen as the very apogee of reason. And for some the vision was still radiantly bright, opaque with brilliance. But for others, somehow, in the interim, the light had faded just enough, for shapes and outlines to appear, for them to see. And what we thought we glimpsed, then knew we saw, was corpses.

And if unreason led to piles of corpses, and if reason led to piles of corpses, too, then where were we to go?

And where we did go was the place that we'd been all the time, but not been of, the very place our fathers came to all those years ago. And to our great surprise, we found that we were welcome in the country of our birth, we were offered places at its seats of learning, on its journals of distinction, in its arts. And everything was fine.

Until that is, we realised there was a price to pay for this as well. And the price was information, on our brothers and sisters who'd been left behind, still in the cold. And as the questions were barked out, and answered, as careers were ruined and lives broken, we closed up our eyes, tight shut, and tried not to admit to anybody, least of all ourselves, the guilt we felt that we weren't there.

But then the winds abated, as winds will, and we could settle down to writing — sometimes, we proposed a mild reform or two; to administration — sometimes we disposed as well; and most of all to teaching, values of compassion, morality and justice, to other people's children and our own.

But then, there came the final, dreadful irony. Our children, without our blessing or encouragement, decided to avenge us. And to wield those self-same weapons, of compassion and morality and justice, against the country that, they thought, had persecuted and excluded us. But when they realised that what they were avenging was not our persecution, but our silence, not our suffering, but our desperate guilt, they turned those weapons on us.

And they kicked away the ladders we had climbed. And even spurned the books we'd read to them. And although there was so much we could remember of ourselves, there was a kind of madness and unreason in their fury that we couldn't recognise.

But you were, as you so often pointed out, you were our children.

Directly to CATHY:

And for a while, it was just you. But pretty soon we noticed you'd got company. The company of spoiled brats, from swanky homes, whose families had never known one day of poverty.

To MARTIN:

You see, friend, you discover that the rich are very greedy. It's not enough that they have money and possessions. They want virtue too. They want to feel they're spiritually superior. And to get that feeling in a form that lets you think that everything is someone else's fault, that you are not responsible to anybody or for anything, well, boy, that's truly wonderful.

He finds a piece of paper and scribbles a number. He gives the paper to AMANDA.

Look, that's my number for the week. Try and have her call me there, OK?

He goes.

MARTIN. Please tell me, why does everyone assume —

CATHY. He's right, of course. We blew it, kiddies, literally.

She takes a small tab from the pendant that CLARK *left her.*

But still . . . we made the news today, oh boy.

MARTIN. What's that?

CATHY. What do you think it is?

She takes the tab. She puts on the headphones. She puts on the record player.

PHIL. The error was the weedkiller. We should have trashed the fucking thing. Burn, babies, burn.

He flails out. CATHY *half hums, half sings along with the record she is playing to herself. Meanwhile, upstage a transformation is beginning: red flags wave, red banners swirl, smoke billows. The roar of railway engines.*

AMANDA. Today is May Day. We must all remember all the May Days. The Paris Commune and the General Strike. The Prague Spring and the May events in France. Red Barcelona. Red Bavaria.

MARTIN. I want to join. I never want to think, or feel, or be, like that.

AMANDA. We must remember, we must absolutely not forget the superhuman things that human beings can and have achieved.

MARTIN. I want to be a traitor to my class.

AMANDA. You want to join?

MARTIN. This May Day of all May Days.

AMANDA *goes and finds a membership card. Upstage, a small prisoner detail enters on one side, an MVD OFFICIAL on the other. The* PRISONER *is* LERMONTOV. *The banners and flags decorate a Moscow railway station. The smoke is the steam of the engines.*

OFFICIAL. Prisoner detail, halt! Name!

LERMONTOV. Lermontov.

AMANDA *gives* MARTIN *the membership card. He fills it in, as:*

OFFICIAL. First name and patronymic!

LERMONTOV. Pavel Mikhailovich.

OFFICIAL. Term! Article!

LERMONTOV. Three years. One nine oh one.

OFFICIAL. Don't say that no one warned you, comrade. Happy May Day.

The OFFICIAL *turns and walks out. The* DETAIL *remains.* MARTIN *hands the card to* AMANDA.

AMANDA. Well? What does it feel like?

MARTIN (*deflated, but smiling*). I have no idea.

CATHY *pulls off her headphones.*

CATHY. It's May Day. Mayday Mayday.

Act Two

Marxism can effect a dissociation from personal identity very like that experienced by the protagonist in tragic drama. Having entrusted his imagination, his centre of reality, to the historical process, the Marxist revolutionary trains himself to accept a diminished range and validity of private regard. The logic, the emotional authority of the historical, even where it entails destruction and humiliation to his own person, surpasses the claims, the intensity of the self. Doom is accepted, almost acquiesced in, as being part of the historical truth and forward motion in which individual existence anchors its meaning . . .

George Steiner, *Language and Silence,* **1969**

I allowed myself to be forced into the position of feeling guilty not only about my own indecisions, but about the very virtues of love and pity and a passion for personal freedom which had brought me close to Communism. The Communists told me that these feelings were 'bourgeois'. The Communist, having joined the Party, has to castrate himself of the reasons which made him one.

Stephen Spender, *The God that Failed,* **1949**

Whatever the shades of individual attitudes, as a rule the intellectual ex-Communist ceases to oppose capitalism. Often he rallies to its defence, and he brings to this job the lack of scruple, the narrow-mindedness, the disregard for truth, and the intense hatred with which Stalinism has inbred him. He remains a sectarian. He is an inverted Stalinist. He continues to see the world in white and black, but now the colours are differently distributed. As a Communist he saw no difference between Fascists and social democrats. As an anti-Communist, he sees no difference between Nazism and Communism. Once, he accepted the Party's claim to infallibility; now he believes himself to be infallible. Having once been caught by the 'greatest illusion', he is now obsessed by the greatest disillusionment of our time.

Isaac Deutscher, *Heretics and Renegades,* **1955**

ACT TWO

Scene One

Spots tight on PHIL. *He reads from a used stencil.*

PHIL. One.

Karl Marx was wrong. The working class has not become more immiserated and thus more conscious of itself. It has become richer and less conscious of itself. Two.

What has happened is that capitalism has mutated. Mass production has led to an increasing, stultifying, numbing universe of things. A stereo in every fridge. A family saloon in every tumble-dryer. Three.

We begin to grow aware of movement behind PHIL. *Men and women running, and taking up positions.*

This we call the society of the spectacle. The theatre of struggle has thus shifted from the factory to the supermarket. The ideology of consumption is the consumption of ideology. The working class is owned by what it buys. Four.

Behind this system of constraints there lies an increasingly sophisticated state machine of co-option and repression. Five.

The old left is trapped in old ideas. The real revolutionaries in our society are blacks, gays and women, disaffected youth who demand the right not to be forced to work, the so-called mad refusing to accept the 'logic' of an insane world. Six.

Sirens begin to wail. More people moving in behind PHIL.

To unite these groups we must provide examples of the possibility of change. The bullet and the bomb are not the real revolution but they are real metaphors of revolution. Seven.

An action of guerilla warfare serves to show that the
power of the state can never be invincible. Such action will
destroy this myth, even if we are destroyed ourselves thereby.
We are the harbingers of the coming storm. We are the
whirlwind.

*Suddenly, the stage is flooded with the light of car
headlamps.* PHIL *is surrounded by armed* POLICEMEN *and*
WOMEN, *their handguns aimed directly at him.*
    A DETECTIVE *steps forward.*

So I wrote this?
You are claiming that I duplicated this?
What's wrong with that?

DETECTIVE. Well, for a start, because it's crazy, Phil.

Scene Two

*The Hospital Camp in Dubrovlag camp complex in Mordovia,
the Soviet Union. Autumn 1971. Evening.*
    A row of naked light bulbs. Two PRISONERS, *in grey
quilted jackets, sit on a bench in the outer area of a guardhouse.
In front of them, on the ground, a stretcher, on which lies a*
PRISONER *under a rough blanket.*
    One of the sitting prisoners is a young man called
KOROLENKO. *The other is* LERMONTOV.

KOROLENKO. Dubrovlag. Oak Forest Camp. Garden of Eden.

He looks at LERMONTOV, *who says nothing.*

Hey. Adam and Eve. First communists. Know why?

LERMONTOV *looks at* KOROLENKO.

No clothes, one apple between them, and they thought they
were in paradise.

KOROLENKO *laughs.* LERMONTOV *a slight smile.*

All right. D'you know what's similar, between the Garden of
Eden and the Great Soviet Socialist Democracy?

LERMONTOV. No, tell me.

KOROLENKO. God creates Eve, says to Adam, go on, choose a woman.

LERMONTOV (*smiles, turning away*). Mm.

KOROLENKO. OK. What will Lenin Boulevard be called in twenty years?

LERMONTOV. I've no idea.

KOROLENKO. You're under arrest.

LERMONTOV *laughs*.

So. What you in for?

LERMONTOV. Me? I spoke to the wrong people.

KOROLENKO. Oh, ar? Different with me. I spoke to the right people.

LERMONTOV. What d'you mean?

An OFFICER *enters briskly.* KOROLENKO *leaps to his feet,* LERMONTOV *stands more formally.*

KOROLENKO. Please, sir. Please, Comrade Sir.

OFFICER. Yes, what?

KOROLENKO. Please, Comrade Sir. We need an escort. To take this patient back to the ward, sir.

OFFICER. Patient?

KOROLENKO. Yes, sir. He's had an operation. The anaesthetic will be wearing off.

OFFICER. An operation? Anaesthetic? What d'you think I am? A doctor?

KOROLENKO. No, sir.

OFFICER. Well, then. There you are.

He strides out. KOROLENKO *looks at the* PRISONER *on the stretcher.*

KOROLENKO. Do you think he's waking up?

LERMONTOV. Don't think so.

KOROLENKO. No.

They sit.

Well, it all started, something of a cockup, really. See, I was working in the coalmines, in Donetsk, you know it?

LERMONTOV. Well, I've heard of it.

KOROLENKO. And there were all kinds of problems. Safety regulations weren't being met. Dangerous build-ups of methane gas. And we weren't being paid our proper Sunday bonuses. So a gang of us, well, got together, and refused to work Red Saturdays. And we all got dismissed.

Well, this didn't seem quite fair to me.

So I went to Moscow. They allow you to, three days. And I went to the offices of the Praesidium of the Supreme Soviet. Huge reception rooms. Hundreds of people, milling round. You mill around for hours.

Then finally you see a grey man in a little booth. And he asks you what you've come to say. And so I did.

And after some time, with me telling and him listening, he calls up another man and he takes me off to hospital. And I say, look, I'm fine, I don't feel ill at all. And they say, yes, well, comrade, that's the point.

They said I had 'a mania for struggling for justice'. And I said, well, so did V.I. Lenin. Didn't he? I mean, if it hadn't been for V.I. Lenin, mania-ing away for justice, we'd still have the tsar. Mean, wouldn't we? And so they tell me I am obviously suffering from 'grandiose delusions' too.

They took me home. To a hospital at home. And injected me with sulphur. And I *did* feel ill, then, very ill. And after three or four months, they released me.

But, still, it didn't seem to me to be particularly fair.

So I started writing letters. Well, I wasn't going to go to Moscow, after last time, was I? So I wrote to Comrade Brezhnev, and to Comrade Kosygin, and the Comrade President Podgorny. And to many other comrades. But, apparently, these comrades, these great men, are of a highly nervous and susceptible disposition, because, lo 'n' behold, I gets hauled up in court *again*, accused of causing 'em considerable agitation. And apparently, I found, there is this cunning little law . . .

But I've only three weeks left. And then I'm free. Look on the bright side, eh?

Pause.

So, who d'you talk to, then?

LERMONTOV. I'm sorry?

KOROLENKO. Said, you talked to the wrong people.

LERMONTOV. Yes. I assembled a petition. And I sent the text to *Pravda*. They decided that they didn't have the space to print it, so I gave it to the *New York Times*.

KOROLENKO. Oh, we'll They don't take kindly to that kind of thing, now do they?

LERMONTOV. No. There are several cunning little laws.

A WOMAN DOCTOR, in civilian clothes, enters briskly, KOROLENKO leaps up. LERMONTOV follows.

KOROLENKO. Ah, doctor. Comrade Doctor.

The DOCTOR carries on.

Comrade Doctor!

The DOCTOR turns.

DOCTOR. Yes?

KOROLENKO. We are the stretcher party, Comrade Doctor. We need an escort, for this prisoner. To return him to his ward.

Slight pause.

DOCTOR. Am I a doctor?

KOROLENKO. Yes?

DOCTOR. Am I an escort?

KOROLENKO. No?

DOCTOR. Do you need a doctor, or an escort?

KOROLENKO. Well —

The DOCTOR goes quickly out. The PRISONER moves slightly.

He's coming round! He definitely moved!

Silence.

LERMONTOV. What was his operation?

KOROLENKO. Oh, an ironmonger's job.

LERMONTOV. I'm sorry?

KOROLENKO. Kettle spout. Spoon handle. Bits of barbed
wire. Stuff like that.

Slight pause.

Not for the first time, either. This one, once swallowed an
entire set of dominoes.

He sits. LERMONTOV *sits. Pause.*

You writing in here, then? Things for the West, in here?

LERMONTOV *says nothing.*

I sometimes think, if people only knew . . .

Pause.

LERMONTOV. Then what?

KOROLENKO. It wouldn't happen.

LERMONTOV. No?

Pause.

Look, I have a friend. In Moscow. His name's Leonid
Pugachev. And it's a good name, because there is a squat and
ugly English dog, a snub-nosed little creature, but with great
energy and affection, they call a pug-dog. Well, that is my
friend. And he's a university professor: and he has most of
what our society can offer; a good job, good apartment,
foreign travel, even, sometimes, to the West, to conferences,
and symposia . . . And he knows. Of course he know.

KOROLENKO. Think so?

LERMONTOV. And I think also of a writer whom I don't know
personally and I doubt if I ever shall. Called C.I. Kaminskaya,
who writes articles in *Izvestia*. And who once wrote an article
on me. An extraordinary polemic. Misfit, renegade. And my
fear is that C.I. Kaminskaya really is the trumpet of this

people. That the dumb hatred she expresses really is the general will.

KOROLENKO. Oh, yes?

LERMONTOV. And there is someone else who occupies my mind.

KOROLENKO. Who's that?

LERMONTOV. My friend. Apparently, they say, that somewhere on the further reaches of this wilderness of camps, there is a prisoner who fought at Kronstadt. Who has been here ever since that sailors' rising was put down by Trotsky, fifty years ago. And that old man has seen Utopia's refuse pile up all around him, all those years: all those generations of class enemies, class traitors, ists and iks and ites: adventurists, capitulationists, and Mensheviks and schizophrenics; Trotskyites, Bukharinites and Titoites . . . Until the pile of shit and sewerage, the effluent of paradise, rose up to drown the spires and steeples of the city . . . And through all of them this old man passes, like a ghost, our Holy Fool. And having seen it all, says nothing.

Pause.

KOROLENKO. So you are writing then.

Pause.

Writing things like that down, for the West.

Pause.

I'm out in three weeks, me.

Slight pause.

LERMONTOV. What is your name?

KOROLENKO. I'm Anatoly Korolenko.

LERMONTOV. From Donetsk.

KOROLENKO. That's right. And your name?

LERMONTOV. Pavel Lermontov.

Pause.

How can a human being not trust someone?

KOROLENKO. That's the spirit.

Pause. A CHIEF OFFICER enters. KOROLENKO leaps to his feet. LERMONTOV follows, quicker.

Chief Officer! Chief Comrade Officer! Two prisoners require an escort to transport this prisoner to his ward, Comrade Chief Officer Chief Sir.

Pause.

CHIEF OFFICER. Is this — are you complaining?

KOROLENKO. No, sir!

CHIEF OFFICER. Do you want the cooler?

KOROLENKO. No, sir!

Slight pause.

CHIEF OFFICER. Right.

The CHIEF OFFICER goes out. The two men remain at attention.

KOROLENKO. I think you're wrong. I think there's millions out there. Misfits. Sure.

Two clangs — a hammer on a rail. Slight pause. Two more. KOROLENKO breaks his stance. Outraged:

And now it's Lights Out. *Lights Out.* We're still *here.*

He throws himself on the bench. The PRISONER coming round.

PRISONER. Uh? Wha?

LERMONTOV. My friend. How often must you be betrayed, before you feel despair?

Blackout.

Scene Three

JEREMY CROWTHER's *house in London, February 1972. Darkness — we're in the middle of a power cut.* JEREMY,

*now forty-four, appears with a lit candelabra. MARTIN — now
twenty-seven — is there too.*

JEREMY. The university gave it to me. I put it round, I already
  had a watch.

MARTIN. Yes, I think I get one as an heirloom.

  Slight pause.

JEREMY. Look, would you like a drink?

MARTIN. No thanks. Unless you've got a bitter lemon, or a —

JEREMY. Well, I'm sure I've something on those lines.

  JEREMY *goes to the drinks table.*

MARTIN. It's my effort at revolutionary discipline.

JEREMY (*pouring drink*). Oh, yes. I see.

  Slight pause.

  I don't recall you as a person that amenable to discipline.

MARTIN. Well, people change.

JEREMY. Indeed, they do.

  He brings over MARTIN's *drink.*

  So, you're in London now?

MARTIN. That's right. Stoke Newington.

JEREMY. Of course. And did you finish your MA?

MARTIN. Uh — no.

JEREMY. I see. So, what —

MARTIN. Oh, I'm doing it full time.

JEREMY. The revolutionary bit.

MARTIN. That's right. I've got this small trust fund, and it
  seemed the only thing to do.

JEREMY. Rather than give away fivers to the starving in the
  street?

MARTIN. Indeed.

JEREMY. It being so tricky, nowadays, to find them.

MARTIN. Certainly round here.

JEREMY. Well, it is your money.

MARTIN. Yes, that's what we felt.

JEREMY. Oh, is there a Mrs Glass?

MARTIN. The Party.

The lights come on. JEREMY lives in a comfortable house, with a distinct country feel. MARTIN takes it in during the following.

JEREMY. Ah, splendid. So. The Party.

MARTIN (*handing JEREMY a paper*). Well, it's more 'a group'. Please, do have a paper.

JEREMY. Thank you. Now, you would be — Maoists?

MARTIN. More like, sort of Trots.

JEREMY. What sort?

MARTIN. Well, we don't believe, if Trotsky farted in the spring of 1934, then it stays true for ever and for aye.

JEREMY. Do people think that?

MARTIN. Sure. Had one or two of them ourselves, in fact, until they got chucked out.

JEREMY. I see.

Slight pause.

Yes, I think I saw your leader on the box the other day. James — Grain? He was going on about this bloody coal strike. And dragging in the Londonderry business too, which struck me as, inopportune . . . But tell me, you know the toiling masses so much better than I do, I mean, I'd assumed your average flying picket wouldn't give the time of day to an Irish psychopath, or would he? I merely ask for information.

Pause.

Your cigarette's the wrong way round.

Which it is. MARTIN reverses it.

MARTIN. Yes, I think you're right. But, it's remarkable how

fast things move. I mean, who'd have thought a year ago,
eleven thousand engineers, all over Birmingham, would down
tools, march across the city, close down a coke depot, and
win a miners' strike? Who would have believed the poor old
working class, written off by everybody, right and left,
would actually, suddenly, behave like heroes?

JEREMY. Ah, yes, is it not Lennon who reminds us —

MARTIN. And who's to say, in twelve months' time, they
wouldn't do the same to get British imperialism out of
Ireland. I'm sorry. You were saying. Lenin.

JEREMY. Lennon, actually.

He notes that MARTIN's *glass is still full. He goes to help
himself.*

Forgive me. Whenever I hear the word 'imperialism', I reach
straight for the bottle. John Lennon, isn't it?

MARTIN. What is?

JEREMY. 'A working class hero's something to be'?

He stands, sipping his drink.

Why did you come and see me?

MARTIN. I'm sorry, I don't know what's happened.

JEREMY. Well, you rang up, and you asked me if I'd mind —

MARTIN. I meant, to you.

Pause.

JEREMY. You could say, I was brutally assaulted by the real
world.

MARTIN. I have a friend who was recently, and brutally,
assaulted by the real police.

JEREMY. I'm sorry.

MARTIN. And has just been jailed for ten years.

JEREMY. Good God. Whatever for?

MARTIN. For running off a stencil on his duplicator.

JEREMY. Oh, yes. The bombings trial. They tried to blow up,

what was it? A cottage in the Cotswolds? Belonging to some ludicrously junior Minister of State?

MARTIN. Yes, Hugh Trelawney. Man who wrote the Housing Bill.

Slight pause.

There's an appeal. And a campaign. And that's actually why I came to see you.

Pause.

JEREMY. Oh. Oh, dear.

MARTIN. It being thought, in fact by me, distinguished man of letters, record of support for various progressive causes . . . silly of me.

JEREMY. Well, you really should read other newspapers.

Pause.

I'm sorry. How embarrassing for you. D'you think he's innocent, your friend?

MARTIN. I've really no idea.

JEREMY. I've just stopped being sorry.

MARTIN. Was there a moment? Road to Damascus, sudden burst of light?

JEREMY. No, I don't think so . . . Shall we say, the hyphen linking 'socialist' and 'democratic' stretched and stretched, and eventually snapped.

Slight pause.

For all the usual boring reasons.

MARTIN. Name some.

JEREMY. Oh, must I? They all sound so commonplace and lame . . . Well, I suppose I realised, that you can't reduce the diversity of people to a mathematical equation, that in the end the only way to make men uniform is to put them all in one, that come the crunch there is always what you would doubtless call a fundamental contradiction between the urge to make men equal and the need to keep them free . . .

Which is why idealism, compassion, all those gleaming impulses, will always, *always* mutate into a kind of sullen, atavistic envy, which I am now convinced is the worse and most corrosive of the deadly sins —

MARTIN. You don't think, people are envious as a result of other people's avarice? Lazy because they're greedy? Angry because they're proud?

JEREMY. You've left out lust.

MARTIN. Well, I don't believe the revolution's fucking in the street.

JEREMY. Oh, don't you, any more?
    I think, in fact, now you ask me, yes, there was a moment. A Kronstadt, if you like. It was in October 1969. And there was a sit-in, or a sleep-in, or a be-in, at the university. And the issue was — I can't remember, banning something, somebody recruiting somebody to something, or perhaps a speaker or a lecturer whose views weren't to their taste . . . And I thought, oh no. Oh, here we go again. The same mean, grey, lazy, and, yes, envious distrust of anything that challenged, anything that didn't *fit*. And I thought, oh, come on, Jeremy: this isn't what you meant at all.

MARTIN. Well, it may not have been what *you* —

JEREMY. And then I read a letter in *The Times*, from someone with some unpronounceable East European name, about a Russian dissident who'd been arrested for the crime of circulating a petition. A petition, I may say, not concerned with the right of people to throw bombs at members of the government, or even dump their garbage in my office, but about the right to public demonstration, a privilege which in this country is as you know quite reverently protected.

MARTIN. Do you think it *shouldn't* be quite reverently —

JEREMY. The man was sentenced to three years. For 'discrediting the system'. And then he smuggled out a statement from the camps, about the camps. And was sentenced to another seven. For 'agitation to subvert the state'. And I thought, now, *that's* the type of man that I admire. I'm with the malcontents and the subversives. I don't think I've changed.

Pause.

MARTIN. Well, I'm naturally very sorry.

JEREMY. Naturally.

MARTIN. But one thing's clear, at least.

JEREMY. What's that?

MARTIN. 'A middle-class hero is something to be.'

JEREMY *doesn't know what to say. He shrugs. He opens* MARTIN's *newspaper. He looks at it. He looks at* MARTIN. MARTIN *moves to get his coat.*

Well, I think I'm going now.

JEREMY. I mean, do tell me, if you actually agree — I'm quoting from your organ — that 'the elitists and the snobs will tell you that the only thing that's worth the name of "culture" is grand opera and boring plays about dead kings and queens. What they forget is that we've got a culture too — even if the posh papers don't take brass bands, pigeon racing and club entertainment seriously. The difference of course is that our culture's actually *fun*.'

MARTIN *looks at him.*

I mean, I merely ask —

MARTIN. For information. Yes. You know what strikes me, Jeremy?

JEREMY. What's that?

MARTIN. That I was wrong.

JEREMY. Well, glory be.

MARTIN. I think, in fact, it wasn't so much that you hadn't been to Spain, but that you weren't a red *at Trinity*. To be quite frank. Sir.

JEREMY. Yes.

Pause.

You know the only thing you've said that gives me any hope at all?

MARTIN. What's that?

JEREMY. That this bomber is your friend.

Because that means that your love for the whole of humankind has not yet strangled, quite, your capacity to love the people whom you actually know.

MARTIN. That's hope for what?

JEREMY. That you'll get out, before it does.

Pause.

MARTIN. No need. It won't. There is no contradiction.

Pause.

JEREMY. No?

MARTIN *stays on stage as the set changes around him.*

Scene Four

Outside a meeting hall in London, early February 1974. Six PAPER-SELLERS, of either sex, forming a line up to the door of the meeting hall. PEOPLE attending the meeting thus have to run a kind of gauntlet. MARTIN walks towards the door. EVERYONE muffled up against the cold.

1ST PAPER-SELLER. *The Workers' Week!*

2ND PAPER-SELLER. *The Revolutionary Worker!*

3RD PAPER-SELLER. *The Revolutionary Marxist Worker!*

4TH PAPER-SELLER. *Socialist Vanguard!*

5TH PAPER-SELLER. *Morning Star?*

MARTIN *turns to the* 5TH PAPER-SELLER, *giving the* 6TH PAPER-SELLER *no chance to promote his/her wares.*

MARTIN. No thanks. If I want to do a crossword, then I'll buy *The Times.* Hey, James!

6TH PAPER-SELLER. Um —

He has seen JAMES GRAIN *enter. He hurries over.*

JAMES. Ah, Martin, how —

MARTIN. James, I want to talk to you.

1ST PAPER-SELLER. *The Workers' Week.* Kick out the Tories.

JAMES. *The Worker's Fortnight,* soon, if our print-shop is to be believed.

MARTIN. My article, for the internal bulletin.

JAMES. Yes, what —

MARTIN. It was rejected.

JAMES. Absolutely. It was felt to be politically inopportune.

MARTIN. The *internal* bulletin.

JAMES. Well, exactly.

2ND PAPER-SELLER. *The Revolutionary Worker.* For socialism and a Labour Victory.

JAMES. Make up your mind, I'll buy the paper. (*To* MARTIN.) And 'internal' now means workers, I am glad to say. You know, the people who have shut down British industry two days a week, and are presently engaged —

MARTIN. Did you read it?

JAMES. Yes, of course.

MARTIN. What did it say?

JAMES. Is this a test? It was critical of the Party line, and it contained a number of self-serving distortions of the truth.

MARTIN. Name some.

JAMES. Well, there was the question of the All-Industrial. That did seem to bother you.

MARTIN. It bothered people who were not allowed to put their case.

JAMES. Such as?

MARTIN. The women's caucus.

JAMES. Yes. The conference was, as you know, an attempt to

build a grass-roots workers' faction in the party. The group that you refer to consisted by and large of teachers. One I believed worked part-time in an engineering firm. They were concerned with issues which bore no relation to the subject of the conference.

3RD PAPER-SELLER. *The Revolutionary Marxist Worker*. The paper that supports the miners.

JAMES. Well, you shatter me.

4TH PAPER-SELLER. *Socialist Vanguard?*

MARTIN. Thank you, we subscribe. And there was indeed —

JAMES. And there was indeed the matter of the paper.

MARTIN. Yes.

JAMES. And the Party's policy that it should be accessible to workers.

MARTIN. And the Party's policy to turn it into *Comic Cuts*.

JAMES. Or put another way, the editorial committee's quite correct decision not to publish long and tortuous articles by you about friends of yours in gaol for acts of individual terrorism.

5TH PAPER-SELLER. *The Morning Star?*

JAMES. No, thank you. When I want a recipe, I buy the *Guardian*.

MARTIN. He was — he is a revolutionary.

JAMES. He may think he is a revolutionary. Objectively, he is nothing of the kind. Any more, I am increasingly convinced, than you are. Now, I really think —

6TH PAPER-SELLER. Um —

As MARTIN grabs JAMES' arm and pulls him downstage.

MARTIN. Look. I won't resign.

JAMES. I rather doubt that there'll be any need.

MARTIN. I beg your pardon?

JAMES. After the left current — left, the PC began to consider

its position on the rightward-leaning elements within the
Party. Elements like you.

MARTIN. You can't be serious.

JAMES (*suddenly angry*). Martin, it's very simple. There are
things you won't give up. You still have this antipathy to
working in a group that's led, if just in part, by manual
workers. There is something in you that fundamentally
distrusts the concept of a leadership, particularly if it's on
the surface less articulate than you.

Slight pause.

MARTIN. I stopped. I pulled out the Phil Mandrell thing. I did
what I was told.

JAMES. Eventually.

MARTIN. You see, I feel, that there is no contradiction —

JAMES. As I've said before, I couldn't care less what you feel.
It's what you think and do. And what your present thoughts
are doing is to undermine the seizing of the time through
which we are passing at the moment, which is principally
defined by the fact that the mineworkers are bringing down
the Government.

I'm sorry, Martin, but that's all.

JAMES *quickly upstage and through the door.*

6TH PAPER-SELLER. Um —

MARTIN *following as the lights dim and the setting begins to
change:*

Stick-Up? For Brighter Revolutions?

MARTIN *stops.*

MARTIN. Christ. Are you still going?

6TH PAPER-SELLER. Strong.

MARTIN. Then, yes.

Fumbling for change.

Yes, please . . .

AMANDA *enters, as the scene continues to transform into . . .*

Scene Five

AMANDA's *house, February 1974.*

It is a commune in Notting Hill, empty at the moment, except for AMANDA *herself, who carries two glasses and a half-empty half-bottle of scotch.*

AMANDA. So what did you expect?

MARTIN. Well, not a gold watch, I suppose.

AMANDA. I'm sorry?

MARTIN. Look, is that a drink?

AMANDA (*nodding*). Take your coat off and sit down.

She pours a scotch and tosses the bottle on a chair before sitting on its arm. MARTIN *takes off his coat and sits on the arm of another chair.* AMANDA *taps her shoulder.*

Well, here it is.

MARTIN *looks at her and smiles.*

MARTIN. Do you know what struck me? Very forcibly? I've spent four years of patient toil, trying to make SV the Government. And I looked at him, as he put the knife in me, with all the tact and understated charm of Jack the Ripper, and thought: come on, do you really want this man to run the country? James Grain, the man who put the 'rot' in Trotskyism?

AMANDA. And the 'rat' in apparatchik.

MARTIN. Yes.

Slight pause. Clicking:

Oh, yes.

AMANDA. Well, hon, I'm full of sympathy, but if you ask me, you're well out of it. When I left, my feelings were of pure relief. No more, the desperate scramble through the paper, trying to suss out this month's line. No longer, last month, 'smash the Labour Party's stranglehold', and this month, 'build united fronts with social-democratic elements'. In my time, I took up more positions than the Kama Sutra.

MARTIN. You jumped. I was pushed.

Pause. AMANDA *sips her scotch.*

And actually, I rather like the twists and turns. Trying to bend and coil the dialectic, just so far it wouldn't snap.

AMANDA. Well, hon, whatever turns —

MARTIN. And then, today of all days . . . when the working class is actually behaving in a way that it's supposed to, siezing history by the throat, when our fucking rhetoric comes real . . .

Pause.

AMANDA. It's not the end.

Slight pause.

Why should it be the end?

Pause.

Why should it be the only place to be?

Pause.

MARTIN. Well, here you are. In your collective living situation. A pageant of the future, acted out within the very belly of the monster.

AMANDA. Well, we like to think that it's at least a dummy run.

MARTIN. So where's the gang?

AMANDA. There's a squat in Lissom Grove. The pigs gave notice of a bust, and everybody's round there, manning barricades.

MARTIN. And you?

AMANDA. I'm on child-minding duty. Holding coats.

MARTIN. Ah. I see.

Slight pause.

AMANDA. Have you no other shoulder?

MARTIN. Why, do you want me to —

AMANDA. No, no. Just wondered.

MARTIN. Well, there is a she.

Slight pause.

An actress, as it happens, working with a theatre group that calls itself The People's Chemistry. Their present show's called Lock-Out, and in it she plays Mrs Mope, the Daughter, Second Seamstress and the Concept of the Falling Rate of Profit. Her name's Linda Lazonby.

AMANDA. I haven't seen her act.

MARTIN (*enjoying himself now*). Neither have I. She sleeps a lot, though, does that well, which isn't actually bad news, because it means she isn't talking. I mean, politically, you wouldn't classify her as 'advanced'. In fact, she thinks that realpolitik's a Spanish football team, and that the National Front's a meteorological phenomenon.

AMANDA stands.

AMANDA. Now, Martin, will you stop that, please.

MARTIN. I'm sorry?

AMANDA. So you should be. Perhaps you ought to —

MARTIN (*slightly blurted*). Look, look, Mand — would you like to go out? For a meal, or something? Talk of old times, weep into our Rogan Gosht?

AMANDA. Martin, I am in charge of three small —

MARTIN. Then tomorrow, when the gang's all back?

Pause.

AMANDA. No, tomorrow there's a tenants' meeting.

MARTIN. Friday?

AMANDA. Women's group.

MARTIN. The weekend?

AMANDA. I would have to check, but I think we're blocking Westway.

MARTIN. Mand. How can I put this.

Slight pause.

Rearrange the following into a well-known phrase or saying . . . Something I've You Always Rotten Fancied.

Pause.

AMANDA. I am tempted to reply, 'Off Fuck'.

MARTIN. Resist it.

AMANDA. Then, quite simply, 'On'.

Slight pause.

MARTIN. 'On'? What? The floor, the sofa? Top of the wardrobe?

AMANDA. 'On' is 'no' spelt backwards.

MARTIN (*going to* AMANDA *and taking her hands*). No, you haven't got the point, it must be actual words, like, um, 'Glass Shouldn't People Stones In Houses Throw'.

AMANDA. *You* haven't got the point. Glass Shouldn't. I should not with Glass.

Pause.

MARTIN. Why not?

AMANDA. All sorts of reasons. Theoretical and practical.

MARTIN. Let's start with practice.

AMANDA. Never on a rebound.

MARTIN. I'm not on a rebound.

AMANDA. No?

Long pause.

MARTIN. The best years of my life.

AMANDA *says nothing.* MARTIN *finds the bottle, and pours himself another scotch. His hands are shaking.*

I tried so hard to please. Did everything that was asked of me. And willingly I gave. I was offered nothing and I wanted to be offered nothing. But now — what's left? How could you do this thing to me?

Pause.

AMANDA. I'm sorry. Know I've always been a good girl. Best girl. Always done what's wanted, always doing what I'm told. But still, I'm leaving, with my little suitcase in my hand.
     I'm sorry. Leaving home. Bye bye.

MARTIN *hasn't listened.*

MARTIN. You what? I'm sorry?

AMANDA. Martin, I used to cry —

Suddenly, a group of LIBERTARIANS — people living in or connected with the house — burst in. A couple of people are bleeding. One carries a crying baby. Another is called RON.

RON. Well, good evening, merry campers. And welcome to the non-stop Revolutionary Cock-Up Show.

AMANDA. What happened?

People rushing around, looking for things, tending wounds.

1ST LIBERTARIAN. They got the fucking time wrong, didn't they? When we arrived the bastards were already there.

2ND LIBERTARIAN (*to the crying baby*). Choo choo. Be quiet, baby.

AMANDA. What, in the house?

RON. All over it. The silly fuckers didn't change the locks. Rule One. Change all the locks.

2ND LIBERTARIAN. Choo choo.

AMANDA. Where's mother?

2ND LIBERTARIAN. In the pig-pen. She went all hysterical.

3RD LIBERTARIAN. Rule Two. Do Not Go All Hysterical.

The 2ND LIBERTARIAN takes the baby out. We continue to hear it cry.

1ST LIBERTARIAN. Does anybody have the name of our tame bent lawyer?

MARTIN (*to* AMANDA). Was this — a real family?

AMANDA. Yes. It was a real, kosher, working-class and homeless, family.

RON *on his way out. He turns back.*

RON. Well, if it isn't Martin Glass. The noted Trotskyite.

The hubbub stops. PEOPLE *look at* MARTIN, *who looks round, nervously.*

Does everyone remember? From 'The Trials of Phil Mandrell'? With Comrade Glass, the great consultant? With his *prima facies* and his *nolle prosequis*? And how we had to have a barrister and we hadn't to be naughty in the public gallery, and take things very seriously indeed?

AMANDA. Look, Ron —

RON. Until that is, The Party tells him Phil Mandrell is objectively a petit-bourgeois individualist. And suddenly, in the middle of a criminal appeal, when he might have been some use, Comrade Glass goes all transparent, and you cannot see him any more.

The 2ND LIBERTARIAN *has reappeared. The baby is still crying.*

MARTIN. That isn't —

RON. And you know what strikes me? That there are certain things that Martin can't or won't give up. Like his deep hostility to working in a group that isn't *led*. Or if it is, is led by everyone. There's something in him, just can't seem to cope with people who are on the surface less informed than him. And I wonder, sometimes, if in fact he's on our side at all.

MARTIN. Please. Please, don't tell me what I think.

RON. Oh, there's nothing wrong with what you think. That's fine. It's what you don't appear to feel.

AMANDA. Leave him alone.

MARTIN. Shouldn't *somebody* do something with that baby?

RON. Why don't you?

AMANDA. Leave Him Alone.

Pause. RON *shrugs, goes out. The others follow.* MARTIN *stands there.*

MARTIN. Thank you.

AMANDA *shrugs. The baby stops crying.*

Red Barcelona.

AMANDA. Pardon?

MARTIN. A kind of code. Me old mate Phil and me.

AMANDA. Go on.

MARTIN. In the beginning, it was just, the communists were saying that the anarchists were wrong. Mistaken. Incorrect.
Then their mistakes and incorrectitude were 'objectively' in the interests of the fascists.
Then 'objectively' the anarchists were fascists.
Then each individual anarchist became an actual, subjective, conscious Nazi.
Ergo, my dog's a cat.

AMANDA. That isn't quite what Ron —

MARTIN. Does it always have to happen, Mandy?

AMANDA. Not unless we want it to.

The baby starts to cry again.

MARTIN. Why did you used to cry?

Slight pause. AMANDA *decides not to say it as she'd planned.*

AMANDA. Because . . . I once asked Tanny, if she knew what socialism was. She said, oh, yes, of course. It's going to meetings. Funny old life I've given her. And me.

MARTIN. I once —

AMANDA. You know, I could — it would be possible to skip the tenants' group.

The 2ND LIBERTARIAN *appears with the crying baby.*

2ND LIBERTARIAN. Could someone . . . There's no milk.
Could someone go . . .

AMANDA (*moving*). Yuh. Sure.

MARTIN. I once caught a cold on a parade ground.

As the scene splits and changes, MARTIN *stays holding his glass of whisky.*

Scene Six

A country vicarage, Christmas 1974.
A comfortable but rather empty room. A little Christmas tree. MARTIN *stands with his glass of scotch. We hear from offstage, a grossly inadequate rendering of the carol 'Good King Wenceslas'. It stops. Pause. Enter* MRS GLASS, MARTIN's *mother.* MARTIN *looks at her.*

MRS GLASS. It wasn't carol singers. Just three grubby boys.

MARTIN. Oh? It sounded like —

MRS GLASS. Not proper carol singers.

MARTIN. Did you give them anything?

MRS GLASS. Oh, no. I ask them if they're collecting, for some charity, and if they say 'no', I don't give a thing. I mean, it's actually begging, isn't it?

Pause.

It starts in mid-November. Actually, I blame the parents.

She goes and pours herself a glass of sherry.

Do you want another sherry?

MARTIN. No. I'm drinking scotch.

MRS GLASS. Well, you can help yourself then.

MARTIN does so.

There used to be the proper carol singers. From the church. With horns and bells. And not just carols either. Real wassailing songs. They'd carry lanterns and we'd have them in. It was bliss.

MARTIN (*under his breath*). Oh, Jesus.

Pause.

MRS GLASS. So you've got a proper job now?

MARTIN. Yes, if you can call the *Islington and Hackney Messenger* a proper job.

MRS GLASS. And you've moved.

MARTIN. Into a state of unwed bliss with a single mother. Yes.

MRS GLASS *does not look at him.*

How long do you keep the vicarage?

MRS GLASS. Oh, just till the New Year, actually. It's kind of them, to let me stay for Christmas. It's been ten months, after all.

MARTIN. New vicar moving in?

MRS GLASS. Oh, no. Nice couple. He's a — captain? Or a 'lieutenant', anyway. But she's British. No, the parish shares a vicar now.

Pause.

It's the upkeep, you see, dear. When it's ten pounds for them to step inside the door, just to *look* at the woodwork, or the guttering. It is the upkeep, really.

Pause.

I suppose it doesn't matter now. Last real Christmas that we'll have. I think, don't you? Before the whole thing falls about our ears.

MARTIN. The whole thing whats?

MRS GLASS. Before your unions bring the whole thing crashing down.

MARTIN. Now, mother, you must stop all that. You know it's only wishful thinking. Wanting it so badly won't bring it any closer.

MRS GLASS *looks at* MARTIN. *Pause.*

MRS GLASS. Do you want to come to midnight mass?

MARTIN. I thought you said —

MRS GLASS. Oh, it's here this year. It's on a kind of rota, actually.

MARTIN. Yes, if you like.

MRS GLASS. I do.

Pause.

I was clearing out some rubbish in the attic, actually. I was thinking about other Christmas Eves.

You and your father sledging in the afternoon. In with a shiver, to the smell of wood-smoke. Mince-pies and mulled claret. And at nearly midnight, crunch across the snow.

I found the crib you and your father made. We've lost a wise man and the ox. And Joseph, actually.

MARTIN. Oh, mother, please, do stop.

MRS GLASS. Stop what?

MARTIN. Saying 'actually' in every sentence.

Slight pause.

Sorry.

MRS GLASS. I didn't know I was.

MARTIN. It never was like that.

MRS GLASS. You won't remember.

MARTIN. Yes I do.

Slight pause.

I remember, every year, three gruesome days of attempting to pretend we were a Christmas card. A kind of seance, trying to raise the nineteenth century. Oh, are you out there, jolly red-faced coachman? Oh, can you hear us, Tiny Tim?

But then it was mother's little yearly treat. Playing at mistress of the manor. With her scarves and wellingtons and fucking mulled red wine.

MRS GLASS *looks away.*

What I do remember, coming back from school, on that

grimy, drafty train, was fantasising how I'd shock the pants off you this year. What I would do or say. To really sear your mind.

MRS GLASS. I know. He did that too.

Pause.

MARTIN. Who did it too?

MRS GLASS. Your father.

Slight pause.

He would say, when I'd worked at something, obviously, all day, at baking, sewing something for the parish, he'd remark: 'Of course, the whole thing's nonsense, isn't it? It's all the silliest pretence, to stop the silliest of people facing up to what's real in their lives.' And he would say it laughingly and kindly, but underneath, such scorn.

MARTIN *goes and fills up his drink.*

Your father was a good man. Noble, in his way. He loved his kind. But not — I think — his kindred. Actually.
    I'm sorry.

MARTIN. Dust.

MRS GLASS. I beg your pardon?

MARTIN. It's a phrase of Trotsky's.

MRS GLASS. Trotsky.

MARTIN. Human dust.

A long pause. Then MARTIN moves downstage, and the vicarage fades away behind him.

Scene Seven

MARTIN *stands there, as we hear the voice of a* RADIO ANNOUNCER, *and* AMANDA *enters to him. She is dressed up, and carries a bottle wrapped in paper.*

ANNOUNCER. This is the BBC News, today, Thursday the first of May 1975, and here are the main headlines. May Day parades have been held in the streets of Saigon, now renamed Ho Chi Minh City, as the new Communist authorities impose severe penalties for looting, prostitution, and 'all decadent cultural activities of the American variety'.

Lights. A private house in North London. A party, at which MARTIN *and* AMANDA *have just arrived.*

MARTIN. Well, this is typical.

AMANDA. What is?

MARTIN. No sounds. This is a party. Where, pray, are the sounds?

AMANDA. There's supposed to be some tapes arriving. Sixties stuff.

MARTIN. They better have the Troggs.

AMANDA. D'you want to get some food?

MARTIN. No, first things first. I never eat on an empty liver.

AMANDA. Fine.

MARTIN *goes off in search of glasses, as* AMANDA *spots* BRIAN, *now in his early thirties, and crosses to him. On his way out,* MARTIN *passes a conversation between a male* SMOKING PARTYGOER *and a female* NON-SMOKING PARTYGOER, *called* MOLLY.

SMOKING PARTYGOER. Well, I can't see how it's a class question.

MOLLY. Well, that's not the point. Though one might point out what the tobacco companies are up to in the Third World.

SMOKING PARTYGOER. I'm not in the Third World. I'm in Muswell Hill.

MARTIN *returns with two beakers of wine. He stops to overhear.*

MOLLY. But the thing I found most interesting was your remark that you smoke at meetings because you're nervous and you're bored.

SMOKING PARTYGOER. Well, I didn't quite —

MOLLY. And it seems to me you're nervous because you're working out some devastatingly impressive speech, to impress your friends, and you're bored because you never listen to what anybody else has got to say. So if it isn't about class, then it's absolutely about gender. No?

She turns and goes. The SMOKING PARTYGOER *is left there. He has half an inch of ash, can't see an ashtray. He flicks the ash into his jacket pocket.*

MARTIN (*to* BRIAN *and* AMANDA). My God, it's like St Crispin's Day back there.

AMANDA. What do you mean?

MARTIN. Revolutionary nostalgia, rampant in the kitchen. With reference the victory of the heroic Vietnamese. I kid you not, there's people rolling up their trouser-legs and showing off the place a police-horse bit their leg in Grosvenor Square.

AMANDA. Now, Martin, you remember Brian?

MARTIN. Yes, of course. Are you still in the —

BRIAN. No. In fact, I've joined the Labour Party.

MARTIN. Heavens. Old Bri, sustaining the illusions of the working class in the strategy of electoral reformism?

BRIAN. Well, that isn't quite the way I'd put it.

MARTIN. No?

BRIAN. I'd put it as recapturing the party of the working class for the principles of democratic socialism.

MARTIN. Which are?

BRIAN. Well . . . the aspirations which were clearly demonstrated by the act of bringing down the Tory Government.

MARTIN. But you don't think that in fact the fundamental role of social-democratic parties like the Labour Party has been precisely to prevent the working class from the achievement of those aspirations, by deviating their mass action down the channels of . . .

Pause.

The channels of —

BRIAN (*to* AMANDA). Um?

MARTIN. Sorry, it's completely gone.

BRIAN. What's gone?

MARTIN. I can't remember what comes next. No matter.
Bound to come back to me.

He smiles. His glass is empty.

I think I'm going to try and liberate our bottle.

He goes.

BRIAN. What's with —

AMANDA. Excuse me, please.

She catches MARTIN *up.*

Martin, what's wrong?

MARTIN. There's nothing wrong.

AMANDA. That is palpably not true.

He looks at her. She changes tack, puts her arms round his neck.

Lovey, it's happened lots of time before. The stage of history
is littered with people who have passed the age of thirty,
doing the most wonderfully exciting things. I can think of
literally dozens of examples.

MARTIN. No, it isn't that.

AMANDA. What is it, then?

MARTIN. It's nothing.

He takes her arms away, turns and goes. She returns to
BRIAN.

AMANDA. I'm sorry. It's our thirtieth tomorrow, and we're
taking the whole thing very badly.

BRIAN. Are you two — I didn't think, in Birmingham . . .

AMANDA. No, a recentish development. Oh, hell the what,
   say I.

BRIAN. Beg pardon?

   JAMES GRAIN *comes to* AMANDA.

JAMES. Amanda.

AMANDA. James.

   MARTIN *has re-entered with a bottle of wine. He is smoking.*
   He stumbles slightly, nearly into MOLLY, *who is engaged in*
   conversation with a small knot of people.

MARTIN. Excuse me. Sorry.

MOLLY. Please, don't smoke that thing at me.

   MARTIN *passes, but turns back.*

MARTIN. Uh — 'plead you to me, fair dame?'

MOLLY. Fuck off.

MARTIN. You what?

MOLLY (*turning back to her conversation*). You heard.

   MARTIN *to* JAMES, AMANDA *and* BRIAN *as:*

JAMES (*raising his glass*). Well. Victory.

MARTIN. Who is that woman?

AMANDA. Which one?

MARTIN (*gestures to* MOLLY). That one.

AMANDA. She's called Molly something. Wages for Housework,
   I believe.

MARTIN. Wages for *what?*

   Slight pause.

AMANDA. Wages for Housework. It's a group —

MARTIN. That's what I thought you said.

   Slight pause.

JAMES. So, Martin, how's the bourgeois press?

   MOLLY *is passing.*

MARTIN. You know, if you think about it, what has really liberated women is the invention of the vacuum-cleaner, the tumble-dryer and the fridge. Well, I think so.

MOLLY stops, listening.

AMANDA (*quietly*). Martin, I'm not sure that I'm presently that interested in what you think.

MARTIN. You see, I feel the problem does come down —

AMANDA (*quietly*). Or what you feel.

MARTIN. I mean, assuming that that slogan is, despite its self-evident absurdity, a serious and practical demand —

AMANDA. I am increasingly convinced, in fact, despite my better judgement, that the problem does come down to what you are.

Pause.

MARTIN. I'm sorry?

Slight pause.

What d'you mean, 'to what I am'?

AMANDA. Martin, do something for me. Please. Stop talking for five minutes and consider, really try to imagine what life would be like if you didn't have a cock. I think that would be really helpful. Actually.

Pause. MOLLY laughs. She goes off. MARTIN and AMANDA look each other in the eye.

MARTIN. Everywhere I turn.

AMANDA. 'What Do You Mean?'

Pause.

BRIAN. Yuh, well, I think that basically the left has underestimated the —

MARTIN. Well. James. Now, is the rumour true, your paper is accusing the Vietnamese of selling out *already*?

JAMES. No, I don't think so.

MARTIN. No? There was excited comment in the drinks queue,

on how many Trotskyists were bumped off by Ho Chi Minh.

JAMES. Well, that's certainly the case.

MARTIN. So what's your prediction, then, for revolutionary Vietnam? Another Stalinist degeneration?

JAMES. Well, I wouldn't be surprised.

MARTIN. Not 'Peace in Vietnam' but 'Victory'?

Slight pause.

JAMES. Martin, what follows is at primer level, suitable for six years and below. We supported Ho Chi Minh because that Stalinist and, as you point out, murderer, was the only person, led the only party, which could win the war.

MARTIN. 'Objectively'?

JAMES. Correct. In the same way as we unconditionally support —

MARTIN. I think in five years time we will all cringe at the memory of tonight.

Pause. A few people have heard this. The buzz of conversation dying, as:

At least, I hope so. Cringe and blush and fidget. Try to change the subject. Hope we will.

Almost EVERYONE now listening. The odd laugh, as if it's a joke:

When this one goes all wrong too. And the walls are built and the barbed wire is in place and our dear old rolly-moley midwife has brought forth another bug-eyed basilisk, I hope we'll cringe. Don't you?

Silence.

JAMES. Oh, dear.

MARTIN. But I doubt it. What I imagine will occur is another alibi, like the last time, and the time before, the ravages of civil war, you can't build socialism in one country, oh, if only Stalin hadn't packed the Politburo in 1924 . . . And as once again the proofs pile up that we are catastrophically wrong, we change the question. Or indeed, having predicted that the world will definitely end on Tuesday, we spend Wednesday morning arguing that all this proves is that the apocalypse is bound to roll along by the weekend. That all the stillbirths, all the monstrous misbegottens with no legs or stomachs but with all those twitching ears and beady little eyes, that they're the deviation, and that *therefore* somewhere in the future there must be a norm.

You see, I just no longer can believe, that a third of humankind is living in an aberration. Any more than I believe the workers of the West are straining at the leash to bite their way to communism, if only we could crack the chains that bind them to their masters. I can't understand this crazy nightmare world we've fashioned for ourselves, where devilish social-democrats conspire to muzzle discontent by day, and dastardly reformists plot to deviate the proletariat by night . . .

Whereas it might be possible, might just be possible, that the putative tin soldiers in our class-war game have seen the future, and they don't believe us when we say this isn't what we meant at all . . .

You see, I don't think it's just Stalin, or even Lenin. I think it is the whole idea. That our childlike sense of justice and compassion and fairplay, the thing that got us here, that we must hone and beat it down, from a ploughshare to a sword; that there's no morality except the interests of the revolution, that to be a communist you must purge yourself of the instincts and beliefs that made you one.

And what it leaves us like. We're right and everybody else is wrong, and so we're arrogant; and the fewer of us that there are, the more insufferable we become. But paradoxically, too, we want the world to listen, and they won't, and so we're mean. And the compound, I think, is this terrible unfocussed fury that we seem to nurture in ourselves, that burns us up, and which we beam about us like a blowtorch, branding everything we touch or see.

And what's it all for, in the end? What is it we're disguising when we say, Marx doesn't give a blueprint, we don't know, the process of the struggle will throw up the forms, etcetera . . .

It's a Golden Age. The dialectical return, to some primitive, communal, blissful — something. A Great Leap Backwards, to the childhood of humanity. It's nowhere.

And, for the sake of that, I don't believe, I can't believe, I actually refuse to be required by anybody to believe, that anyone is human dust.

Pause.

They say that every generation has its Kronstadt. Well, today is mine.

Pause.

I feel a great deal better.

MARTIN *goes quickly to the exit. He bumps into the entering* RON. *There is a beat between them. Then* MARTIN *goes out.*

JAMES (*to* AMANDA). I'm sorry.

AMANDA. Well, I suppose . . . it's only rock and roll.

RON. Uh — evening, comrades.

Um . . . Met a young person on the doorstep. Her Renault Five had broken down on the North Circular. She's covered in apology. She's brought the sounds.

Rock music from off.

JAMES. And there they are.

BRIAN (*to* AMANDA). Do you want to dance?

AMANDA. No, I don't think so. Thank you very much.

BRIAN. They better have 'A Whiter Shade of Pale'.

Scene Eight

Frankfurt Airport. Late 1978. Bare stage.

An OFFICIAL *quickly leads in* PAVEL LERMONTOV, *followed by a large gaggle of* REPORTERS *and* CAMERAMEN. *The* REPORTERS *shriek questions in several languages.*

The CAMERAMEN *flash away.*

LERMONTOV *looks totally bewildered, as the* OFFICIAL *leads him into a space where a microphone is set up, waiting. All this very fast:*

PRESS (*variously, and in various languages*). When were you released, Mr Lermontov?
> When did they tell you?
> Please look over here, Mr Lermontov.
> What does it feel like, to be in the West?
> How long ago did you know?
> Mr Lermontov, just turn your head, please —
> What do you feel about being exchanged for a Russian spy?
> Did they tell you in advance?
> Did you want to be exiled to the West?
> Just look this way, Mr Lermontov —
> Do you have any family left in Russia?
> When are you flying to England, Mr Lermontov?
> Which hotel are you staying at?
> How long will you be staying there?
> How long are you going to stay in England?
> Do you have any immediate plans?

They are now at the microphone. The jabber goes on, as the OFFICIAL *tries to get silence.*

OFFICIAL. Please, please, ladies and gentlemen —

PRESS. Why did you choose to come to Frankfurt?
> Here, please, Mr Lermontov —
> Did you have any idea before today?

OFFICIAL. Please, ladies and gentlemen.

The jabber subsides.

Mr Lermontov.

Pause.

LERMONTOV. Well. Well.

Pause.

Look, um, I — Look.

Slight pause.

There is, a saying in our country. That it seems foolish to spend so much time, as we do, learning to speak, when one . . . When one is not allowed subsequently to do so.

Slight pause.

Now I can speak.

Slight pause.

Now I am free to say what I like.

Slight pause.

I find . . . I have no words to say.

Slight pause.

You will forgive me.

He leaves the microphone. Before the jabber can restart, we see MIKLOS PALOCZI, *now forty-three years old.*

PALOCZI. Pavel.

LERMONTOV (*confused*). I'm sorry —

PALOCZI. Pavel. Miklos Paloczi.

LERMONTOV *doesn't remember.*

Hungary.

LERMONTOV *remembers.*

LERMONTOV. Oh, no. Oh, no.

LERMONTOV *embraces* PALOCZI. *He is crying.*

Oh, no . . .

And the flashbulbs flash around them.

Act Three

If one were to probe into the hearts of many potential and actual Tory supporters — and others besides — one might discover that what worries them most about contemporary Britain was not so much the lack of freedom as its excessive abundance; not so much the threat of dictatorship as the reality of something unpleasantly close to chaos . . . and for Mrs Thatcher to tell a party indignant at the collapse of all forms of authority, and longing for the smack of Firm Government, that the country is suffering from a lack of liberty makes her seem out of touch with reality . . .

Peregrine Worsthorne, in *Conservative Essays,* **1978**

The defence of individual rights has reached such an extreme that society itself is becoming defenceless against certain individuals. And in the West it is high time to defend, not so much the rights of individuals, as their duties.

Alexander Solzhenitsyn, *Harvard Speech,* **1978**

ACT THREE

Scene One

Autumn 1978. A public place. MARTIN *and* JEREMY *meet. They look at each other.*

JEREMY. Three years ago.

MARTIN. That's right.

JEREMY. So long.

MARTIN. I wanted to be sure.
    It does take time. You must remember that. You shove two fingers up the dialectic, bound to get a shock.

JEREMY. Indeed. But, now . . .

MARTIN. What, now?

JEREMY. You're sure?

   MARTIN *takes a piece of paper from his pocket. He reads.*

MARTIN. 'The red blood splatters both the
        cities and the plains of the
        beloved fatherland
    The sublime blood of the workers and
        the peasants, revolutionary fighters
        of both sexes . . .
    That red blood liberates us all from
        tyranny.'

Etcetera, etcetera.

He puts the paper away.

The anthem of the Khymer Rouge.

Slight pause.

Oh, absolutely sure.

JEREMY. Then — welcome.

JEREMY puts out his hand to MARTIN, who takes it. Lights fade. In the darkness, MARTIN's voice:

MARTIN (*voice over*). And I looked from face to face, from 'Trotskyist' to 'Libertarian' to 'Democratic Socialist', and I realised that all these faces, from the harshest to the most benign, were set like flint against the way that human beings really are.

Scene Two

During MARTIN's speech, a spot fades up on JAMES GRAIN, reading a copy of 'The Times'. Then, general lights. We are on the far edge of an anti-racist rally-cum-rock-festival, in an open public place, in the autumn of 1978. Upstage, a few people, watching the concert that is taking place further upstage. A few people holding lollipop shaped placards, with slogans in the red and yellow of the Anti-Nazi League. Similarly coloured balloons as well. AMANDA comes downstage. She wears a steward's armband.

AMANDA. Well, James.

JAMES. Amanda. Hallo.

AMANDA. Now isn't this delightful?

JAMES. Isn't it. Have you seen this?

He waves the paper.

AMANDA. Yes. Yes of course I have.

Pause.

Well, as they say —

JAMES. Some fashionable words. We'll hear a lot of them today, I'm sure. The ra-ra words of the bright new ra-ra left. 'Open'. 'Tolerant'. And 'pluralistic'.

AMANDA. Well, yes —

JAMES. Tolerant of *him?*

AMANDA. I rather doubt if he'll turn up. Too busy
supergrassing on his past.

JAMES. Of people who in five years time will be doing the same
thing?

Pause.

AMANDA. You know, I once attempted, unsuccessfully, to tell
Comrade Glass a little about being me.

JAMES. Well, yes —

AMANDA. I tried to tell him how I used to cry. Me and my
child, our noses pressed against the lighted windows,
watching the 2.4 kids playing round the Christmas tree.

Why me? Why couldn't *I* accept things as they were? Why
did *I* have to feel it was all wrong, and that I was put into the
world to set it right?

Well, you know as well as I do. All those opportunities,
those bold bright schools and gleaming universities. That our
folks had never had themselves, but had been through a
slump and then a war to win for us. And if we didn't finish
it, if we didn't get it right, this time, if we didn't actually
complete the building of the New Jerusalem, for them, for
us, then what the fuck were we about?

And I left your party when I realised the one absolute
condition of my membership was checking in those feelings
at the door.

JAMES *is about to reply when* JUDY *strides down from the
upstage group, bearing a clipboard, and also wearing a
steward's armband.*

JUDY. Ah, Mandy.

AMANDA. Jude.

JUDY. The International Brigade.

Slight pause.

AMANDA. I'm sorry?

JUDY. Where are they?

AMANDA. Barcelo — ?

JUDY. The Band. They are on next and not here.

Slight pause.

AMANDA. Well, I'm very sorry, Judy, but —

And BRIAN *has also come in, harrassed, carrying a sensible toy.*

BRIAN. Judy. There is a minor riot in the creche —

JUDY *bangs her forehead with the flat of her hand.*

JUDY. I try to combat bourgeois cultural hegemony.

She strides off.

JAMES. You know . . .

Something in his tone makes AMANDA *and* BRIAN *turn to him.*

There is a moment, and it's not a pleasant one, when you do begin to realise . . .

Slight pause. He changes tack.

There is shortly going to be a General Election. And in our view the Conservatives will win. They will win in part because the working class has been betrayed, not least by those whom we have always said were really on the other side, and who now appear, in their true colours, so to be.

Pause.

The moment, is the moment when you realise that what you've always said is true. When the enemy looks like the enemy. The moment when your rhetoric comes real.

He looks at them a moment, then tosses 'The Times' to AMANDA *and goes out.*

BRIAN. He's got problems with the crossword?

AMANDA. No. Revenge.

BRIAN. I'm sorry?

AMANDA. Old mate Martin. Taking his revenge.

A YOUNG MAN has appeared. He wears a hideously ripped and pinned Mao jacket, and tiny rectangular glasses with white rims. His hair consists largely of spikes. He carries a guitar case.

YOUNG MAN. Uh — scuse —

AMANDA and BRIAN look at him and then at each other.

BRIAN. For me, it all went off with Elton John.

Scene Three

December 1978.
 A suite in a hotel in Kensington. Hightech, tubular design. We are in the sitting-room part. MARTIN sits making notes on a pad. JEREMY is reading newspapers. MIKLOS PALOCZI is on the telephone.

JEREMY (*reading from a newspaper*). The University of Loughborough is planning to spend £20,000 researching something they describe as 'pinball art'.

PALOCZI. That's Andreyushkin? Why not Griboyedov?
  Well, I'll have to speak to him about it.
  Yes, that's right, Paloczi.

He puts the phone down. It rings immediately. He picks it up.

Hallo?

JEREMY. There is a body called 'The Free Media Campaign', which is presently 'demanding' that the NUJ expel from membership all journalists whose work 'uncritically promotes ideas of racial, class or sexual superiority'.

PALOCZI. No I'm afraid that Mr Lermontov is already booked for interview.
  The *Sunday Times*. Today.
  That's right. Exclusively.

He puts the phone down. It rings.

Hallo?

JEREMY. And apparently, it's been proposed that the Inner London Education Authority provide free creche facilities for schoolgirl mothers.

PALOCZI. What, actually in the lobby?

JEREMY. Free in the sense of 'on the rates', of course.

PALOCZI. No, they must ring. Please tell them, they must telephone.

JEREMY. The idea is being given serious consideration.

PALOCZI. And now, please hold all calls.

He puts the phone down as PAVEL LERMONTOV enters. He looks well brushed and scrubbed, in new clothes.

JEREMY. Sometimes I think they print these things, deliberately, just to outrage me.

LERMONTOV. Hallo.

PALOCZI. Pavel.

MARTIN *and* JEREMY *to their feet.*
   A note: Although LERMONTOV's *English is good, when he and* PALOCZI *speak alone, we assume they are speaking Russian. There are also moments in conversations with other people when* LERMONTOV *will slip into Russian: usually, as later in this scene, when he cannot remember an English word. So, when he is groping for the word 'blur' later on, the words 'dimness, hazy, foggy' are, as it were, the Russian words for blur, rather than English synonyms. It is important for later events that this device is established in the scene.*

LERMONTOV. Now, these are —

PALOCZI. Now, Pavel, meet —

LERMONTOV. Mr Crowther?

JEREMY. Jeremy.

LERMONTOV. And —

MARTIN. Martin.

PALOCZI. Glass.

JEREMY. Look, I can't tell you how delighted —

MARTIN. I'm terrifically pleased to —

LERMONTOV. There's a man out there. A man, out in the street. I've been watching him for half an hour.

PALOCZI *a quick move towards the other room.*

He is selling newspapers.

PALOCZI *turns back to the smiling LERMONTOV.*

All different shapes and sizes, and of all complexions too, I'm sure: left ones and right ones, clever ones and stupid ones, serious and trivial — and he seems as pleased to sell one as the other. Pleased to please. Like a card-sharper, with his papers and his change. A real entertainer. They say that we, we 'dissidents', see the West as our hero. Well. I think I have found mine.
 Were all those calls for me?

PALOCZI. Yes. Do you want to hear about them?

LERMONTOV (*sits*). Please. It's such a novelty.

PALOCZI (*reading from his notebook*). Well, there's a group, based at the London School of Economics, campaigning against psychiatric torture. They want you to address them. I said yes.

LERMONTOV. Good, good.

PALOCZI. Then the BBC World Service people rang. They want you for an interview. They tried to fob us off with a man called Andreyushkin, but I told them where they could put that. They're calling back.

MARTIN. What's wrong with Andreyushkin?

PALOCZI. Soft. In the section, he is called 'Kerensky'.

LERMONTOV. Ah.

PALOCZI. And then there were lots of papers, but I said the *Sunday Times* . . . And various cranks and crazies whom you needn't bother with.

LERMONTOV. I'm sorry, cranks and crazies?

PALOCZI. Well, you know, the type —

LERMONTOV. No, I'm sorry, I don't know.

PALOCZI. Well, like —

Slight pause.

Pavel. There are in Britain, groups, campaigns, committees, with high-sounding titles, all for freedom, liberation, civil rights — but which, if they actually achieved any real influence or power, would put you in a camp again.

LERMONTOV. I see.

Slight pause.

Well, now. Miklos informs me you are taking me to lunch.

JEREMY. Indeed we are.

LERMONTOV. And interviewing me.

MARTIN. That's right.

LERMONTOV. The *Sunday Times*.

PALOCZI. Correct.

LERMONTOV (*to* MARTIN). And you, a former Trotskyite? Is that unusual?

PALOCZI. Um, well —

MARTIN. We tended to prefer 'Trotskyist'.

LERMONTOV. And now? What type of 'ite' or 'ist' are you?

Slight pause.

MARTIN. Well, in fact I find most 'isms' pretty hard to —

LERMONTOV. Oh, come on. Please, tell me. I am interested. After all, I too am, what you might call, a defector.

Slight pause. MARTIN *looks to* JEREMY *for confirmation, and gets it.*

MARTIN. Well, in a sentence, I suppose I realised that men and women are only equal in the prison or the graveyard.

LERMONTOV. Yes?

MARTIN. And that — that all attempts to force them to be equal, every increase in the power of monopoly, the closed shop and the state, lead ultimately to the concentration camp.

LERMONTOV *still looking questioningly at him.*

And that the only social value which means anything is the right of individuals to forge their destinies, uncoerced and undirected, as they will.

PALOCZI. Ah, but do you think they really want it? Freedom?

MARTIN. Who?

PALOCZI. You see, I sense complete contentment. The nation sitting on its quango, with one hand held out for its girocheque, the other filling in its VAT return.

MARTIN. Content?

PALOCZI. Now, freedom *from* is one thing, freedom from want and hunger and disease, they'll vote for that . . . But those who believe that human rights don't *end* with breakfast, those who believe in freedom *for* . . . A small minority. The merest speck.

MARTIN *looks to* JEREMY, *then back to* PALOCZI.

JEREMY. Yes, you know the thing that I can't understand?

MARTIN. What's that?

JEREMY. How it was possible for us to think that if you opened up the sluice-gates, then the lower water automatically bubbles to the level of the higher. Genuinely thought, a couple of good education acts, a few bright modern city libraries, and within a three-month sturdy sons of toil will all be reading Thomas Mann amd whistling Dvorak. Whereas, what actually happened was, a kind of rising silt. Of bingo, dogs, and, pinball. Hardly need 'The Revolution' any more. This is how the world ends, actually: not with a big bang, but a whippet.

MARTIN. You don't think that's unnecessarily pessimistic? You see, I think, that if you really set the people free, if you really broke the shackles of the state, you'd be amazed how many flowers would bloom.

PALOCZI. You think so? Really?

LERMONTOV. What is a whippet, please?

Slight pause.

MARTIN. It's a kind of dog. I'm sorry —

LERMONTOV. What, like a pug?

PALOCZI. No, nothing like a pug.

The phone rings.

And I did say no calls.

LERMONTOV, *who is nearest, answers the telephone.*

LERMONTOV. Hallo?
Yes, yes, hallo?

He hands the phone to PALOCZI.

You had better take it. It is apparently a man of some importance. Hence, his getting through.

PALOCZI. Yes, who is this?
Oh, I'm sorry. Yes. Hallo.

LERMONTOV. It's very odd.

PALOCZI. Yes, that was him.

LERMONTOV. We used to talk in English, in the camps, because of course the guards were not well educated, and they couldn't understand us.

PALOCZI. Well, yes, sometime next week?

LERMONTOV. But now I'm here, surrounded by it, and it's just a — (*To* PALOCZI.) Dimness, hazy, foggy?

PALOCZI. Yes, absolutely. Both of them.

He puts the phone down. LERMONTOV:

That's 'Just a blur'.

LERMONTOV. A Blur.

PALOCZI. There is a body, called the Committee in Defence of

Liberty. They want to give you an award. Big dinner, and
you make a speech. That was the chairman. He's a former
member of the Government, now a Provost of a Cambridge
College. He wants to invite you there. To meet him. Have a
chat. Discuss the matter.

LERMONTOV. An award?

PALOCZI. You know, a statuette, or something.

LERMONTOV. And 'liberty' means freedom?

PALOCZI. Yes.

Slight pause.

LERMONTOV. Then, of course. I'd be most privileged.

Slight pause.

And now, to lunch?

PALOCZI. To lunch!

*He claps his hands. Bustle. They go out. MARTIN lingering.
PALOCZI and LERMONTOV have gone.*

MARTIN. Look, Jeremy.

JEREMY. Yes, what?

MARTIN. Who is that man?

JEREMY. Miklos Paloczi. Writes for the Economist.

MARTIN. I mean, *who* is he? What's he doing?

JEREMY. Well, what he's done is to spend eight years
campaigning for our friend to be —

MARTIN. I mean, what is he doing now?

Slight pause.

JEREMY. Look, Martin. The man does have impeccable
credentials. In fact you could say, that unlike me, he left
Hungary, over the Party.
Now, shouldn't we —

MARTIN. And 'The Committee in Defence of Liberty'?

JEREMY. It's a pressure group. As its name implies. I think I'm on its council.

MARTIN. And this Provost?

JEREMY. Is a man called Hugh Trelawney. Martin —

MARTIN. Hugh Trelawney.

PALOCZI has re-entered to find out the reason for the delay.

PALOCZI. A tragic story, in a way. Poor bloke got kicked upstairs. There was some, well, unpleasantness, surrounding the enactment of his Housing Bill.

MARTIN. I know.

PALOCZI. But I think you'll find, an interesting man.

MARTIN. I'll find?

PALOCZI. Well, I hope you're coming too.

Scene Four

The Provost's rooms, a Cambridge College, January 1979.

An upstage and downstage area, divided — we imagine — by doors or a curtain. The downstage area, with a roaring fire, and comfortable chairs, is presently empty. Upstage, LERMONTOV is being introduced to a group of well-wishers, dons, undergraduates and others by PALOCZI. JEREMY is there too, as is MARTIN, who is in the downstage area, looking for an ashtray. JEREMY nods to the College Provost, HUGH TRELAWNEY, and the two men come into the downstage area.

TRELAWNEY. Now, Mr Glass?

MARTIN. That's right.

JEREMY. Martin, meet Hugh Trelawney.

MARTIN. How do you do?

TRELAWNEY. Delighted you could make it. Filthy weather.

MARTIN. Not at all.

Slight pause.

TRELAWNEY. Have you been to Simeon before?

MARTIN. No, I haven't.

TRELAWNEY. We are very proud of —

MARTIN. It is most agreeable.

Slight pause.

TRELAWNEY. I read with interest your piece on Lermontov, where was it?

MARTIN. *Sunday Times.*

TRELAWNEY. Great interest. As with your pieces on your own, trajectory, the series in — the *Standard?*

MARTIN. No, the daily *Times.*

TRELAWNEY. Indeed.

Slight pause.

JEREMY. Um, Martin. Hugh was saying —

TRELAWNEY. Hugh will say.

He gestures MARTIN to sit. MARTIN perches on the edge of a sofa.

In fact, Hugh thought of offering you a job.

MARTIN. What kind of job?

TRELAWNEY. Our little, group, requires a full time officer.

MARTIN. To do —

TRELAWNEY. We had in mind, the preparation of a kind of, manifesto.

MARTIN. For?

TRELAWNEY. To outline what, in our view, the priorities of the next Goverment should be.

Slight pause.

That is assuming, naturally —

MARTIN. Of course. I'd need to know, precisely, where you —

TRELAWNEY. As would we.

Pause.

MARTIN. You first?

TRELAWNEY. Well, where to start?

> TRELAWNEY *smiles. A slight nod to* JEREMY, *who withdraws a little upstage, and sits. We begin to lose a sense of the upstage area.*

> It's an outworn phrase, of course, but the next election will, in my view, be the most important since the war. The showdown, if you like. The polity a pyramid, the electorate a silver ball, perched on the top, unsteady, could roll either way.

MARTIN. A pyramid has several sides.

TRELAWNEY. Of course. And the side that you are on — the side that you are *now* on — is very clear. Unless we want to end up in the Gulag, stop the clicking ratchet of the state.

MARTIN. That's right.

TRELAWNEY. Health warnings off the packets, nanny off our backs. Free, adult men and women in a free, grown-up society.

MARTIN. Correct.

TRELAWNEY. And if people want to buy pornography or drugs, and if they're offered on the market at a price they are prepared to pay, then nobody, and least of all the state, should interfere.

MARTIN. I'm glad that you agree.

TRELAWNEY. I think — about your article — the word I used was 'interesting'.

> *Pause.*

MARTIN. Go on.

TRELAWNEY. Well, the fact is, on a cursory inspection of your output, I have noticed that the word 'right' — as in 'human right' — has graced your columns, oh, a hundred times. But I've only seen the word 'duty' once. In a sentence starting, 'In the free world, we have a duty to . . .', protect our threatened liberties, or something of that ilk.

MARTIN. What's wrong with human rights?

TRELAWNEY. That so often they're not balanced by a corresponding consciousness of obligation.

MARTIN. You tug my forelock, I'll tug yours?

TRELAWNEY. Well, if you like.

MARTIN. I see.

TRELAWNEY. I'm not convinced that's so.

Slight pause.

My Party has an interesting history. In the nineteenth century, the age of liberalism, it stood for land, tradition, church and state, against the rising tide of *laissez-faire*. Against the collapse of ancient hierarchies, and indeed the obligations that went with them, kindness, charity: against, in short, the cold and calculating face of commerce.

MARTIN. And the liberties that went with *that*.

TRELAWNEY. Indeed. Whereas, in our own century, things changed. Because the enemy had changed. Now it was socialism. Grey, monolithic, smothering. As you say, the Nanny State. Her charges guarded against every challenge, from the cradle to the grave. Her nursery the council house, her schoolroom a closed shop. Her motto, 'I want always gets'. And against *that*, we stood up for enterprise, for the brisk, chill wind of competition, for individual liberty. And there are, in the Party, many, like yourself, who think that battle is still on.

MARTIN. You don't?

TRELAWNEY. I think it's won. I think that socialism, as a reputable intellectual concept, is quite dead. A 'wasm' in our times.

MARTIN. Well, honestly, you could have fooled —

TRELAWNEY. In the form of state control of the means of production, distribution and exchange.

MARTIN. There is another form?

TRELAWNEY. Well, more a residue. A kind of putrefaction, left there, breeding in the body politic. Which it is now our party's task to purge.

MARTIN. I see. And so, what antidote do you prescribe?

TRELAWNEY. Well, in a word: Authority.

Pause.

MARTIN. Well, I'm sorry, Mr Trelawney. But I think I've spent quite long enough believing that the choir of humankind sounds best in unison. I'm really very sorry.

TRELAWNEY. Not unison — so much as harmony.

MARTIN *is about to say something, but* TRELAWNEY *goes straight on.*

Look, I do — I think I understand. How hard it is.

MARTIN. How hard what is?

TRELAWNEY. What you have had to do. Remake your life. Both for you and Lermontov. You have both been through the centre of the fire. You've both been branded by the century.

MARTIN. Him just a little more than me.

TRELAWNEY. Which is why you are both such expert witnesses. It is why your testimony is uniquely credible. Because you *know.* Because you have *seen* the future, and you *know* it doesn't work. Which is why whoever said the final struggle will be between the communists and the ex-communists, was right.

MARTIN *looks at* TRELAWNEY.

But I must be frank with you. If the only lesson you have learnt in all those years is that men need liberating *from* the state instead of *by* it, then your usefulness to us, to me, is pretty limited. But a defector who would stand up publicly and argue not for the roll-back of the state but for the reassertion of its full authority . . . Well, there's a man whose testimony would be listened to.

MARTIN *a slight laugh.*

But, of course, I understand, old loyalties . . .

MARTIN. That wasn't what I said.

TRELAWNEY. The sense of loyalty, old friends. That, I completely understand.

MARTIN. Please don't. Call my commitment into question. I know all about commitment. I once had a friend, for instance, committed to assassinating you.

Pause.

TRELAWNEY. Exactly.

PALOCZI *comes into the downstage area.*

PALOCZI. I'm sorry, Hugh. I've lost Pavel. Has he been through here?

TRELAWNEY. No, I don't think so.

JEREMY. In fact, we shouldn't be too long. It's snowing and of course the bloody gritters are on strike.

TRELAWNEY. Yes, yes, of course.

PALOCZI. The latest is, apparently, the gravediggers.

TRELAWNEY. The what?

PALOCZI. Good NUPE men. It's comic, in a way. You drive because there are no trains, you crash because the roads are ice, and if you're killed, you lie unburied.

TRELAWNEY. Yes. My friend here thinks that basic problem in this country is too much authority.

MARTIN (*to* JEREMY). Do you agree with this?

JEREMY. With what?

MARTIN. With what this man's been saying?

JEREMY. Why, don't you?

Pause.

MARTIN. I merely ask, for information.

JEREMY. Martin, of course, it was the state that bred it.

MARTIN. What?

JEREMY. The idea that every appetite is an entitlement.
Society an open mouth, the state a ladle.

But you know, it strikes me, something else has happened,
happened in the sixties, what you liberteenies actually did,
despite your efforts to the contrary, was not to abolish the
free market, but to take it over. Win it for your side.

Pause.

MARTIN. Go on.

JEREMY. 'Do your own thing.' 'If it feels good, fondle it.' And
if it doesn't, fondle something else.

MARTIN. Well, I can live with that.

JEREMY. Or someone else's.

And, of course, permissiveness implies permission, and
even licence must be licensed, by somebody or another. But
what has changed now is that it's the market sells the slop
that's poisoning us all and commerce that's provided the long
spoon.

A video-machine in every Porsche. A Magimix in every
microwave. And, yes, a pick-up in every lavatory. A fix in
every vein. The Prostitution Ethic. Mine, mine, mine.

Well, I don't call that liberalism, though some might, nor
socialism, though it's socialism's mutant child. I'd call it
nihilism, and unless it's understood that our disease is not
too little freedom but too much, it will destroy us all.

Pause.

TRELAWNEY. Hear hear.

Pause.

MARTIN. I see.

Pause. LERMONTOV *has come in, unnoticed by the*
OTHERS.

MARTIN. 'I'm with the malcontents, I haven't changed'?

JEREMY. Well, that does depend a bit, of course, on which
malcontents you mean.

MARTIN. There's no 'of course' about it, Jeremy.

JEREMY. Then just one question, Martin. How do you think they will react? The people who've been breastfed on the milk of social kindness all these years? When the teat is pulled away? When the plateglass is put up between them and the goodies they've been promised as of right?

I listen to the future and I'm hearing broken glass. I look into my crystal ball, and I see London burning.

With a gesture towards TRELAWNEY:

And the falcon, plotting to assassinate the falconer.

MARTIN. Now, come on, Jeremy —

PALOCZI. You know, it's very strange, to come here, from a country which has never had political or economic freedom, in the sense we understand it. It is very strange, initially, to discover that a country which has both of these good things seems to care so little about losing them. Until you realise the paradox that unless it is built on the foundations of what one might call the ultimate realities, then all freedom actually consists of is the absence of restraint. An empty canvas on which anyone may scrawl whatever vile graffiti they desire.

MARTIN. What 'ultimate realities'?

LERMONTOV. I have been looking at the pictures in your dining-hall.

The others turn to him.

Quite remarkable. So many faces, of so many dead.

It must be, I have always thought, that the condemned are blindfolded, not for themselves, but for the executioner. So he can't see their faces.

Pause.

TRELAWNEY. Was it Chesterton who said, we are fleeing from the faces of our ancestors, because that is what they are.

Long pause.

MARTIN. Look.

Slight pause.

Look, the point is, that I didn't mean . . .

As the lights fade, and the set begins to change, a picket-line crosses the stage, shouting slogans:

PICKETS (*variously*).
   What do we want? Revolution!
   Where do we want it? Salvador.
   When do we want it? Now!
   Hands off Cuba, Hands off Cuba!
   Smash Pin-Pinochet! Smash Pin-Pinochet!

WEINER *crosses the stage towards the set that is beginning to build behind the picket.*

   CIA — out! CIA — out! CIA — out!
   Sandinistas — in! Sandinistas — in! Sandinistas — in!
   The People — United — Will Never Be Defeated.
   The People — United — Will Never Be Defeated.
   El Pueblo — Unido — Nunca Será Vencido!
   El Pueblo — Unido — Nunca Será Vencido!

And by now, WEINER *has arrived, and the* PICKET *runs out.*

Scene Five

A reception room adjacent to a banqueting hall in a large and expensive London hotel. Drinks and a telephone on a small table. A large, dark, early seventeenth century painting on the wall. There are two exits: one, left, into the banqueting hall, and the other, right, leading to the rest of the hotel.

   TEDDY WEINER *stands, alone. He has a drink in his hand. Like all the men in this scene, he wears a dinner jacket.*

   TRELAWNEY *enters, quickly, right.*

TRELAWNEY. Professor Weiner. Hugh Trelawney.

WEINER (*looks at his watch*). Well, hallo.

TRELAWNEY. Look, I'm so sorry, we've completely lost — Do you have a drink?

WEINER. I helped myself.

TRELAWNEY. Well done.

Pause.

Um — presumably you managed to evade the welcoming committee?

WEINER. What? Oh, sure. A quick chorus of 'Smash Pinochet' and 'Hands off Nicaragua' and I was through. I think your British picket-lines are wonderful.

TRELAWNEY. Yes.

He gets it.

Oh, yes.

A noise in the corridor.

Aha.

He turns to the right entrance as PALOCZI *and* LERMONTOV *come through it.* LERMONTOV *is in a strange, distant mood.*

PALOCZI. Hugh, Pavel was at Bush House, it over-ran two hours, I had to pick him up and change him in the cab —

WEINER (*To* LERMONTOV). Hallo, I'm Teddy Weiner. It's a privilege.

LERMONTOV *and* WEINER *shake hands.* TRELAWNEY *hands out sherry.*

LERMONTOV. We had our main problems with the tie.

PALOCZI. I know, I should have got you one of those elasticated jobs.

TRELAWNEY. Heaven forfend. A terrible American invention. Outdone, in my view, only by the verb 'eventuate'.

He realises his faux pax. WEINER *smiles.*

WEINER. As they say, America, the only country in the world to pass from barbarism to decadence without an intervening period of civilisation.

TRELAWNEY *and* PALOCZI *laugh.*

PALOCZI. Whereas, of course, where Pavel and I come from,

it's precisely opposite.

TRELAWNEY *and* WEINER *laugh.*

LERMONTOV. I did an interview today, with the BBC Russian Service. The interviewer was a man called Griboyedov. Very strange. He seemed to think we fought on the wrong side in the war.

Slight pause.

TRELAWNEY. Who's we?

LERMONTOV. You are.

Slight pause.

PALOCZI. He said nothing of the kind, Pavel. He wasn't talking about Germany.

LERMONTOV. He was talking about fascists.

PALOCZI. He was talking about Chile and Brazil.

LERMONTOV. And they're not fascists?

PALOCZI. Ask Professor Weiner. He has written quite extensively on that very subject.

LERMONTOV *turns to* WEINER.

LERMONTOV. Well, then. Perhaps he will explain.

WEINER *a quizzical look to* TRELAWNEY, *who makes no reaction.*

WEINER. Well, I've been known to advance the view that the West cannot afford to be too, well, fastidious about its choice of friends.

Slight pause.

LERMONTOV. Go on.

WEINER. If we are not to end up living in a country like your country, Mr Lermontov.

LERMONTOV. I see.

Slight pause.

Yes, yes, I see, that's very clear. I'm sorry. You will

understand, it is a whole new — (*To* PALOCZI). Parlance, idiom?

PALOCZI. Vocabulary?

LERMONTOV. Yes.

TRELAWNEY. Well, now, perhaps —

LERMONTOV (*draining his sherry*). Indeed.

The phone rings. TRELAWNEY *picks it up.*

TRELAWNEY. Hallo?

He puts his hand over the receiver.

There's somebody in the lobby, 'needs' to speak to Mr Lermontov.

PALOCZI *takes the phone.*

PALOCZI. Hallo, now what is this?
    No, I'm not Lermontov, Mr Lermontov is about to go into dinner.
    No, I'm sorry, but he cannot possibly —
    Can't you hear what I'm saying? Do I have to spell it out in semaphore?

After a moment, he slams the phone down.

People so slow and *stupid* in this country.

LERMONTOV *goes to the phone, picks it up and dials.*

LERMONTOV. Hallo, front desk? This is P.M. Lermontov. I would like the person who has come to see me sent up, please. (*To* TRELAWNEY). Where are we now?

TRELAWNEY. The Jacobean Suite. Um, I . . .

LERMONTOV (*down the phone*). The Jacobean Suite. Thank you.

He puts the phone down.

You will understand, in the Soviet Union people spend much time, waiting in lobbies to see influential men.

Slight pause.

Please, start without me. I will miss the soup.

TRELAWNEY *and* WEINER *look at each other. An unspoken agreement. They go out by the left door.*

PALOCZI. Pavel —

LERMONTOV (*suddenly angry*). Do I have to spell it out in semaphore? Please, go away.

Pause. PALOCZI *takes out a pile of postcards, on which* LERMONTOV's *speech is written.*

PALOCZI. We didn't have enough time in the taxi. You should look through this.

He hands the cards to LERMONTOV *and goes.* LERMONTOV *gets another drink. He starts to look through the cards. His bow-tie is uncomfortable. He fiddles with it, it comes apart. A knock, right.*

LERMONTOV. Come in.

LERMONTOV *shrugs, pulls the tie off, undoes the top button of his shirt, pockets the cards. He turns to see a Russian* WOMAN, *in her mid-forties, who has entered.*

Good evening, I am Lermontov.

WOMAN. I know.

LERMONTOV. So, who are you?

WOMAN. I'm sorry to disturb you. It was in the paper, you were here tonight.

LERMONTOV. I've only got a moment, I'm afraid . . .

WOMAN. My name is Kaminskaya.

Pause.

LERMONTOV. What?

WOMAN. I work for TASS in London. Formerly a correspondent of *Izvestia*.

Pause.

And formerly to that, attached to the Military Intelligence Division of the Soviet Army. As — as a stenographer.

Pause.

Clara Ivanovna.

LERMONTOV. Oh, no.

CLARA. Do you remember?

LERMONTOV. You're in *London*?

CLARA. Yes. I wanted a new job. That work I was doing on *Izvestia*. There's only so long, you can do that stuff. I imagine it's the same here, writing the letters to the *Daily Mail*.

LERMONTOV. I don't believe this.

CLARA. How do you find it? I find the most striking thing is the trivia. Not the pornography, just the torrential triviality, each way you turn.

LERMONTOV. I just do not believe this.

CLARA. And the lack of books in people's houses. Working-class people. You would think, at least a set of Dickens, Rudyard Kipling —

LERMONTOV. This is — *preposterous*. The man is — *in there*.

CLARA. Who's in there?

LERMONTOV. The boy who I released, in Budapest. Who threw the hand-grenade.

CLARA. What hand-grenade?

Pause. LERMONTOV *looks at* CLARA.

LERMONTOV. I am aware that there are rules. Grades of invective. 'Childish, scurrilous and egotistical' for signing a petition, 'hoarse, malicious and unsavoury' for an interview with Western correspondents, 'slanderous, corrupt and cynically treacherous' for a pamphlet published in the West. But what was visited on me broke all the rules. That wasn't from some well-thumbed manual. That wasn't faceless. It was sharp and real, and *personal*.

CLARA. Yes. It was personal.

LERMONTOV. Then — *why?*

CLARA. Because —

LERMONTOV. Why did you come here?

CLARA. Because you were coming here. Because you have been seduced into the camp of the most bellicose cold war imperialists. And I did want to know —

LERMONTOV. 'The camp of the most bellicose —'

CLARA. Yes, the language is a little arch. A little coarse and breathless. It's the vocabulary, in fact, of people who until quite recently were stupid peasants, working with wooden ploughs. Until they were all sent off to school, and taught at least a kind of language.

LERMONTOV. At what a cost.

CLARA. One of the great achievements, you may think, of the Great October Revolution. A victory comparable with that of the Red Army in the Civil War.

LERMONTOV. Oh, please —

CLARA. Or indeed the five year plan. Those thousands upon thousands of young party cadres, laying pipelines across Russia's freezing wastes.

LERMONTOV. These words —

CLARA. Those superhuman tasks. Against all odds. At any cost.

LERMONTOV. I have, I have read the picture books. I do, I know these words —

CLARA. You see, it just isn't true, that the only way that people will do anything is if they're bribed or forced at the point of a revolver. There are times, Pavel Mikhailovich, when it just isn't true.

LERMONTOV *looks at* CLARA.

It's just, at other times . . . Most times . . .
   People get tired. They can't go on. Suddenly, the odds seem stacked too heavily against them, and the cost appears too great. Even the most heroic superman flops down onto the ground, and realises that he's just a normal human being after all.

And turns his tired eyes to people who will tell him what
to do. And sullenly, resentfully, submissively, does what he's
told.

Returns to normal life.

Pause.

LERMONTOV. So?

CLARA. So, you don't pretend it never happened.

LERMONTOV. This is just absurd.

CLARA. What is absurd?

LERMONTOV. I am standing in a suite in a hotel in London,
being lectured by a woman who put me in a labour camp.

CLARA. Well, now I have a face.

LERMONTOV. You knew *I* had a face.

CLARA. You're right. I'd seen it.

LERMONTOV. But you still —

CLARA. I'd seen it sneering in contempt, at a stupid girl from
a Russian village, who knew nothing about music, who had
never seen a city and who didn't always understand when
people shouted at her very loud.

Pause.

LERMONTOV. I see.

Pause.

Eight years.

Pause.

I see.

TRELAWNEY *and* PALOCZI *enter.*

Well, there he is. The boy who I released. Who was
exactly who we thought he was. To whom I gave a
hand-grenade.

CLARA *looks at* PALOCZI, *then quickly to* LERMONTOV
and then goes out quickly.

PALOCZI. Pavel, who was that woman?

LERMONTOV. You don't know?

PALOCZI. Please what is going on, Pavel?

LERMONTOV. I might ask you, the same question. I might ask you, what has happened to the brave young revolutionary, full of dreams, who understood why peasants brought free food to feed the cities, and who clearly doesn't understand that any more.

PALOCZI. Please, what is this about?

LERMONTOV. And who will tell us — *now* — what he thinks that *that* was all about?

Pause.

PALOCZI. It isn't very difficult. It's very simple. For a man who came here from a country which has not possessed a real border for a thousand years. Quite simple. God save Hungary.

Pause.

LERMONTOV. That wasn't what you said.

PALOCZI. It wasn't what I thought. But it was what I felt.

MARTIN *enters quickly*.

MARTIN. I'm sorry. Look, am I very late?

LERMONTOV. I would like to know, I would like to be informed. Exactly what is happening here today.

TRELAWNEY (*with a glance at* PALOCZI). I'm so sorry. Didn't anyone explain?

Slight pause.

The Committee in Defence of Liberty, is a body dedicated to the simple notion that we face two enemies, in Britain, one without and one within. Without, we face a rapacious military power, bent on conquest and subordination; while within, we see a society so soft, so feeble and degenerate that we fear it may have lost, quite literally, its will to live.

And despite the fashionable nostra of the day, we do suspect that the economics of the corner grocer's shop, while admirable values in themselves, may not prove quite sufficient as a means to reassert the basic, fundamental instincts of the nation.

And so — resistance to aggression from without; the reassertion of authority within. You are speaking to the next Government of Britain, Mr Lermontov. Which is why we are so keen to hear what you have got to say.

Pause. LERMONTOV *reaches in his pocket, takes out the pile of cards which* PALOCZI *gave him. He glances at them. He realises he still holds his black tie in his hand.*

LERMONTOV. Could someone help me, please?

Scene Six

The top table of a banquet. Flowers bedeck, white linen gleams. Behind the table sit — from left to right — JEREMY, TRELAWNEY, WEINER, LERMONTOV, PALOCZI, MARTIN. A statuette in front of WEINER. TRELAWNEY stands, and speaks into the microphone.

TRELAWNEY. Professor Weiner. (*He sits.*)

WEINER (*stands*). Gentlemen, I hope you will forgive me, if I address what I have to say, on your behalf, directly to Pavel Mikhailovich. Because I feel that what ought to be said must take the form of an apology, an apology which must be made by us, the West, to those brave men who have stood up for their beliefs in Budapest, in Prague, in Warsaw and indeed in Moscow, whom I think we have betrayed.

And I don't mean just by lack of military support, though that's important, but by a kind of lie that we've been living, about what we are and what we have become. Most of all, a lie about those people out there in the street, who are as we well know the same ones who ten years ago were marching for the US to get out of Vietnam, and for Black Power, peace and love and indeed the whole shebang. And in your presence it behooves us — those of us who argued for so long that those folks were at least idealists, at least sincere — to put ourselves in the witness box, to test that testimony, to tell it how it really is.

Pause. A little cough. Then:

To affirm that agitation's agitation, even if it's published quarterly in learned periodicals, and that subversion is subversion, even if the subverters of our culture are distinguished film directors, poets, writers and musicians. And that treachery is treachery, even if the traitors to our country have no need of telephoto lenses, tape-machines and microfilm, but ply their trade as smart left lawyers, clever linguists, and conscience-striken academics.

And, for I think these matters are connected, that mobs of hooligans are mobs of hooligans, even if they happen to consist of college students, teachers and professors. And that parasites are parasites, whether they are feeding off the state as clients, or as members of that army of administrators who, with such precious, finely-honed compassion, dole out our largesse.

PALOCZI *has been looking at a particular card in the pile. He removes it from the pile. He writes another card.*

And even worse than that, to admit that it's our fault. To confess that in order to assuage our overwhelming sense of guilt, we spawned a generation so soft and so effete, so resistant to responsibility of any kind, that it is not prepared to die, or even really live, for anything beyond its own sense of material and moral satisfaction. And, worst of all, that we snatched away from them at birth the only antidote there is to the sickly and corrosive culture of appeasement and surrender they've created. I mean, a sense of who they really are. I mean those gut emotions, instincts, prejudices even, that are in fact the only things that men have ever really found worth living or worth dying for. I mean . . .

I mean that it has taken me some time: it has taken me the best part of a lifetime, to admit, without embarrassment or hesitation: that I belong to the nation of my birth.

Pause.

And if I may say so, Pavel Mikhailovich, it has taken you and people like you, voices issuing from the darkness of a nationhood suppressed, to convince me of that fact.

Pause.

And so — please accept our welcome, and our admiration, and our thanks.

Applause, as WEINER *hands the statuette to* LERMONTOV. LERMONTOV *stands to receive it. As* WEINER *sits and passes the microphone,* PALOCZI *hands* LERMONTOV *the cards.* LERMONTOV *coughs and begins to speak.*

LERMONTOV. Thank you. May I say first of all how good it is to spend an evening discussing freedom. Particularly as, in my country, no one is free to hold such a discussion. May I also thank the organisers for providing such a — (*To* PALOCZI.) What's this?

PALOCZI. Sumptuous.

LERMONTOV. Sumptuous — repast; and Professor Weiner for such a generous and indeed inspiring speech. I think the phrase is, 'follow that'.

He turns to a new card written by PALOCZI *during* WEINER's *speech. As he does so, an ad lib:*

Well, I will do my best.

I was particularly struck by his remarks on the surrender of the West and those people who have made a career of promoting this surrender. I would — *morely?*

PALOCZI. Merely.

LERMONTOV. Merely remark in passing, to those who would be rather red than dead, that there are many graves where I have recently come from, which confirm that they may not have the option.

Turns cards. Back on the pre-written text.

And I must thank those gentlemen who selected me as a recipient of this award. I am most honoured. But I must say that I do not view this award as mine alone. I view it as being for all the zeks, in all the camps, the living and the dead.

New card.

For the seventies and the one-nine-oh-threes, the one-nine-oh-ones and the two-oh-nines, the two-sixties and the sixty-fours, the violators, great and small, of the Criminal Code of the Russian Federated Socialist Republic.

He turns the card. The next card is not the one he expects. He realises that PALOCZI *has removed it. He sees it on the table. He picks it up quickly and reads:*

From the agitators and subversives, violators of the public order, slanderers and hooligans and parasites and traitors, of the Soviet Corrective Labour Colonies.

Pause.

Who up until their sentences were teachers, physicists, academicians and administrators. Writers and poets. Actors, film directors and musicians. Workers and trade union officials. Linguists and lawyers. Publishers. Professors.

Pause.

People who, resist.

A very long pause, as LERMONTOV *looks through the rest of the cards. Then he looks up.*

I appear — to be expected — to advance the view — that the bombing of my country, and of yours — is preferable to the greater evil — of, surrender.

Pause. He places the cards on the table.

It is not of course the same. It is not —

To PALOCZI:

— equivalent, to be compared with?

Pause.

PALOCZI. Comparable.

LERMONTOV. Comparable. Of course. You have no camps. Your 'dissidents' are free. It is no way comparable.
  And yet.
  I wonder, can there be anything as bad as telling someone that they only think the things they think because they're

'cranks' or 'crazies'? How, um —

To PALOCZI:

Caustic, eaten into, rust, decay?

PALOCZI. I don't know —

LERMONTOV (*with a gesture to* WEINER). Yes, *corrosive*, of a human being's dignity?

Pause.

I'm sorry. I have not fulfilled my duty. Pavel Mikhailovich has not reminded you of what he was supposed to. He has not affirmed 'the ultimate realities'. But he will nonetheless say something. It is this.

He breathes deeply. Then:

That if you really want to see a nation, strong and tough and virile, marching to a single rhythm, banged out with a hammer on a rail, then — please, gentlemen — come to my country.

   It is not that it's the same.

   It's just — that it does appear to be — the same variety of people — who applaud it on their own side — but oppose it on the other. People for whom, the ultimate reality is not in fact resistance, but —

To PALOCZI, *as it were in Russian:*

Control, administration? People in control?

PALOCZI. I'm sorry?

LERMONTOV. You know. Police, the army, running things?

PALOCZI. What do you mean, Pavel?

LERMONTOV (*gesturing at* TRELAWNEY). He used the word. I heard him use the word.

PALOCZI. Pavel, you are behaving like a child!

   LERMONTOV *remembers. In 'English'.*

LERMONTOV. 'Authority'.

He turns out front. Back in 'English':

I'm sorry. Slight problem of translation. Yes.

You see, I look around this room, and I don't see faces which have ever seen the world through wire. Yours are not gaolers' faces. But perhaps they are the faces of the people who employ the gaolers.

Faces which cannot remember, if they ever knew, the superhuman things that people can achieve, when for a moment they forget what they've been told they are.

Pause.

I'm sorry. How embarrassing of me.

He picks up the statuette.

And I am most honoured. Most —

He can't find the synonym. A glance to PALOCZI. *He changes his mind.*

Most honoured.
    But I have decided. No.

He puts down the statuette.

You will I hope forgive me.

LERMONTOV *goes. Long pause.* PALOCZI *stands, abruptly, and goes out too. Pause.* TRELAWNEY *looks at his watch. Then, almost as if he'd just remembered some pressing engagement, he stands and goes.* WEINER, *rather efficiently, as if it was the end of the event, tidies his napkin, pockets his notes, and goes.* MARTIN *stands.* JEREMY *stands.* MARTIN *and* JEREMY *alone.*

JEREMY. Martin, he's wrong. Just because he's suffered, just because he's brave, a hero, doesn't mean he can't be wrong.

MARTIN. I stood there for an hour. Stood across the street. Those faces. Couldn't move.

Outburst:

I mean, come on, Jeremy, with hand on heart, do you really want a man like that to run the country?

JEREMY. Who?

MARTIN. Trelawney?

JEREMY. Yes.

MARTIN. We sack the nanny, hire a governess? Her motto, heed the mystic voices of our ancestors?

JEREMY. Well, that's certainly one way of —

MARTIN. So, then, what do you predict, for Hugh Trelawney's brave new world? The rope? The cat? The censor? Military conscription?

JEREMY. Well, I wouldn't be at all —

MARTIN. 'In the end the only way to make men uniform is to put them all in one?'

JEREMY. Martin. What follows, surely, even you can understand. That man is like he is because those people in the street are like you were. Because what he says has got to happen is indeed the only way to win the war.

MARTIN. 'Objectively'?

JEREMY. Correct. In the same way that —

MARTIN. Why does this matter quite so much to you?

JEREMY. Because you're right.

MARTIN. Well, glory be.

JEREMY. In a way, yes, I do wish I'd been a Red at Trinity. Wish that instead of having to betray my class, I could have, merely, come in from the cold.

And if *I* can sacrifice that whey-faced child who thought the toiling masses were about to rise and forge the New Jerusalem, then why the hell can't you?

Pause. He changes tone.

You see, you come to realise, it really is the little things. The sensual things. The smell of woodsmoke. Mulled wine, warming chilly fingers. The family's Wellingtons, all lined up in the hall. But that come the crunch, you'll take up arms, you'll maim and kill, to keep those things. The past that you rejected, but I never had, you see.

Pause.

MARTIN. What should I do?

Pause.

JEREMY. Take the last step, Martin. And Go Home.

TRELAWNEY stands there.

TRELAWNEY. They've gone.

JEREMY. Who've gone?

TRELAWNEY. The Barbarians Without The Gates.

Pause.

JEREMY. Is it not Leon Trotsky who reminds us, there is such a thing as human dust.

TRELAWNEY goes out. Behind him stands a child in her early teens, wearing a portable stereo. She wears a CND badge. It is TANIA, AMANDA's daughter. Darkness on MARTIN and JEREMY.

Scene Seven

Summer. The early 1980s.

Green hangings, representing trees and foliage. TANIA sings along with the song she's hearing on her stereo.

Upstage, a YOUNG MAN cycles on. He wears a slouch hat and a long mackintosh. He looks a bit like a gangster.

The YOUNG MAN comes to a halt, gets off his bike, and leans against it, waiting for something or somebody.

TANIA turns and goes out as a second CYCLIST enters, a slightly seedy, middle-aged man. It is PUGACHEV. The first cyclist calls out to him. It is KOROLENKO.

KOROLENKO. Well. Comrade Pugachev.

PUGACHEV comes to a quick halt.

PUGACHEV. Uh — yes?

KOROLENKO. What a pleasant chance to meet here, in the park. How are you?

PUGACHEV dismounts and lays his bicycle on the ground.

PUGACHEV (*bemused*). Oh, I'm — very well.

KOROLENKO (*no change of tone, still light and conversational*). I've been looking for you a whole week. My pass ran out four days ago. I'm Anatoly Korolenko.

PUGACHEV (*taking out a cigarette*). Pardon?

KOROLENKO (*lighting PUGACHEV's cigarette*). I'm a friend of Lermontov. Your friend.

PUGACHEV *drops his voice.*

PUGACHEV. What do you want?

KOROLENKO (*drops his voice*). I'm told you travel. Other countries.

PUGACHEV. Sometimes.

KOROLENKO (*light and conversational again*). I'm a miner. I was exiled to Vorkuta in the Northern Urals. They introduced new schedules in the pits. The workers told them they were crazy. Big explosion. Fifty died.

PUGACHEV (*low voice*). What has this to do with me?

KOROLENKO. There's this little group. In Leningrad. Donetsk. some other places. We're a kind of unofficial union. We've got this manifesto. We want to get it out.

PUGACHEV (*low voice*). I don't travel to the West. Well, not that often. Mainly the DDR, and Hungary and Poland. Places like that.

KOROLENKO. Exactly.

Pause.

Will you take it, then? The manifesto?

PUGACHEV. No, of course I won't.

KOROLENKO. It's titled 'For our freedom — and for yours'.

Pause.

PUGACHEV. Look. I'm a Professor at the University of Moscow. I'm not that good at thinking on my feet.

He looks round, warily.

Particularly, in the middle of the day.

KOROLENKO mounts his bike. Briskly:

KOROLENKO. Right, then. At nightfall. We will meet.

Looks at PUGACHEV.

And then you'll tell me.

AMANDA (*off*). Tania! Tanny, where are you?

Lights fade on PUGACHEV and KOROLENKO. A wire fence falls between them and the entering AMANDA. Lights only downstage now. MARTIN follows AMANDA on to the stage.

Tanny!

She turns back to MARTIN.

They're some of them so frighteningly young.

MARTIN. Indeed.

AMANDA. But very brave.

MARTIN. That doesn't mean they're right.

Two WOMEN, one of them in her 40s, enter from stage left. The older WOMAN has a map. They look around and go out right.

Well, obviously not *all* —

AMANDA. Oh, no. In fact, I was surprised, how various —

MARTIN. And you are seriously considering, yourself —

AMANDA. I've not made up my mind.

Slight pause.

It was Tanny, really. She was desperate to come.

TANIA has entered.

MARTIN. And here she is, by all that's wonderful?

AMANDA. She is indeed. Hey, Tan —

TANIA is wearing headphones, so can't hear.

Hey, Tanny —

TANIA *spots* AMANDA's *wave and takes off her headphones.*

D'you remember Martin?

Pause.

TANIA. Oh, yuh. 'Course.

With a grin.

'That fucking renegade.'

Slight pause.

AMANDA. Yes. That's the one.

The two WOMEN *enter from right.*

1ST WOMAN. There's a kind of copse. It's sheltered by the trees. We'll set up there.

They go out left.

TANIA. Well, still . . . It's only rock and roll.

She grins, turns, and follows the two WOMEN *out.*
AMANDA *breathes deeply.*

MARTIN. You know, there's this little, stained-glass St Anne, in the Lady Chapel of our church, the spit —

AMANDA. You go to church?

MARTIN. I'm the anchor of the baritones.

Slight pause.

We only get a service every other week, but the padre is a sound, no nonsense chap. Soup only to the conspicuously needy. Lucky, because in Lower Purley they've this bloke who appears to think Pol Pot was basically sound, just a little soft on the urban middle class.

So what's your present bag, then? Apart, that is, from Battered Lesbians Against the Bomb?

Pause.

AMANDA. I'm running a resources centre.

MARTIN. Well well well. I run a XJ12.

Pause.

AMANDA. There's gold in them thar Tory think-tanks, then?

MARTIN. Well, silver, certainly. What in God's name —

AMANDA. Well, I say 'run'. It's more of a collective.

MARTIN. Naturally.

AMANDA. We produce a kind of newspaper. Do have a copy.

MARTIN (*taking a copy*). Thanks.

The TWO WOMEN, *a* 3RD WOMAN, *and* TANIA *cross the stage, carrying camping equipment. They go out right.*

Well, this is all quite clear. 'Facilities.' 'Advice bureaux.' The Women's Movement. Peace Groups. 'Black Defence Campaigns.' From whom does who wish to 'reclaim the night?' What in the name of all that's holy is 'alternative technology?'

The 2ND WOMAN *crosses the stage from right to left.*

AMANDA. Oh, you know, finding ways of making things that people actually need. Like, ploughshares, as opposed to swords.

MARTIN. I see.

AMANDA. Oh, Martin, what the fuck's gone wrong with you?

The 2ND WOMAN *has re-entered left, dragging a huge sheet of polythene. The* 1ST *and* 3RD WOMEN, *and* TANIA *have come in stage right to help her.*

2ND WOMAN. They've closed the south gate. And they're clearing space around the hangers. That usually means there's an alert.

MARTIN. That always means there's an alert.

1ST WOMAN. Oh, yur? How do you know?

MARTIN. I live here. You are dragging polythene across my property.

Pause.

3RD WOMAN. Who is this creep?

TANIA. Oh, it's this bloke who used —

AMANDA. He's what he says he is. He lives there, in that house. It used to be his father's house. And he's just bought it back.

1ST WOMAN. I thought he was a friend of yours.

AMANDA. He was. Now he's the person who could call the police and have you all removed.

MARTIN. Now can I ask, of whoever is in charge here —

2ND WOMAN. Look. The land was common. The land between 'your land' and the perimeter of the US Air Force property. Last week, the Council repossessed the land, and sold it to the base. So, yesterday, at dawn, we were ejected, *that* was built, and hence, today —

MARTIN. I have fairies at the bottom of my garden.

Pause.

I was thinking more in terms of an injunction.

3RD WOMAN. Wouldn't work.

MARTIN. You wanna bet?

1ST WOMAN. Injunctions require names. We have no names.

MARTIN. Is this a metaphysical —

3RD WOMAN. Or put another way, you find our names and the court may order us to go. And go we will. But others will take over. And the same thing will keep happening.

Slight pause.

We — in the sense of this — we have no names.

1ST WOMAN. No membership.

2ND WOMAN. And no committees.

3RD WOMAN. No printing press. No postal code. No phone.

2ND WOMAN. And I assure you — nobody 'in charge'.

Pause.

MARTIN. Well, you got it all worked out.

1ST WOMAN. No, not 'it all'. Just this.

The WOMEN *go out.*

AMANDA. It doesn't actually need working out.

MARTIN. Oh, no?

AMANDA. Any more than for all my silly people with their weird and wonderful campaigns.

MARTIN. You're sure?

AMANDA. And of course you may say that the urge to stop the planet being blown to blazes is a form of brute, material self-interest —

MARTIN. Well, that's certainly an argument —

AMANDA. Or that to want these aeroplanes to be removed is merely good old British national pride —

MARTIN. Well, nobody likes Yanks —

AMANDA. But I think in fact that in the end what they are doing, what we all are trying to do, in our many different ways, can only be accounted for by something in the nature of our species which resents, rejects and ultimately will resist a world that is demonstrably and in this case dramatically wrong and mad and unjust and unfair.

And I wonder, Martin, if you ever really felt like that. Or, if you did, if you can still remember.

MARTIN. No.

Pause.

No, as it happens, I don't think I do.

Pause.

AMANDA. So. Are you going to call the police?

MARTIN. Tomorrow. Are you going to stay?

AMANDA. Tonight.

Suddenly, a LOUDSPEAKER *blares, as the lights quickly fade.*

LOUDSPEAKER. Scorcher. We have Scorcher. I repeat, we have

a Scorcher.

Sirens begin to wail. Dogs bark. Beyond the wire, searchlights and running men. Huge doors open, revealing headlamps. Engines rev.

Cresta Run. We are go for Cresta Run.

The headlamps — of trucks and motorcycles — career downstage, up to the wire. The lights beam through the wire, dazzling the audience. The lights flash. Engines revving wildly.

Kiss. We are kiss. Repeat, all units. We are kiss.

The sirens fade. The headlamps die, as the 'vehicles' reverse away.
     Silence.
     But just before it's total, two cycle headlamps, illuminating PUGACHEV *and* KOROLENKO *on their bicycles.*

KOROLENKO. Well, then?

PUGACHEV. How long.

KOROLENKO. How long?

PUGACHEV. Do you think you'll last? A week, a month, a year?

KOROLENKO. Maybe. Who knows? 'May Days.'

That Summer

The action of *That Summer* is set against the background of the 1984-5 miners' strike. The play is a work of fiction and its characters are invented. But it nonetheless owes much to many Rhondda miners and their families in particular to Pat and John Bates and Tony and Maudie Gazzi; and most of all to their daughters Karen and Lisa.

That Summer was first performed at the Hampstead Theatre, London on 2 July 1987. The cast was as follows:

CRESSIDA, *early 30s, a chiropractor*	Jessica Turner
HOWARD, *early 40s, a university lecturer*	Oliver Cotton
DANIEL, *16, Howard's son by his first marriage*	Edward Rawle-Hicks
ALUN, *mid 30s, a miner*	Gareth Morris
MICHELE, *15, Alun's daughter*	Caroline Berry
FRANKIE, *15, Michele's friend*	Catherine Tregenna
TERRY, *mid-30s, a schoolteacher*	Mick Ford

Directed by Michael Attenborough
Designed by Sue Plummer
Lighting by Gerry Jenkinson

The play is set in a holiday house in North Wales, in August 1984.

The set consists of the living room of the house, and a terrace, connected (we imagine) by french windows. In the living room is a selection of fairly basic furniture, including easy chairs, a dining table and dining chairs.

There is a large vase on a side-dresser. On the terrace is a bench and table.

At the back of the living room are two doors: one leading to the hallway, the other to the kitchen and the other interior rooms of the house.

From the terrace, it is possible to walk down to the beach. We imagine an extension to the terrace on the same side.

ACT ONE

Scene One

On the terrace, the bench and table. Also, a canvas garden-chair, recliner, and a free-standing barbecue.
At first, CRESSIDA is alone, with everything else in darkness. As she speaks, late afternoon sunlight lightens the terrace and the living-room.
Indeed, the light is so bright that CRESSIDA, who wears a some-what tent-like Japanese kimono, looks over-dressed, an intruder from another time.

CRESSIDA. In fact, it wasn't smaller. I mean, they say that when you go back to a childhood place, then everything looks smaller. But for me, this time, if anything, I saw the photograph enlarged.

DANIEL, CRESSIDA's sixteen-year-old step-son, throws back the hallway door, and strides in, with his suitcase and sports bag. He looks around.

DANIEL. Oh, Jesus.

He drops his cases and walks back out.

CRESSIDA. I think, you see, it was a matter of perspective. Before, I'd never raised my eyes above the water line. Nothing mattered if it didn't wriggle and you couldn't catch it in a net.

CRESSIDA's husband HOWARD marches into the living room from the interior of the house. He carries a duplicated document — the owner's description of the house and its facilities. He looks round the living-room.

HOWARD. I see.

He goes out.

CRESSIDA. Even the sun was by reflection. Just a shiny penny glinting in a rockpool.

HOWARD (*calling*). Cressida! I've found the master bedroom with twin beds and shower en-suite!

CRESSIDA. That's when there was a sun of course. Personally, I've never bought the sundrenched summers of our youth.

HOWARD. There's also what purports to be an annexe with bunk beds and put-u-up where we could put your little friends . . .

CRESSIDA. My memories are all of plastic wellingtons and pac-a-macs.

HOWARD. That's if Terry doesn't mind the 'vestibule'.

CRESSIDA. So this time, for the first time, I could look along the headland, to the village. Down the scrubby cliff-path, to the beach. And crumbs. The sky. The sea.

CRESSIDA drifts away as HOWARD and DANIEL re-enter, simultaneously, through their previous doors. DANIEL has two carrier-bags of food.

HOWARD. Danny, you're up top. It claims to be an ample attic space, but I'm afraid it's more a sort of loft. Had we brought the cat, it would be hazardous to swing her.

DANIEL. Kitchen?

HOWARD (*points to the door to the interior*). Thataway.

DANIEL goes out towards the kitchen. HOWARD looks at the room.

Well, by process of elimination, this must be the well-proportioned and attractive lounge with easy chairs, convertible settee and dining area.

He looks askance at the vase. He goes on the terrace. He looks at the document, and looks up.

HOWARD. I would have thought 'verandah' should imply some class of canopy or awning. I'd call this 'terrace'. (*He glances at the document.*) If not 'patio'.

HOWARD goes back into the living room as DANIEL reappears.

HOWARD. You found the kitchen?

DANIEL. Yes. The fridge is full.

HOWARD. Well, yes. It isn't very —

DANIEL. It is full of film.

HOWARD. And food.

DANIEL. And tennis balls.

HOWARD. Danny, you know, you may have seen, at Wimbledon, when they ask for new balls, and the ballboys go and take them from a kind of cabinet —

CRESSIDA *enters from the hallway. She is dressed in a more summery fashion. She carries a case of wine.*

DANIEL. It's Dan*iel.*

HOWARD. All right then, Dan*iel,* you may have seen at Wimbledon —

CRESSIDA. Where shall I put the wine?

HOWARD. Oh, in the kitchen. On the left.

CRESSIDA. Presumably there is a fridge.

HOWARD. Why don't you put it in the pantry for a moment?

CRESSIDA. Fine.

She's on her way.

DANIEL. Seeing as how the fridge is full of Howard's balls.

CRESSIDA. I'm sorry? What was that?

DANIEL. Because, you see, at *Wimbledon* —

CRESSIDA *puts the wine down near the door.*

CRESSIDA. Is full of *what?*

Slight pause.

HOWARD. All right. In the modest to minute refrigerator, there is a box of half a dozen tennis balls. And a small amount of photographic film. I would point out there is also a great deal of food. For instance, there are several plastic boxes stuffed with chops and ribs and other toothsome segments of dead animal, which have been gently marinading in a rich array of sauces, stocks and glazes all the way from Oxford, and which I intend to barbecue tonight.

CRESSIDA. Already marinading. That's my man.

HOWARD. In fact, I think I'll start the charcoal. In anticipation of the Minerettes' arrival.

He goes out on to the terrace, looking for a suitable spot.

DANIEL. The miner — who?

CRESSIDA. It's what your father calls our little guests. And it's what he mustn't call them when they're here.

HOWARD *has re-entered the room.*

HOWARD. Firelighters.

CRESSIDA *throws him a packet of firelighters.*

Ta.

HOWARD *goes out to continue his search. He finds a spot to the side of the house, which need not be visable, where he sets up and lights the barbecue.* CRESSIDA *has picked up the wine.*

CRESSIDA. Right then. The pantry.

DANIEL (*as a car door slams, off*). Cressida —

CRESSIDA. Oh, cripes. That can't be them.

She goes and looks through the hallway door. Then, to DANIEL:

Get Howard, will you, dear?

She looks round for somewhere to put the wine and puts it on the dining table. Then she hurries out into the hall. After a moment, DANIEL *goes on to the terrace and shouts:*

DANIEL. Hey, Howard! Dad!

HOWARD. Yes? What?

DANIEL. The Minerettes.

HOWARD. Yes, what about them?

DANIEL. They've apparently arrived.

HOWARD *quickly appears. He wears leather gauntlets. He goes into the house.*

HOWARD. They've what?

DANIEL (*following* HOWARD). And, pr'aps, now, someone will explain —

HOWARD (*a little impatient*). I'm sorry?

DANIEL. Why 'our little guests'.

Pause.

HOWARD. Well, 'apparently', they've found it difficult to place them.

DANIEL. Place them.

HOWARD. Yes. The boys will go alone, you see, but the girls insist they have a friend or confidante —

DANIEL. No, no. I *meant,* why have you asked two perfect strangers on your holiday at all?

HOWARD. Our holiday. You. Your father. And his wife.

As HOWARD *continues,* ALUN *enters. He carries two suitcases.*

Well, as it happens, it was her idea. Via her friend Terry. Who knows one of their fathers. Who's a miner.

DANIEL. Oh, of *course.*

HOWARD (*quite sharply*). And I don't know if they actually take the papers in this — seminary your mother's packed you off to, but since March there's been this coal strike —

ALUN. Well, so they say. But then again, you mustn't go believing everything they tell you in the papers.

CRESSIDA *comes in with a radio-cassette player and another case.*

HOWARD. Alun. This is Daniel, my son.

ALUN. Well, hello, Daniel. And you're Howard. Very pleased to meet you.

*He puts out his hand to shake. HOWARD's still got his
gauntlet on.*

HOWARD. Barbecue. For which we hope you'll stay.

CRESSIDA. Indeed.

ALUN. Well, that's very kind of you, but I ought to get on really.
I'm supposed to be in Preston by tonight. But the offer's most
appreciated.

HOWARD. Drink, at least.

ALUN. A cup of tea'd go down marvellously well. Now, where's
those girls?

HOWARD. Um, they can't have got —

CRESSIDA. Or even, there's some fizzy wine —

HOWARD. There is a rather classy Cava —

ALUN. Um, no. No, thanks. I think the bobbies got my
registration, see, and at present they don't need much excuse.

HOWARD. Yes, of course. Now, Daniel, could you pop the
kettle on?

*CRESSIDA picks up the case of wine and hands it to
DANIEL.*

CRESSIDA. And put that in the pantry.

*DANIEL throws a look, but then he goes. HOWARD looks
through the hallway door.*

I'm afraid that Terry's late. I don't know where —

ALUN. No matter.

HOWARD. Well, you say that, but he's got the salads.

CRESSIDA. So, shall we 'take tea on the terrace'?

ALUN. It would be a pleasure.

*CRESSIDA gestures to ALUN, who goes out on to the terrace.
She's following, when she sees HOWARD, who has turned
from the door and is slumped against the wall in a mock
indication of total astonishment. During the following, ALUN
looks out to sea, notices the smoke from the barbecue, and
goes to look at it.*

CRESSIDA. Howard?

HOWARD. It's them.

CRESSIDA. Who's them?

HOWARD. The Minerettes. I mean, there's no dispute. They are precisely how I . . . There's a fair one, and a dark one, and they're wearing . . .

CRESSIDA. *Howard.*

A head pops round the door. It's MICHELE's.

MICHELE. Um — excuse me. Beg your pardon. But can we come in, please?

CRESSIDA. Oh, yes. Of course. Indeed.

MICHELE *turns to the other girl, not yet visible.*

MICHELE. See, I told you, it's okay.

MICHELE *and* FRANKIE *enter. They are both 15.*
MICHELE *wears a white T-shirt with the slogan* 'FRANKIE SAYS' *in big letters.* FRANKIE's *T-shirt says* 'RELAX'.

Um — I'm Michele. And this here's Frankie.

HOWARD. Goes to Hollywood.

MICHELE. No, really. That's her name.

CRESSIDA. And this is Howard.

MICHELE. And are you Cressida?

CRESSIDA. Well, Cressida. Or — Chris.

HOWARD. In fact.

CRESSIDA. And your father's on the terrace.

HOWARD. Or verandah.

DANIEL *comes in with the tea.*

CRESSIDA. And here's tea. Daniel: Michele and Frankie.

MICHELE. How d'you do?

She nudges FRANKIE.

FRANKIE. Hello.

Slight pause.

DANIEL. Hello.

DANIEL *takes the tea out and puts it on the table on the terrace.*

HOWARD. Right then.

HOWARD *and* CRESSIDA *lead* FRANKIE *and* MICHELE *on to the terrace.*

Everyone arrives as ALUN *returns from the barbecue.*

ALUN. Ah, there you are.

CRESSIDA. Please, do sit down.

MICHELE *sits on the bench.* FRANKIE *was about to sit on one of the garden chairs, but notices this in the nick of time and sits by* MICHELE. DANIEL *sits on the recliner.* HOWARD *starts pouring the tea.*

HOWARD. Does anybody not take sugar?

MICHELE. No. I mean — no sugar, thanks.

DANIEL. No milk or sugar.

HOWARD. Right.

Pause.

So — was your journey —

ALUN. Fine. Bit of a snarl-up, round Dolgellau.

HOWARD. Ah.

Pause.

CRESSIDA (*with a glance at the sky*). And is it, um — like this, down where you are?

ALUN. The weather? more or less.

Pause.

Now, Howard, is this right, I hear you're a historian?

HOWARD. Yes. Yes, I am.

ALUN. And are you, like . . . researching anything particular, at present?

HOWARD. Well, at this very moment, I'm, um, sort of moonlighting. I mean, I'm, by profession, I'm a don — a lecturer. But at this moment, as I say, I'm working for a television company. There's a series on the 30s, 'Red Decade', all that, and I'm helping with the episode about the British left and Spain. How people like John Strachey, Harold Laski, how they responded to the Civil War. George Orwell. People of that ilk.

ALUN. Well, you've picked the year for it.

HOWARD. Indeed. Though of course it won't go out in 1984. In fact, the notion is to coincide —

ALUN. Well, no, I meant the strike. Over a hundred South Wales miners fought in Spain, I'm proud to say.

HOWARD. Oh, yes, indeed. I'm sorry.

ALUN. No need to apologise.

HOWARD. A glorious chapter in your history.

ALUN. Well, if you like.

HOWARD. I mean, it must be — very close to you.

ALUN. Well, yes.

CRESSIDA. Were there any from your village?

Slight pause.

ALUN. Yes. I believe so. One or two.

Pause.

In fact, if I'm honest, what appeals to me, by way of history, goes much further back than that. In archaeology. The ruins of old cultures, crumbling into dust, then rediscovered after centuries. Like, the Book of Nahum. You know, Nineveh and Tyre.

CRESSIDA *smiles and shrugs.*

CRESSIDA. No chapel childhood, I'm afraid.

ALUN (*with a shrug*). No. School.

Pause.

HOWARD (*looks at his watch*). Now, look, I really ought to make a —

CRESSIDA. Come. We will watch Escoffier.

HOWARD. Momento.

> HOWARD *goes out to the kitchen.*

ALUN. He's a dab hand at the cooking, is he, eh?

CRESSIDA. And needs to be. He made a foolish marriage. Wife can't boil an egg. Well, that's not absolutely true. The real disaster's scrambling. As he says, they tend to end up stood in peaks. Like the Grand Tetons.

ALUN. Sorry?

CRESSIDA. Mountains, in America.

> HOWARD *has reappeared with a pile of plastic containers, plates, spatulas and other implements.*

HOWARD. Wyoming. (*To* DANIEL.) Bottom shelf is free.

DANIEL. *Thank* you.

HOWARD (*as he goes towards the barbecue*). You know, young Terence better not be too much longer.

CRESSIDA. Why?

HOWARD (*obvious*). He's bringing half the food.

CRESSIDA. Oh, yes.

> HOWARD *goes out to the barbecue.*
>
> You might say, just the weeniest bit obsessional. Like taking his own mayonnaise to restaurants. Banning Heinz tomato ketchup from the house.
>
> CRESSIDA *gestures* ALUN *to go with her to the barbecue.* DANIEL *makes to go into the house.* CRESSIDA *gestures to him, indicating that he should stay and talk to the girls.* ALUN *and* CRESSIDA *go.* DANIEL *stands there. He drums the back of a chair with his fingers.*

DANIEL (*eventually*). Um — how was your journey?

> MICHELE *and* FRANKIE *nod, smile and shrug.*

MICHELE. All right.

FRANKIE. Fine.

Pause.

DANIEL. You come from — South Wales as I gather. From the south.

MICHELE. Correct.

FRANKIE. You know — the valleys.

Pause.

DANIEL. Mm. The Rhondda.

His rounded, hard-d pronunciation pushes the girls over the edge. They crack up. DANIEL is furious.

Yes?

MICHELE. It's — Rhondda.

FRANKIE (*with an odd, offhand gesture*). Rhondda Valley.

DANIEL *can take no more.*

DANIEL. Right, then.

He strides out through the living room. FRANKIE and MICHELE look at each other, a shared moment. Then:

MICHELE. Hey, Frankie. D'you like, know where we are?

FRANKIE. I dunno. Gwynedd?

MICHELE. Oh.

Pause.

FRANKIE. Hey, Michele. You seen a telly?

MICHELE. No.

FRANKIE. Hey, s'pose they haven't got one? What the hell we going to do?

Pause.

MICHELE. I heard there's some got holidays in Georgia. You know, Russian Georgia.

MICHELE *looks at* FRANKIE. FRANKIE *looks around.*

FRANKIE. Some people, all the luck.

Enter CRESSIDA.

CRESSIDA. The latest news is dinner in ten minutes. If you want to wash or anything.

MICHELE *and* FRANKIE *nod and stand.*

MICHELE. Yes, please.

CRESSIDA (*looks round*). Um — Daniel!

DANIEL *comes into the living room from the kitchen.*

DANIEL. Yes?

CRESSIDA. I think the girls are in the 'annexe'.

DANIEL *goes to the interior door and opens it with a gesture.*

And their bags are there.

DANIEL *goes and picks up the bags.*

DANIEL. Pliz valk zis way, mamzelles.

FRANKIE *and* MICHELE *look at each other and follow* DANIEL *out.* ALUN *has re-entered with his tea. He nods back, in the direction of the barbecue.*

ALUN. Miraculous.

CRESSIDA. It keeps him off the streets.

She sits. ALUN *follows.*

So what's in Preston?

ALUN. There's a power station. Well, nearby, as I understand it. Place called Heysham.

CRESSIDA. Ah.

ALUN. Bringing the day closer when she's calling us 'the enemy within' by candlelight.

CRESSIDA. You think that's how it's going to end?

ALUN. It's going to end in victory.

CRESSIDA. No, I meant, *that way.* Industrially. By closing down the power stations. Stopping trains.

ALUN. Oh, there's no doubt about it, to my mind. It'll finish when the lights go out, like last time. That's my prediction.

CRESSIDA. Hence the trip to Heysham.

ALUN. Right.

CRESSIDA. Do you enjoy it? Picketing?

Pause.

ALUN. Well, it can be a bit boring. Or by contrast, p'raps a little over-hectic, on occasions. But by and large I'm having a great time.

CRESSIDA. The travel. And all that.

ALUN. Exactly. Bit of a — magical mystery tour, this strike, if you take my meaning. A temporary suspension of one's usual obligations.

CRESSIDA. Footloose and flying free.

ALUN. That's right.

ALUN's *picked up a note in* CRESSIDA's *tone.*

Now tell me. I'm not in the presence of a dreaded Oxford feminist, or am I?

Slight pause.

CRESSIDA. Sorry?

ALUN. You know, the dungarees and everybody's really lesbian brigade. Notorious throughout the length and breadth, they are.

CRESSIDA (*uncertain*). Um — may I ask, what makes you think —

ALUN. 'Footloose and Fancy Free.' You sounded as if you didn't quite approve.

CRESSIDA. Oh, no. That wasn't what I meant at all. (*Pause. Briskly.*) I mean, don't get me wrong. I mean, I kind of work and everything . . . But as far as being, dungarees . . . No, that stuff gets right up my nose. (*Slight pause.*) I mean, I collect food, for food parcels, outside supermarkets, and aside from the didactic dieticians, you know, tons of wholewheat pasta and no tins, apart from them, the ones who really irk me are the women who give nothing that a man can use at all. All baby food and tights and tampax. Which is of course all very well and useful but — it seems to miss the point. To me.

A head pops round the hall door. It belongs to TERRY. *He's from Yorkshire. During the following he brings in his luggage in two loads: the first is a suitcase and portable TV, the second two large bowls with plates on top and a plastic carrier-bag.*

ALUN. What do you do?

CRESSIDA. I'm sorry?

ALUN. When you kind of work.

CRESSIDA. Oh, I'm a sort of doctor.

ALUN. What sort?

CRESSIDA. Chiropractor.

ALUN. Pardon?

CRESSIDA. I do work on backs.

ALUN. What, like an osteopath?

CRESSIDA. Well, in that we manipulate. But osteopaths knock you about more, and they tend to concentrate only on the bit that's hurting, while we're more concerned with the whole spine. Howard calls osteopathy chiropractic Marxist-Leninist. The delusion that you can build socialism in one vertebra.

ALUN. Yes. I see. (*Slight pause.*) And is it Howard brought you in to all of this?

CRESSIDA. What, to the strike? Oh, no. Well, not directly.

Slight pause.

No, in fact this time it's been more me.

TERRY. That's more you what?

CRESSIDA. Hey, Terry. Where d'you creep in from?

TERRY *comes on to the terrace with his carrier-bag.*

TERRY (*taking a bottle from his bag*). Beware of creeps bearing gifts.

CRESSIDA. Sambuca!

ALUN. Hello, Terry.

TERRY. Alun. I'm sorry I'm so late. The roadsigns are in Sanskrit.

HOWARD enters from the barbecue, carrying plates of cooked food, en route through the living room and out to the kitchen.

HOWARD. Well, he'd better have the salads. That's all *I* can say.

TERRY. Well, yes, in fact, and though I says it —

HOWARD. You got *five* from *now*.

He's gone.

TERRY. Well, hi there, Howard. (*To* CRESSIDA.) So. You two been forging links?

CRESSIDA. Alun's been telling me about the dreaded Oxford feminists.

TERRY. Ay, well. You've got to understand that Alun's what you might call a mite unreconstructed on the women question —

ALUN. Oh, come on now, Terry. I told you, all that fuss about the May Day rally? And we had to have equal speakers, male and female? And we must invite a gay and we've got to have a lesbian?

TERRY. See what I mean —

During the following HOWARD enters the living room with plates and cutlery and starts laying the table.

ALUN. One meeting, Cressida, I said the NCB was turning miners into what you might call industrial gypsies. And so half the fems jump up, saying, 'So, what's wrong with gypsies?' Apparently, I'm showing chauvinism to our gypsy brothers. Gypsy sisters. Well. Ridiculous, to my mind.

HOWARD calls from the living room:

HOWARD. Heartily agree.

ALUN. But you must have your supper.

CRESSIDA. No, really, we can have it any time . . .

A look from HOWARD, *who's passing back en route to the barbecue.*

ALUN. No, I should have been off already, anyway. I'll just go and tell the girls goodbye.

TERRY. Well, if you're sure . . .

CRESSIDA. I'll show you where they are.

She takes ALUN *through the living room and out.* TERRY's *alone on the terrace. He goes and gets his casseroles, picks up a pair of wooden spoons from the table, and comes back out. He opens one of the casseroles — which contains potato salad — finds a screwtop jar in his carrier, opens it and dresses the salad with the contents, tossing with the wooden spoons.*

Enter DANIEL.

DANIEL. Terry.

TERRY. Danny.

DANIEL. Daniel. Did you bring the television?

TERRY. Yes.

DANIEL. Thank God for that. The Olympic track and field kicks off on Friday.

TERRY. Right.

HOWARD *crosses with another plate of barbecued food direct to the living-room table.*

HOWARD. Right then.

TERRY (*to* DANIEL). I think it's suppertime.

HOWARD. Just waiting for the salad monitor.

CRESSIDA *and* ALUN *come back into the living room.*

CRESSIDA. Well, they might have let you in.

ALUN. Oh, no. Can't interrupt the preparations.

CRESSIDA. What?

ALUN. Howard, you know, if you're studying the Spanish
   Civil War . . . You should ask Frankie how she got her name.
   If you get the chance.

HOWARD. Yes, sure. I will.

   DANIEL *and* TERRY *come into the living room.*

ALUN. Well, then. Good luck with 'em. Don't take no nonsense,
   mind.

CRESSIDA. We won't.

TERRY. And give 'em hell at Heysham.

ALUN. Right.

HOWARD. Take care. It's good to meet you.

   DANIEL *gives a little wave.* ALUN *goes to the hallway door.*
   He turns back.

ALUN. Now, look. I know I don't have to tell you, but there's
   still lots of people talk as if this strike's about wages and
   conditions. Who don't understand that it's about survival.
   Not just for us, but for our kids. So they don't end up — well,
   you know. And to my mind, if we're going to stand a chance,
   we've got to show *we* can survive. So I hope it don't need
   saying. But, you know . . . How grateful we all are. (*Slight
   pause.*) 'Cos if not, she might as well just flood the valley,
   turn the bloody thing into a reservoir. In my opinion, anyway.

   Slight pause. He smiles, goes to TERRY *and lightly punches*
   him on the shoulder. TERRY *mirrors the gesture: clearly this*
   is a ritual.

   So. So long, our Terry. (*To the others.*)

   All of you.

   He goes.

CRESSIDA. She?

TERRY. Goes without saying.

CRESSIDA. Yuh.

   Pause.

HOWARD. Right. Action. Daniel. There is souvlaki in the oven, dips and relishes are on a tray. Oh, and the wine.

CRESSIDA *is looking at the meat on the table.*

CRESSIDA. What's this?

DANIEL *goes out.* TERRY *collects his salads and brings them to the table.*

HOWARD. It's spareribs. What's it look like. Terry . . .

CRESSIDA. Howard . . .

TERRY (*putting his salads on the table*). Potato salad. Spinach.

CRESSIDA. . . . you are convinced . . .

HOWARD (*handing* TERRY *an empty serving plate*). Looks wonderful. There's chicken tikka on the barbecue.

CRESSIDA. . . . they'll actually *like* . . .

As TERRY *goes out,* DANIEL *comes in with the tray.*

DANIEL. Your meat. Your wine.

HOWARD. The girls.

DANIEL *turns round, hands the tray to* CRESSIDA *and goes back out.* HOWARD *puts the stuff from the tray on the table.*

CRESSIDA. . . . they'll actually eat this stuff?

Slight pause.

HOWARD. I'm sorry? What d'you mean?

CRESSIDA. You are convinced they'll eat the food.

HOWARD. Whyever not? (*Pause.*) Why, what do you think they'd like?

CRESSIDA. Well, burgers, I'd imagine. Hot dogs. Things like that.

HOWARD. This establishment does not serve things like that.

Enter TERRY *with chicken tikka, still on skewers, on the plate.*

CRESSIDA. Would you say that about culture? Would you say they can't have Coronation Street, they must have Turandot?

TERRY (*putting down the plate, to* HOWARD). Your move.

HOWARD. Coronation Street is part of a genuine popular narrative tradition.

CRESSIDA. Well, Crossroads.

HOWARD. Arguably just the same.

CRESSIDA. The Price is Right.

HOWARD. They will have pork ribs in Hoisin sauce and like it. (DANIEL *comes in during:*) Look, just because their fathers are on strike, you treat them as if they're refugees. They are perfectly normal, no doubt actually fairly average, contemporary teenage girls —

DANIEL. Ahem.

He gestures theatrically to the door, through which come FRANKIE *and* MICHELE. *They have dressed up for dinner, and look quite extraordinary. In particular,* MICHELE's *hair is in spikes, and* FRANKIE's *a frightening new shade. They stand there.*

CRESSIDA. Well . . . Hi there. Supper. Hope you like barbecue.

The girls sit at the table, noting the television.

Now, this is Terry. Have you met?

They nod.

TERRY. We've briefly met.

CRESSIDA. And would you . . . like some wine?

They nod. Everyone else sits. Wine is poured.

And . . . chicken tikka?

They look bemused at the skewers.

HOWARD. It is mildly curried.

They shake their heads.

TERRY. Spareribs? You eat them with your fingers.

FRANKIE *and* MICHELE *look at each other and shake their heads. The souvlaki has been de-threaded.*

CRESSIDA. Um — grilled lamb?

MICHELE takes a very small piece of lamb. FRANKIE does the same.

Potato salad? Spinach?

They take small portions and hand the casseroles on. As the conversation continues, everyone else helps themselves, pulling pieces of chicken off the skewers, and munching the ribs in their fingers. Part of the problem for MICHELE and FRANKIE has been not knowing how much to take, so as the others serve themselves with ample portions they glance at each other.

CRESSIDA. It was nice to meet your dad, Michele. After all we've heard from Terry.

HOWARD. I was very glad to hear that he's refused to be transfixed by the loopier outreaches of Oxonian feminism.

CRESSIDA. What reaches, Howard?

HOWARD. Well, while he was talking, I was thinking about your buddy Hobbes.

CRESSIDA. She's not my buddy and her name isn't Hobbes.

HOWARD. I imagine Terry knows the type. Permanently furious at what she assumes you're going to say next.

TERRY. Why do you call her Hobbes?

CRESSIDA. You only don't like her 'cos she's so overt.

HOWARD. The latest outrage was a friend of mine, whose marriage broke up, and whose ex was charmed into the Hobbesian embrace — I don't think literally — but who accused my mate, when he wanted access to their child, of — wait for it — 'biologism'. (*Pause.*) She affects poverty. She ought to be in solitary. And she is indisputably nasty, brutish and short.

Pause.

TERRY. So what you up to, Danny?

DANIEL about to correct him.

Daniel.

DANIEL. Nothing much.

HOWARD. We're at present into bodies beautiful.

TERRY. Oh, whose?

HOWARD. Our own.

CRESSIDA. He's training.

TERRY. Right.

HOWARD. A project which appears to justify the daily calorific intake of a smallish Indian village for a year.

CRESSIDA (*to* MICHELE *and* FRANKIE). And presumably you two have just done CSEs?

MICHELE. O level.

CRESSIDA. Right. And how d'you think you've done?

MICHELE. Dunno. Okay.

CRESSIDA. And — what are your favourite subjects?

Pause.

MICHELE. Well, as it happens, I like history best.

CRESSIDA. Well, there's a hap—

MICHELE. But Frankie, she likes English Lit. Now don't you, Frankie?

Pause.

FRANKIE (*very quietly*). Yes. I do.

Pause.

HOWARD. So what . . . What books, particularly?

MICHELE *gesturing and encouraging* FRANKIE *through the sentence.*

FRANKIE. Well. I did like 'Romeo and Juliet'. And 'David Copperfield'. And the selected poems of John Keats.

Pause.

HOWARD (*to* FRANKIE). And after your results, what then?

Pause.

FRANKIE. Well, we'll be back at home.

HOWARD. No, I meant, you know, what does the future hold?

FRANKIE *looks round in panic.*

FRANKIE. Uh, I —

MICHELE (*suddenly*). Now, *my* ambition lies in archaeology.

Slight pause.

HOWARD. I'm sorry?

MICHELE. I have always been, like, fascinated by the history of ancient times.

CRESSIDA. What, like your dad?

MICHELE. Correct.

HOWARD. Well you've come to the right place. We'll hotfoot it to a castle or a monastery first thing.

MICHELE. I would like that very much.

TERRY. So what's it really like?

MICHELE. Beg pardon?

TERRY. What's it really like for you? I mean, it must be pretty tough. (*Pause.*) With no new clothes. No records. Treats. It must be hard.

MICHELE (*aggressively*). Well, we're not starving, anyway. (*Pause.*) I mean, those things, they're not important. So, we had to send the video back, but the house is still kept nice and tidy. It's not like we're in, you know, real poverty.

TERRY. What do you mean by that?

MICHELE. I mean, it's not like no one taking proper care of things. It's not like scrawling on the walls and business in the lifts and water coming through the roof and everybody lying round on pot and heroin. I mean, we've not descended to that level. We're not tramps or thieves. We've kept our pride.

Pause. FRANKIE *kicks out her feet. She wears pink trainers which, now we notice them, look a bit odd with the rest of her outfit.*

FRANKIE. Well, here they are.

TERRY. What's that?

FRANKIE. Me mam bought me new trainers for the holiday. Last new things till we won. (*Pause.*) Look silly with this, really.

Pause.

CRESSIDA. Look. Do have some more. (*Pause.*) We don't want anyone to think we're starving you . . .

TERRY *helps himself to a large helping of potato salad and then hands it to* MICHELE *and* FRANKIE.

TERRY. Go on.

FRANKIE *helps herself.* MICHELE *helps herself.* TERRY *helps himself to spareribs and passes them. Again, they help themselves to large helpings. Following* TERRY, *they pick the ribs up with their fingers and eat.*

Blackout.

Scene Two

The following week. Morning. In the living room, the television is set up on a small table, the radio-cassette is on the floor, surrounded by cassettes and presently playing the morning news in Welsh. We hear words like 'Sheffield', 'Arthur Scargill', 'N.U.M.', 'Los Angeles' and 'Daley Thompson'. On the table is the first 'load' of breakfast crockery and cutlery. CRESSIDA enters from the interior side, in her dressing gown. She looks a little furtive. She goes to the big vase, feels in it, and takes out a small transparent plastic cube with some mechanism inside. She's about to go back out when she hears voices. She quickly goes out on to the terrace and hurries round the side of the house. HOWARD and DANIEL enter from the kitchen with cereals, fruit juice and coffee.

HOWARD wears tennis whites and DANIEL wears running gear. He has a walkman — the phones are presently round his neck. As they argue, HOWARD switches off the radio, pours cereal and

coffee, and takes them through on to the terrace, followed by
DANIEL, *who contents himself with orange juice.*

DANIEL. I mean, Duran fucking Duran.

HOWARD. I'm sorry?

DANIEL. What?

HOWARD. The reference escapes me. Duran who?

DANIEL. They purport to be a pop group.

HOWARD. There's a group called Duran fuck—

DANIEL (*imitating the girls*). And 'I got the latest Wham
   cassette, d'you wanna hear it, Daniel' and 'Oh no I can't go
   swimming with my skin, it blisters something dreadful' and
   'Ooh Terry, you'll have to help me round the battlements,
   I got this terrible vertigo' and that's not to mention all those
   hours in the bathroom and the constant getting ready and
   'Ooh don't you like Duran Duran, Daniel, I think they're
   really great —'

HOWARD. You're only peeved about the castle because Michele
   knew King John preceded all the Edwards.

DANIEL. That's just not fair. What I found peeving was —

HOWARD. In fact, she appeared to have remarkable command of
   the epoch as a whole.

DANIEL. If you want to know, I'm peeved because I don't know
   why they're here. And I don't know why *I'm* here. At all.

   Enter CRESSIDA, *with all the insouciance of someone whose
   last entrance was successfully undiscovered. She wears a
   colourful, vertically striped T-shirt, long French-type shorts
   and tennis shoes.*

HOWARD. You're here because your mother's in New York.

DANIEL. Not for two weeks.

HOWARD. And because she thinks the three of *us* should get a
   little closer.

DANIEL. Ha!

   Pause.

CRESSIDA. Frankie's agreed to doubles. Could you wake them, please?

After a slight pause, DANIEL turns to HOWARD.

DANIEL. Howard, what does your dear wife think she's wearing?

CRESSIDA. Um —

DANIEL. I'll go wake Frankie.

He goes into the living room. He's on his way to the interior door, when he sees the cassette player and cassettes. During the following, he inserts two or three cassettes into his walkman, so he can test what they are without being overheard. The first he rejects. The second he looks at quizzically, and pockets. The third he smiles at, takes out of the walkman, puts in the cassette player. He picks up the player and goes out. This process can take up to TERRY's entrance.

HOWARD. One sees his point.

CRESSIDA. I'm dressed for tennis.

HOWARD. No, you're not. You may be dressed in what you plan to wear to play the game, but dressed for it you're unequivocally not.

CRESSIDA. Howard, it is a recrea—

HOWARD. Rather like those students I remember who thought that wearing dirty jeans and odd socks proved their proletarian credentials, whereas, in fact, the real working class —

CRESSIDA. Howard. Don't take him out on me.

Enter TERRY from the beach. He's been swimming, and wears a beachrobe. He breathes.

HOWARD. Good morning, Terry.

TERRY. Morning. You know, all in all, gravity's a mixed blessing. Is that breakfast?

He goes into the living room and gets breakfast. HOWARD follows.

HOWARD. Terry, the court is booked at ten.

TERRY. Ah, yes. Now, Howard, I'm not sure —

HOWARD. Terry, it's taken a week of patient negotiation —

TERRY (*pouring coffee*). Sure, I know, it's just I think I may
have pulled —

*Suddenly, very loud music, DANIEL shouting, and even the
odd shriek from FRANKIE and MICHELE. CRESSIDA comes
into the room.*

DANIEL (*off*). Wake up! Wake up! Show a leg there! Eight bells
called! Bring out yer dead! Awake!

TERRY. What the hell —

CRESSIDA. It's Daniel. I asked him to —

*DANIEL enters with the cassette player still blaring. He
switches it off.*

DANIEL. Girls woken. I'm off running. Tra.

*He puts down the cassette player, puts on his earphones, and
goes out to the hall.*

CRESSIDA. What's wrong with him?

*HOWARD goes out to the terrace with CRESSIDA, followed
by TERRY.*

HOWARD. His mother's just back from Manhattan. He's in
Gwynedd. What d'you think?

TERRY. What's with the Daniel?

HOWARD. He was born in 1968.

That's not a total answer.

Danny Cohn Bendit. Paris. May events.

That's still not an explanation.

I think, you could say, he's engaging in a heartfelt but
inchoate act of protest —

TERRY. Right.

HOWARD. He should be glad we didn't call him Stokeley or
Fidel.

CRESSIDA. Or Peace or Love or Freedom.

TERRY. And do we yet know why Frankie's Frankie?

CRESSIDA. No. I tried to ask. But she doesn't seem to want to say.

Slight pause.

TERRY (*mock conspiratorial*). I'll get her on her own.

MICHELE *and* FRANKIE *enter.* FRANKIE *wears a skirt and sports shirt, but not matching.*

MICHELE. Good morning, all.

CRESSIDA. Hi, girls. Do you want some breakfast?

MICHELE. Not for me.

FRANKIE *goes and gets cereal.* MICHELE *puts on her dark glasses as she comes out on to the terrace.*

TERRY. But . . . But . . . You're *beautiful* —

MICHELE. Oh, Terry!

CRESSIDA (*looking at the weather*). Well, can this last, I ask myself.

TERRY. No problem. Weatherwise, we have it absolutely sorted.

HOWARD. How?

TERRY. The slightest puff of cloud appears, we sacrifice Michele.

MICHELE. Oh, you . . .

FRANKIE *appears with her cereal.*

FRANKIE. Oh, I didn't know we'd got to dress up like.

Slight pause.

CRESSIDA. Whereas of course the *real* working class —

HOWARD. It's all right, Frankie. You look absolutely fine. Particularly beside Cressida, who has misread the invitation yet again and come as a deckchair.

TERRY. Or a stick of rock.

HOWARD. Not from this angle.

CRESSIDA. Actually, I think I might, on this one, take a rain check.

HOWARD. Some day that phrase will be explained to me.

CRESSIDA. I mean, if Terry's pulled his — well, I hardly like to ask —

TERRY (*to* MICHELE). My lips are sealed.

CRESSIDA. Then why don't you play singles?

Pause.

HOWARD. Yes, why not. I'll get my racket.

He goes into the living room, followed by CRESSIDA *and* FRANKIE.

CRESSIDA. Frankie can use mine. It's got a thinner grip than Daniel's.

HOWARD *goes to the kitchen, returning with tennis balls and his racket, as* CRESSIDA *gives* FRANKIE *her racket and* MICHELE *and* TERRY *converse.*

TERRY. Are you going to go?

MICHELE. Oh, sure.

TERRY. You needn't.

MICHELE. Oh, I couldn't let her go *alone.*

FRANKIE (*calls*). You ready then, Michele?

MICHELE (*to* TERRY). 'My lips are sealed.'

TERRY. No one need ever know.

MICHELE. Oh, *you!*

MICHELE *goes into the living room with* HOWARD *and* FRANKIE. *The three go, as:*

HOWARD. Now, in fact, you'll notice that my forehand's rather weak, which is because I pulled a shoulder while of all things mounting tiles . . .

As soon as they're gone, CRESSIDA *hurries quickly out to the kitchen.* TERRY *notices. He stands, looking into the living room.*

TERRY. Cressida? Chris?

CRESSIDA *appears again. She is affecting unconcern.*

CRESSIDA. Well. Peace.

TERRY. Mm.

CRESSIDA *joins* TERRY *on the terrace. She sits on the recliner, lies back in the sun.*

CRESSIDA. So how's your — strain?

TERRY. Well, it could do with some attention.

CRESSIDA. Oh? Like what?

TERRY. Gi'us a massage then, chuck.

CRESSIDA (*shocked*). No.

TERRY. What's this? Professional reticence?

CRESSIDA. Terry. I am a chiropractor. Not a Swedish —

TERRY. Oh, come come. The magic fingers.

Pause.

CRESSIDA. Very well. Lie down and think of Islington.

TERRY *takes off his beachrobe and lies on it on the table.* CRESSIDA *gets up and goes and massages his back.*

TERRY. So how's it going?

CRESSIDA. Oh, fine, I think, don't you? Daniel is being pretty bolshie, but I think . . . he would be anyway. And the gels are starting to come out at last.

TERRY. You mean, socially? Or is Frankie finding hidden urges —

CRESSIDA. I can't understand why on earth they find you funny. All your jokes are way beneath their level.

TERRY. It may be that the alternatives are Howard's.

CRESSIDA. Howard is very droll. It's just his taste in humour has to be acquired.

TERRY. If not contracted. No, I meant — how is your strain?

Pause.

CRESSIDA. I see no reason to revise my answer. Fine.

TERRY. The academic life? The constant sherry?

CRESSIDA. Well, just listen to the darling dodo. Lapsang Souchong. Perrier.

TERRY. And living in North Oxford?

CRESSIDA. Smashing.

TERRY. You're serious?

CRESSIDA. Crumbs, yes. Over half the population suffers from some form of chronic inflammation of the lumbar spine — they claim it's poring over their word processors but I blame all that bicycling. My acupuncturist and I met on our basic Alexander course, we read the Tarot on our nights off, and I'm blissfully content.

TERRY. And do you see — the former Mrs —

CRESSIDA. Gillian? Not often. Met her, obviously. She's big in TV movies. Package, deal and megabuck.

TERRY. So did she get Howard this — this telly thing?

CRESSIDA. No, not directly. Look, who's doing this? The masseur asks the questions. Not the massagee.

TERRY. Well, just the one.

CRESSIDA. I need only give name, rank and number.

TERRY. Why did you run off to the kitchen when they'd gone?

Pause.

CRESSIDA. Just now?

TERRY. Uh-huh.

CRESSIDA. My test is in the pantry.

TERRY. Eh? What test?

CRESSIDA. For what. For pregnancy.

Pause.

TERRY. Congratulations?

CRESSIDA *shakes her head.*

TERRY. Why, wouldn't Howard —

CRESSIDA. No, not wouldn't. Couldn't.

TERRY. Pardon?

CRESSIDA. On account of his vasectomy.

Pause.

TERRY. Um . . . Do you know . . . ?

CRESSIDA. Oh, just about. I mean, I've narrowed it down to half a dozen.

TERRY. Sorry.

CRESSIDA. Awful irony. It was the strike. A talent contest. At some social. Quite excruciating. And eventually, escaped. In the most delightful company. (*Pause.*) He's a sort of Trot at Cowley. Lovely fella. Lovely time.

TERRY. It's over?

CRESSIDA. It has — run it's natural course. Or at least, I thought it had. (*She realises she's stopped her massage.*) I'm sorry. Where was I?

TERRY *sits up.*

TERRY. So what's the news?

CRESSIDA. Dunno. You've got to leave it for an hour, undisturbed, for the hormone or whatever to react. I did one Tuesday, actually, but it seemed to have got jolted when we put the cereals away.

TERRY *looks bemused.*

You see, the only place that I could think to put it was the pantry shelf.

TERRY. The pantry —

CRESSIDA. Cool and dry. But naturally, concealed. Behind the fettucini.

TERRY. Cressida.

CRESSIDA. Yes, Terence?

TERRY. Had . . . Had Howard had, was Howard, when you married him . . . ?

CRESSIDA. Oh, yes. (*Pause.*) You see, I didn't . . . don't want babies. And they refuse to do the operation if you haven't had one. Absolutely. No exception. So Howard was the perfect choice. In every way.

TERRY. You mean, you chose to abrogate your right to choose.

Pause.

CRESSIDA. Yes. I suppose so. Yes. In fact. As I watch the thundering stampede of what-me-nevers rushing to get their ankles through the stirrups, before they hit the danger zone, you know, thirty-eight or nine . . . Yes, I wanted a locked door behind me. No internal catch. An — an irrevocable decision.

Pause.

TERRY. And now?

CRESSIDA. Oh, absolutely. On that question, there is none.

TERRY. And on the other one?

She smiles, squeezes his shoulder, stands, moves away. TERRY sits up. She looks back.

CRESSIDA. Look. (*Slight pause.*) It is important, Terry, that you understand about my husband. When we met. For he was wonderful. I mean, I really hadn't done a thing — I'd been on half a dozen marches, I suppose, done some street theatre . . . But he'd done it all. Knew everything. And could do, anything. So clever, so experienced, committed, *clear* . . .

TERRY. So what went wrong?

Pause.

CRESSIDA. Dunno. (*Pause.*) I *do* know. That since — this little thing about which we will drop no hint however slight of any kind to anyone, that since that, I've been flying free. In a way I haven't been for years. And it is — magical.

Pause.

TERRY. Well. We'll keep 'em crossed then, eh?

*DANIEL runs round the side of the house, on to the terrace.
He comes to a halt, bends over and breathes heavily.*

Hi there, Daniel.

DANIEL. Well — at least I beat them up the road.

CRESSIDA. Beat who?

DANIEL. Howard. The Minerettes.

CRESSIDA. Already?

DANIEL. Right. I'm going to have my shower.

*He goes into the living room. Seeing the cassette player, he
remembers something. He checks his pocket, finds he still has
the cassette he took earlier, picks up the recorder and takes it
through the interior door.*

TERRY. In fact, though, if you think about it, there's something
pretty bizarre about calling your child Cressida.

CRESSIDA. It was a pun. Ironically enough. I was the result of
what was incorrectly thought a false alarm.

TERRY. 'As false as Cressida'.

CRESSIDA. You got it.

TERRY. No wonder you're at home.

CRESSIDA (*looks at her watch*). Ah. Which reminds me —

*She's going through into the living room as HOWARD,
FRANKIE and MICHELE come in from the outside.*

So. How went the day?

*She looks to HOWARD, who gestures to FRANKIE.
FRANKIE waves her arms, a little gauchely.*

FRANKIE. I won, I won.

HOWARD. She's very good.

FRANKIE. Oh, it was luck, mind. Howard's shoulder. Stuff like
that.

HOWARD. That's true. But I'm certain, if you took some
lessons, got your backhand sorted out, you could be really . . .

He realises FRANKIE's *face has fallen.*

FRANKIE. Lessons. Well.

HOWARD. I mean, to firm up your technique, I didn't mean —

FRANKIE. Thanks for the game.

She goes off into the interior of the house.

HOWARD (*to* MICHELE). What's wrong?

TERRY. I think, it may be, that they can't afford —

MICHELE (*improvising*). I think, you know, you sounded like her mother. I think that's what upset her. Think you sound like her.

HOWARD. 'What you need is some nice chicken soup'.

MICHELE. Beg your pardon?

HOWARD. It's a joke. This guy says to his shrink — psychiatrist — doctor, 'I seem to think that everyone's my mother.' Shrink replies: 'Don't worry. What you need is some nice chicken soup.'

MICHELE's face is frozen into an expression of pleasurable anticipation. CRESSIDA *looks to* TERRY, *who moves in.*

TERRY. Or even — there's the guy who's spent his whole life searching for the meaning of the universe . . .

CRESSIDA isn't sure this is a good idea.

CRESSIDA. Ah. Now, perhaps —

But MICHELE *has transferred her attention — and expression — to* TERRY.

TERRY. . . . and his search takes him all over, and eventually he hears that there is but one person in the world who knows the total meaning of the universe, this guru on this mountain in Tibet.

TERRY pauses, impressively. CRESSIDA, *prompting, to hurry it along.*

CRESSIDA. And so, sells up his business, mortgages his house . . .

TERRY. . . . that's right, he sacrifices everything, and sets off to seek this mountain . . .

CRESSIDA. . . . finds it, climbs it . . .

TERRY. . . . thank you, yes, and at the top there is this little wizened man, and he, the guy, says, 'Oh great guru, I'm reliably informed you know the meaning of the universe, the answer to all questions,' and the old guy says, 'That's right, I do, the answer to the question of the meaning of the universe is simple. It is "chicken soup".'

Pause. MICHELE doesn't move a muscle.

And the guy says, 'You old bastard. I have spent my whole life searching for the secret of the universe, I've sold up everything I own, I've trekked across the world, I've climbed this fucking mountain, and you have the nerve, the immortal gall, rind and temerity to tell me that the answer's *chicken soup*?'

MICHELE has stopped breathing.

And the guru says, 'You mean it isn't chicken soup?' (*With a little music-hall gesture:*)

Bu-boom.

Everybody laughs.

HOWARD. Well, it's good to greet old friends.

Holding up his box of tennis balls.

Now, yielding to not inconsiderable pressure, I shall put these in the pantry.

HOWARD *goes out to the kitchen.* CRESSIDA *has got the giggles, which* MICHELE *is finding mildly infectious.*

TERRY (*to* MICHELE). It's the way I tell 'em.

CRESSIDA's *laughter propels her on to an easy chair.*

Well, it wasn't — quite, that . . .

CRESSIDA. No, it's not your stupid joke . . . It's just that Howard's going to put his balls . . . in a cool . . . dry . . .

Suddenly she realises where HOWARD's *going to put his balls.*

Crikey.

She's on her feet when MICHELE *starts her contribution.*
CRESSIDA *is captured in the glare.*

MICHELE. There's this poof, see, who comes back from the
office, right, and there's his friend, you know, sitting with his
bottom in the fridge. And the first poof says, 'Hey, what you
doing with your bottom in the fridge? And the second poof
says 'Well I thought, that after a hard day' . . .

TERRY. . . . 'you'd want something cool to slip into.'

MICHELE (*with* TERRY'*s gesture*). Bu-boom. (*To* CRESSIDA.)
He knew it.

CRESSIDA. Sorry.

She runs to the door, just as HOWARD *comes through it. He
is very exercised.*

HOWARD. Cressida —

He sees MICHELE.

MICHELE. Well, I'd better — go and see to . . .

She hurries out.

HOWARD. Cressida. I have to talk to you.

CRESSIDA. Oh — yes?

TERRY. Um, should I — ?

CRESSIDA. Don't you dare.

HOWARD. It's a — what one might call the ultimate, loco-parental
nightmare.

CRESSIDA. What? Parental?

HOWARD. Look, the fact is, one of them appears to be —

FRANKIE *and particularly* MICHELE *start screaming off.*

What's that?

The door bursts open and DANIEL *enters followed by*
MICHELE *and* FRANKIE. DANIEL *has the cassette player,
on which is playing the cassette he listened to and pocketed
earlier, which is — as we will discover later — a tape made by*
MICHELE. MICHELE *is desperate to get the machine, and*

FRANKIE is eager to help. The chase goes round the room, over the furniture, and culminates on the terrace.

MICHELE. You give that back. Just give that back, Daniel —

CRESSIDA. Now, what's going on?

FRANKIE. Come on now, Daniel, give it to Michele.

HOWARD. For heaven's sake —

MICHELE. You bastard. Give that back. It's private.

TERRY. Frankie, what is —

DANIEL. No!

MICHELE. You fucking *bastard.*

FRANKIE (*explanatory*). Her cassette, you see . . .

The chase has reached the terrace. HOWARD realises the phone has been ringing.

HOWARD. What's that?

CRESSIDA. The phone. Remember — telephones?

HOWARD. Where is it?

TERRY. Kitchen.

HOWARD runs out to the kitchen, as MICHELE corners DANIEL and starts hitting his chest, as DANIEL holds the recorder over his head.

MICHELE. Bastard. Shit. Give it here. Give — it — to — me —

TERRY. Stop that, Michele.

Somewhat surprisingly, MICHELE stops hitting DANIEL.

Now, everyone, calm down. Michele, leave Daniel. Daniel, give me the machine.

MICHELE leaves DANIEL. DANIEL hands the machine to TERRY, who switches it off.

Now. What is this?

FRANKIE. It's a cassette. It's something Michele wrote. About the castle. It's a poem.

TERRY. Right. So it's Michele's.

He hands it to MICHELE.

CRESSIDA. I'd like to hear it.

MICHELE *looks alarmed.* TERRY *shakes his head.*

I'd like to hear it, please.

Pause. FRANKIE *takes the recorder from* MICHELE, *rewinds and plays:*

MICHELE'S VOICE (*on tape*).
The castle stands upon the hill,
In ruins now, all stark and still.
But as we mount its towers high,
We can imagine days gone by,
And how it must have been to climb
These high steep steps in Arthur's time,
And on the battlements catch sight
Of the shadow of a noble knight,
Or on a turret faintly hear
The voice of Launcelot or Guinevere.

MICHELE *gestures to* FRANKIE *to switch the tape off. But* FRANKIE *doesn't get to the button in time to miss:*

MICHELE'S VOICE. This poem's for Terry.

FRANKIE *switches the tape off.*

CRESSIDA. Thank you. That was very nice.

MICHELE. The last line doesn't match.

CRESSIDA. It doesn't scan. It doesn't matter.

She hands the machine to MICHELE.

There.

MICHELE *takes the machine. She and* FRANKIE *go out through the living room.* CRESSIDA *turns to look at* DANIEL. DANIEL *is about to say something, but changes his mind, and goes out as* HOWARD *re-enters the living room, carrying a paper bag.* TERRY *and* CRESSIDA *go into the living room.*

HOWARD. So what was all that?

CRESSIDA. Tell you later.

HOWARD (*taking the plastic cube — a pregnancy testing kit —
from the bag and handing it to* CRESSIDA). Now look,
Cressida, correct me if I'm wrong, but isn't this —

CRESSIDA. A pregnancy predictor.

HOWARD. Yes. (*Pause.*) So one of them is pregnant. Here.

TERRY. Well, they won't have actually *got* pregnant —

During this, CRESSIDA *takes the kit from* HOWARD
*and looks at it. In fact, of course, it's been so jogged about
that it's useless, but she makes great play of looking in the
little mirrored surface at the bottom for the telltale ring.*

HOWARD. Yes, you see, it's wonderfully romantic, take a pair
of utter strangers with us on holiday, being daughters of the
revolutionary masses, as it were, but in the real world they
are actually female adolescents at a particularly tricky age —

CRESSIDA. They are not pregnant.

HOWARD. What?

CRESSIDA. I've had these things before. Neither Michele nor
Frankie has one in the oven.

HOWARD. Are you sure?

As HOWARD *looks impotently at the kit,* CRESSIDA *is able
to shrug at* TERRY, *to indicate she can't tell the result.*

CRESSIDA. Well no doubt, in a day or two, there will be a
confirmation.

HOWARD. Good. Well, I'm sure they'll be relieved.

CRESSIDA. I'll bet.

TERRY. It might be better if they didn't know we know.

HOWARD. Indeed.

He puts the test back in the bag, and makes to go.

CRESSIDA. What was the call?

HOWARD. The programme.

CRESSIDA. Good news?

HOWARD. Don't know. They want me to go back.

CRESSIDA. What for?

HOWARD. A meeting. Day after tomorrow.

CRESSIDA. That's Saturday.

HOWARD. Apparently these people work on Saturdays.

CRESSIDA. Didn't you explain you were on holiday?

HOWARD. Of course. But this is a very long, expensive series, and they will pay me to come back, and this is how these things occur.

CRESSIDA. You mean, in the zippy, zappy world of package, deal and megabuck.

HOWARD. Apparently.

He makes to go.

CRESSIDA. A world I worry you could learn to love.

Pause. TERRY *delicately removes himself to the terrace, where he sits.*

Oh, not the tinsel and jargon and the hype. But perhaps the zip and crackle. Getting on with it. Not loafing round the place complaining about everything. Operating in the real world.

Pause.

HOWARD. It is — it is very refreshing, sometimes, to be with people whose reaction to an ill-run whelkstall is to try and run it better. Who when they see a brewery, say, 'They're on me.' Who if they found themselves inside a paper bag, would seek not for excuses but the exit. (*Slight pause.*) Or if they came across an egg, think, hey, wow, I wonder how you cook this thing.

CRESSIDA. As opposed to oddballs taking strangers' kids on holiday. As opposed to trying to save an industry that in the real world —

HOWARD. I didn't say that.

CRESSIDA. Didn't even think it, shouldn't wonder. But it might
be — what you feel. (*Long pause.*) Well, if you're off,
tomorrow? . . . (HOWARD *nods.*) . . . let's have something
nice tonight. I'm sure you boys can fix up something really
scrumptious.

She goes off towards her room. HOWARD *comes out on to
the terrace.* TERRY *looks up, not sure what* HOWARD's *going
to do or say.*

HOWARD. Lobster. Lobster Thermidor.

Blackout.

Scene Three

Evening. CRESSIDA, HOWARD, TERRY, MICHELE *and*
FRANKIE *sit round the dining table, which has been cleared
after dinner. The girls are dressed up, the adults have changed —
but are dressed informally. Everyone has wine.* TERRY *stands.*

TERRY. Comrades, I give you the complete and total victory of
the National Union of Mineworkers, their struggle for their
pits and their communities . . .

CRESSIDA. Hear hear.

MICHELE. Hear hear.

TERRY. And the utter rout of the armed might of the ruling
class and its lackeys in the National Coal Board . . .

CRESSIDA. Boo! Boo!

FRANKIE. Boo.

HOWARD. That's not to mention all reactionaries, who as we
know are paper tigers.

TERRY. I am content to toss in all reactionaries.

CRESSIDA. Running dogs.

TERRY. Them too. So, victory to the miners, utter rout of the
forces of reaction —

HOWARD. The eternal friendship of our two great peoples —

TERRY. Natch —

> DANIEL *comes in with a tray of coffee.*

CRESSIDA. And of course the chefs, for all the toothsome fare —

TERRY. So I should think —

FRANKIE. And Daniel, for making coffee —

TERRY. Daniel, especially, for coffee *and the rest* . . . But most of all — to us.

ALL. To us.

> *Everybody drinks.* TERRY *and* DANIEL *sit. Coffee is distributed.*

CRESSIDA. Oooh, but he makes a pretty toast.

TERRY. Well, it's all those weddings.

HOWARD. Weddings?

TERRY. Oh, ay. You demonstrate an aptitude, you end up losing rings for half the village. I have read more telegrams in function room up at t'welfare —

FRANKIE. Welfare?

TERRY. Mm.

FRANKIE. You mean, like, miners' welfare?

TERRY. Yuh.

MICHELE. Well, fancy that.

TERRY. Yuh, my father was a deputy. South Yorks. Though, as it happens, I was born in Durham, and he'd been born in Lothian. Gypsies, tramps . . .

CRESSIDA. Tt tt.

MICHELE. And you still live there, do you?

TERRY. No. I moved away.

> *Slight pause.*

Like so many, both before and doubtless since. From the coal face to the chalk face.

FRANKIE (*whispers, to* MICHELE). *Chalk* face?

MICHELE (*whispers, to* FRANKIE). School.

CRESSIDA. So do you do much with the welfare and the union?

FRANKIE. No, no. I mean, occasionally they have a disco. And from time to time I go up for some bingo with me mam.

CRESSIDA. No, I meant, I don't know, trips, or the colliery brass band, or —

FRANKIE. What, the band? You must be joking.

CRESSIDA. Why?

Pause.

FRANKIE. Well, it's a bit naff, really, isn't it? You know, ta-ra-ra-boomdiay.

MICHELE. To be honest, it's the boys that put you off. All a bit poncy, really.

HOWARD. Poncy?

MICHELE. Yuh, you know, a bit effete.

Pause.

TERRY. Near where I was born, there was a pit, which had a lodge, which had a banner, with the slogan: 'Come, let us reason together'. And I thought that was socialism. Reasoning together. But of course that was in the bad old days. Before the reactionaries and paper tigers had this wonderful idea, that the way to stop the people reasoning together was to give them — rather, sell them — music centres, TV sets and videos, and cram their clubs with booze and bingo rather than old-fashioned stuff like billiards and all those boring books, so instead of doing things together they'd get done apart. (*Slight pause.*) Beg pardon. (*Pause.*)

CRESSIDA. Look, I wonder if the time has come — to unveil our party pieces. To underline the festive spirit of the evening.

HOWARD. What a wonderful idea. So who'll kick off, then?

TERRY. Daniel?

DANIEL. Me?

During the following, there is an increasing amount of nudging and pushing between FRANKIE *and* MICHELE.

CRESSIDA. Why not? Didn't Howard say you learnt to tapdance at some stage?

DANIEL. About a hundred years ago. And I was awful.

HOWARD. They must have taught you something at your nice new school.

DANIEL. You leave my mother out of this.

CRESSIDA. Or perhaps we should start off with Terry's folk song.

DANIEL. Folk song?

TERRY. P'raps a little later.

HOWARD. He needs to, like, crank up a bit. Get the old foot stomping. Screw the finger in the ear.

TERRY. My repertoire is drawn from the industrial tradition. We stick our fingers somewhere altogether different.

HOWARD. How quaint.

CRESSIDA. Look, do I detect some pressure being put on here?

FRANKIE *and* MICHELE *realise the attention is on them.*

FRANKIE. Oh, no.

MICHELE. No. Definitely not.

Slight pause.

HOWARD (*carefully*). Of course the point of opening is that once you've done it you can sit back and get pissed and heckle everybody else. Well, that's always seemed the point to me.

CRESSIDA. The principle that one should remain slightly less drunk than one's audience.

HOWARD. Exactly so.

The girls are weakening. TERRY *leans over.*

TERRY. Go on. You show me yours, I'll show you mine.

The girls look at each other. In exaggerated pantomime, they

*begin to suck their lips and shake their heads. But then,
suddenly,* MICHELE *turns back to the company.*

MICHELE. Right then. You're on.

CRESSIDA. That's *wonderful.*

FRANKIE (*checking the running order*). Krrk. Working miners?

MICHELE. Krrk krrk. Margaret Thatcher, working miners, Ian
McGregor —

FRANKIE. Krrk krrk Kinnock?

HOWARD. What's with 'krrk krrk'?

TERRY. As in Delta Foxtrot.

*And we realise the girls have been imitating the little
noise on policeman's walkie-talkies.*

MICHELE. Krrk krrk, Kinnock *then* McGregor.

FRANKIE. Wilcoe.

MICHELE. Right.

MICHELE *stands on her chair, followed by* FRANKIE.

We did this at a talent contest, see. Fund-raiser.

CRESSIDA. That's a nice idea.

FRANKIE. What? It was terrible. Really embarrassing.

TERRY. Did you win then?

MICHELE *looks witheringly at* TERRY.

MICHELE. One, two, three.

The girls sing:

MICHELE *and* FRANKIE.
What shall we do with Margaret Thatcher
What shall we do with Margaret Thatcher
What shall we do with Margaret Thatcher
Early in the morning

Cut her down to size and privatise her
Cut her down to size and privatise her
Cut her down to size and privatise her
Early in the morning

The song continues on the same principle. Everyone except
HOWARD *is drawn into the choruses.*

FRANKIE. ⎫
MICHELE. ⎬ What shall we do with

FRANKIE. ⎱ Neil —
MICHELE. ⎰ Working —

FRANKIE. ⎱ — miners?
MICHELE. ⎰ Sling 'em to the bottom of the nearest pitshaft

What shall we do with Neil Kinnock
Stick him in the flightpath of a flying picket

What shall we do with Ian McGregor?
Hang hang hang the bastard

And, finally:

Burn burn burn the bastards
Burn burn burn the bastards
Burn burn burn the bastards
Early in the morning!

They finish. Enthusiastic applause from TERRY *and*
CRESSIDA, *slightly mocking clapping from* DANIEL.
HOWARD *doesn't applaud, but gets up and goes to get
another bottle of wine, which he brings to the table with a
corkscrew as:*

CRESSIDA. Wonderful.

TERRY. You woz robbed.

CRESSIDA. Well, certainly, the opposition must have been
terrifically impressive.

TERRY. I'd demand a recount.

HOWARD *pointedly opening the wine.*

CRESSIDA. Howard, is there something wrong?

HOWARD. Well, no, not really. It's just, as it happens, I don't
believe in burning Neil Kinnock. He's the leader of the party I
vote for. Nor, actually, do I believe in dropping working
miners down pitshafts, or even hanging Ian McGregor.

The girls don't know how to react.

In fact, I think it's exactly what's wrong with the way this strike's being conducted. Mindless, malicious and macho.

Pause.

CRESSIDA. Howard, it's only —

HOWARD. And I think it would be actually rather condescending, I mean, it would be patronising, just to — clap politely, and say, dears, well that was very nice, now can we change the subject please.

He puts down the corkscrew and sits. CRESSIDA *stands and goes out.* TERRY, *quietly, speaks a verse of the Blackleg Miner*:

TERRY. 'O don't you gan near the Seghill mine
For across the way they'll hang a line
To catch the throat and break the spine
Of the dirty blackleg miner'.

HOWARD. You what?

TERRY. But I suppose that's okay 'cos it's *old.*

HOWARD. No. No, now you come to mention it, I don't agree. I think there is a tendency to sentimentalise the past. In fact, I'm not at all convinced by this idea of yours that it was all Sibelius and quiet evenings boning up on William Morris in t'lodge library, before everybody got brutalised by electronic amplification, Dallas and Keg bitter. I imagine, actually, that an aggressive, tribal and, might we say, machismo culture was just as prevalent in 1926 as 1984.

TERRY. Oh, sure. So how —

Enter CRESSIDA. She has a book, a pad of paper and a pencil.

HOWARD. I mean, how do you *really* think they're reacting to the women, in the villages? To their wives going off to London, Brussels and Turin, addressing meetings, leaving them to mind the kids and cook the tea? I mean, Frankie, what do you think that Alun *really* feels about all that?

To FRANKIE's relief, CRESSIDA interrupts.

CRESSIDA. Over four thousand years ago, when the First
Emperor Fu Hsi ruled all things under heaven, he saw the
bright patterns of the sky, the shapes of the earth, the
distinctive markings in the beasts and birds and living things.
And from these configurations he divined eight sacred
trigrams, from which it is possible to deduce the character of
everything, which is not chicken soup, but does go a long way
to explain the hidden workings of the universe.

TERRY. What's this?

HOWARD. Chris, do you take that everywhere?

CRESSIDA. It never leaves my side.

CRESSIDA *sits, opens the book — which is the 'I Ching' — and
continues to speak.*

For from those trigrams did arise this book, the I Ching, oracle
of change, containing no less than sixty-four configurations,
in the form of hexagrams, in which the ancient forces, yin and
yang, the passive and the active, feminine and masculine . . .

HOWARD. Aha.

CRESSIDA. . . . are set in constant flux and conflict one with
t'other, and through which he or she who would confront the
aforesaid hidden wisdoms of the universe may by the throwing
of three coins six times reveal the mysteries of what is yet to
be. So. Anybody want a go? (*Pause.*) Say — Howard's trip?
Or Daniel's prospects? Will Michele dig up the site of
Camelot? (*Pause.*) Howard. Why don't you kick off, show 'em
how it's done.

HOWARD, *against his better judgement, starts tossing coins,*
CRESSIDA *noting down the results.*

Ah. Yang. (*To the young people.*) You see, I'm rather younger
than these folks. When I went up to university, the 60s had
already gone occult. So at the stage when Howard was
immersed in Mao Tse Tung and Che Guevara . . .

TERRY. . . . obviously not *too* thoroughly . . .

CRESSIDA. . . . I was into Nostradamus, motorcycle

maintenance and sacrificing virgins.

TERRY (*to* MICHELE). Sorry, chuck. That is unless —

MICHELE. Tt — nice!

Now CRESSIDA *is looking up* HOWARD's *hexagram — the 14th — in the sacred book.*

CRESSIDA. Right, then.

DANIEL. So, is Seb Coe going to win the 1500?

CRESSIDA. Daniel, you don't play hoot'n'nanny on a Strad. (*Reading the result*:) Howard, I'm pleased to tell you that your trip will be crowned with progress and success. If you spurn that which is harmful, and avoid all error, you will achieve considerable prosperity. You may even end up crossing the great water, but on that I wouldn't bet. Who's next? (*To* FRANKIE *and* MICHELE:) So. One of you?

The GIRLS *don't look enthusiastic.* CRESSIDA *passes the coins to* TERRY.

Our Terry?

TERRY *passes the coins to the* GIRLS.

TERRY (*pointedly, directed at* HOWARD). Encore.

Slight pause.

FRANKIE (*with a shrug*). OK, then. If you like like.

CRESSIDA. Just throw the coins.

FRANKIE *tosses the coins.*

FRANKIE. What's that mean?

CRESSIDA. Nothing yet. One heads, two tails, that's Yin. Go on, again.

As CRESSIDA *notes the first line,* FRANKIE *throws again.*

Yang. Once again. Six times.

FRANKIE *carries on throwing the coins, as:*

MICHELE. So where you going, Howard?

HOWARD. I've got to go and see these television people.

FRANKIE (*as she tosses*). What, on your holidays?

CRESSIDA. It's a mystery how far these people push their luck.

DANIEL. Why, aren't they paying him?

HOWARD. Yes, they are paying him.

CRESSIDA. So they may have got his body, but can they buy his soul? Right, Frankie, what d'you want to know?

FRANKIE (*tosses for the last time*). Like what?

CRESSIDA (*looking through the book*). Well, anything you want to know about yourself.

FRANKIE. What, like me inside leg?

CRESSIDA. No, it's not a quiz. It's about what's going to happen in your future life. What the future holds for you.

MICHELE *flashes a look to* FRANKIE. *Pause.*

FRANKIE. Okay. What's going to happen in my life? What does the future hold for me?

There is a careless, almost sarcastic tone in FRANKIE's *speech that worries* HOWARD. CRESSIDA *finds the commentary on the 32nd hexagram.*

CRESSIDA (*from the oracle*). All right. The answer lies in the hexagram called Heng, which means 'Of Long Duration'. Its trigrams, Chen and Sun, mean thunder, and a gentle wind. Its meaning is that the earth endows all things, and through the seasons constantly renews itself. The lower trigram warns you that you must not dwell on sacrifice, however painful and however hard it may be to endure, but rather on the promise of good fortune, and the certainty that like the seasons winter will give way to spring. Whereas, the upper trigram —

FRANKIE *stands quickly and runs apart, bursting into tears.* MICHELE *follows quickly.*

Oh, crumbs, I'm sorry —

MICHELE. Now come on, Frankie, it's —

CRESSIDA. What a silly *fool* —

CRESSIDA *and* HOWARD *go over to* FRANKIE
and MICHELE.

MICHELE. Now just try and calm down, now . . .

TERRY (*to* HOWARD *and* CRESSIDA). Just let — just let
Michele —

MICHELE. Now try and think about some nice thing, eh? Think
about Norman.

MICHELE *turns to the adults to explain her strategy.*

She's got a cat called Norman. Don't ask me why. (*To*
FRANKIE.) And about your holiday in Yugoslavia. You
enjoyed that, right? And d'you remember that, that weird
boy, what was his name? Mihallo?

FRANKIE. No, Mihailo.

MICHELE. What?

FRANKIE. Mihailo. And he wasn't weird. Well, not really.

MICHELE (*to* HOWARD). You see, she had this holiday last
year.

FRANKIE'*s recovering.*

(*To* FRANKIE.) Now, just think about Mihailo. And you'll be
all right. (*To* CRESSIDA.) You see, I'm trying to keep her mind
off things'll make her cry. Like the strike. The future. Stuff like
that. (*To* FRANKIE.) Now, shall we go back to the table? Or
d'you want to go off to the room, just for a little while?

FRANKIE. Perhaps. The room.

MICHELE. Okay.

She helps FRANKIE *to go.*

And p'raps, while you're out there, it might be best if I
explained why you're upset.

FRANKIE *looks at* MICHELE.

I think that would be best, you know.

Pause. Then FRANKIE *bursts into tears and runs out.*

FRANKIE. Say what you like!

MICHELE *is making to follow when* HOWARD *stops her.*

HOWARD. Look, Michele, I think there's something that I ought to say.

TERRY. Um, are you sure — ?

HOWARD. Yes. Absolutely sure. Because I think — that Frankie ought to know, that it's all right.

MICHELE. I'm sorry.

HOWARD. She's not pregnant.

MICHELE. Pregnant?

HOWARD. That test. In the pantry. It was negative. So if it's that that was upsetting her . . .

MICHELE. What? Frankie? Thought that she was pregnant?

Pause.

HOWARD. Yes?

MICHELE (*a little offended*). I'm sorry, no. I mean we're friends you see. I'd know that. No, it's nothing of that character, I can assure you.

HOWARD *turns to* CRESSIDA.

HOWARD. Then —

MICHELE. No, it's very simple, really. Like, Frankie used to skate.

TERRY. What, roller-skate?

MICHELE. No, ice-skate. Figure skating. And she was supposed to be, like for her age, well, really ace. Not international level, mind, but if she took it seriously, and got the practice and the ice-time, and the tutoring and stuff like that, I'm not quite sure how it works, like, but there's various levels, and if she really worked at it, and went to stay at Swansea with her gran, like in the holidays, so as she could use the rink, they said she could have got her grades for national competition. And

then, like, she'd not be Jane Torvill, but . . . who knows?
(*Pause.*) She got the skates for Christmas. You know, the
proper standard, all that stuff. But when it was obvious the
strike was going to last, she sold 'em back. And gave her mum
and dad the cash, you see. (*Pause.*) And she doesn't mind. To
be honest, she was really pleased that she could make a
sacrifice. But just, there's moments, like when you asked her
about tennis lessons, or like when the conversation turns to
stuff like what's the future, she does get a bit upset. That's all.

FRANKIE *has re-entered.*

FRANKIE. You told 'em.

MICHELE. Yes.

FRANKIE (*to the others*). I'm sorry.

CRESSIDA. No. No, it's us that should be sorry. Me.

FRANKIE. It's just, you see . . . I know we must look very
backward to you, very immature . . .

CRESSIDA. Oh, no —

FRANKIE. . . . Well, if we do, it's right, we are, I mean, we don't
get half of what you're saying, let's be honest, specially when
you're being clever about reactionaries and running dogs, we
don't know half the time you're being serious, and like when
you ask us things, about ourselves, we're just praying it's a
question we can answer. Or if it isn't, we can make it up.
(*Pause.*) Like, we talk about what we might have to say.
(*Pause.*) Like, Michele isn't really going to be an archaeologist.
She made it up. Spur of the moment, you could say. (*Pause.*)
'Cos, to be honest, kind of future that you think about, the
kind of future that's a normal thing for you . . . for us, it's
just a joke. I mean, like just a fantasy.

Pause.

HOWARD. I think — I think perhaps —

MICHELE. Say what you said.

FRANKIE. Say what?

MICHELE. Say what you said, about her being like a skater.

FRANKIE. Oh —

MICHELE. Just tell 'em what you said.

Pause. FRANKIE *looks to the others, finally to* TERRY.

TERRY. Go on.

FRANKIE. Well, all I said was. That you know they call her 'iron maiden'. But I don't see her in that light at all. (*Pause.*) Like, I see her like those posh girls at the rink in Swansea, gliding so easy 'cross the ice, like they haven't got a care. 'Cos you see, I think, to her, we're only frozen faces. Faces, frozen in the ice, for her to glide upon. I think she skates on people's faces. (*Pause.*) And let's be frank. However much you care, you're the spectators. You are looking on. While we — we're looking up.

Long pause.

HOWARD. Look. Look. (*Pause.*) Look, Frankie, we —

CRESSIDA. Howard, you and I have got to have a conversation.

Blackout.

ACT TWO

Scene One

Sunday 12 August 1984. In the living room, HOWARD *lies asleep on a chair in front of* TERRY's *television. He is dressed informally, but for town. He has dropped off in front of last night's Olympic track and field finals. Now the breakfast programme is recapping the night's events in other sports.* CRESSIDA *enters from the interior of the house, in her nightclothes, carrying a cup of coffee and a magazine, which she intends to take on to the terrace. She sees* HOWARD. *She breathes a little, then goes over, stands in front of him. He wakes. She holds the coffee out to him.*

CRESSIDA. Archery?

    HOWARD *takes the cup and drinks.*

HOWARD. I was eager not to miss the coxless fours.

CRESSIDA. How did Seb do?

    HOWARD *imitates the miler Sebastian Coe's victory gesture.*

    Well, that's good news for all us oldies. Howard, why —

HOWARD. I decided to come back.

CRESSIDA. I wasn't sure if you'd decided that you'd gone.

HOWARD. I meant, earlier than planned. (*Pause.*) No more was I.

CRESSIDA. I'm not — if it's of interest, I don't think I'm pregnant.

HOWARD. Ah. (*Pause.*) This from your apparatus in the pantry?

CRESSIDA. No. I sought professional advice.

HOWARD. That's fast. I thought you had to send off entrails to the hospital.

CRESSIDA. Your friendly local pharmacist will cope.

HOWARD. What, Jones the Truss?

CRESSIDA. More Jones the knowing little wink. He says it's 95 per cent, but it's a little early to be absolutely sure. So if nothing happens by tomorrow, I'll send off another sample to old Doc McWhatsisname.

HOWARD. What, in the post?

CRESSIDA. Mr Jones has an assistant. They're a chatty pair. There is something uniquely demeaning about listening to a long discussion of one's piss in Welsh.

Slight pause.

HOWARD. Did he have a view as to why you're nine days late?

CRESSIDA. Well, the usual diagnosis is some kind of psycho-, some emotional upheaval, isn't it? Either that or a very early menopause.

HOWARD. Now, in what sense could we say that you've been emotionally upheaved?

She senses he wants her to repeat it.

CRESSIDA. Howard. I've just had a love affair.

Pause.

HOWARD. You mean the one with, whatsit?

CRESSIDA. Derek. Yes, of course. (*Slight pause.*) As opposed to what?

HOWARD. Well, all I thought was, all I wondered was if you had got involved with all of this, the strike, because you wanted an affair —

CRESSIDA. What, only in it for the fellas? Howard —

HOWARD. Or whether, rather, the affair came out of what you found inside yourself. Through your involvement with the strike. (*Pause.*) Or rather, even ratherer, what you found within yourself, through it, that you had lost, or never had, with us.

Pause.

CRESSIDA. Point taken.

HOWARD. What if they lose?

CRESSIDA. They won't.

HOWARD. Why not?

CRESSIDA. They can't.

HOWARD. How do you see them winning?

CRESSIDA. Winter. Power cuts. That's how they'll win.

HOWARD. There's a third of them at work.

CRESSIDA. Why don't you want them to?

Pause.

HOWARD. That isn't fair.

CRESSIDA. Oh, isn't it?

Pause.

HOWARD. How could it be?

CRESSIDA. I just, you see, just wonder, with you old 68-ers, if you hadn't got things really rather nicely sorted, with your realignments, new configurations, forward march of labour halted, gourmet socialism, all that stuff. And that, therefore, that all this, and these, these wonderful brave people in their T-shirts and their trainers, up against the helmets and the truncheons and the shields — a bit unwelcome. Uninvited. Tapping at the window. Spectres at the feast. You know?

HOWARD. Oh, yes. I know. I know it well. Indeed, you could say it's something of a *deja vu.*

Pause.

For nearly 4,000 years ago, when even I was young, the prevailing view was very much the same. The proletariat eliminated from the van of history. The workers bought off and sucked in. But then came Edward Heath, and all those dock and rail and coal strikes, and we all thought: hey, perhaps the working class's revolutionary demise has been, well, just a mite exaggerated. Until it became, well, equally transparent that what had actually been exaggerated was their resurrection. That however much we might regret it, we'd been dead right all along. And however much *I* might, and do, regret it now —

CRESSIDA *interrupts. Simply*:

CRESSIDA. Knock knock. Who's there?

HOWARD. Well, even so. And don't — don't feel too good about it. Don't fall into that trap. Because, in fact, it's relatively easy — I mean, in the same way as it's relatively easy to have a nice-and-comfortable, no-ties-on-either-side —

CRESSIDA. Oh, Howard —

HOWARD. — in the same way, it is actually not hard, *that* hard, to run a strike in summertime, in your T-shirts and your trainers. But what happens in the winter, Chris? When it's not that they can't have ice creams, but the parcels have dried up and they're down to baked beans every night and they've outgrown all their shoes?

CRESSIDA. Howard, it will be over —

HOWARD. What, 'by Christmas'?

CRESSIDA. Yes. By Christmas, certainly. All will be crowned with great victory and success.

HOWARD. But if it isn't, Cressida?

Pause.

CRESSIDA. You sound like Gillian.

HOWARD. I don't. She'd say —

CRESSIDA. No, I meant the mode of discourse.

HOWARD. *She*'d say, that if she can overcome those centuries of patriarchy, if she'd cracked PMT, if she'd made it in the world against the odds, why on earth can't everybody else. Your pit's closed? Simple. Why not start up a little graphics firm in Camden Town. That's what Gillian would say.

CRESSIDA. Yes. Yes, she did.

HOWARD. Did? When?

CRESSIDA. Last night. She rang.

HOWARD. Rang? Why?

CRESSIDA. 'Cos Danny had rung her.

HOWARD. Dan- Why? Whatever for?

CRESSIDA. To ask her if she'd come and take him home.

Pause.

HOWARD. I see.

CRESSIDA. There's been, well, some emotion since you left.

HOWARD. That's 'since'?

CRESSIDA. Okay, as well. The girls were mortified about that stuff on Thursday night, kept going on about how awful it had been, to have to make an exhibition of themselves, in front of us.

HOWARD. You did assure them that we are *quite* as capable of making —

CRESSIDA. 'Us' in the sense of, middle-class people.

HOWARD. Christ.

CRESSIDA. Overhearing which, Daniel said just what you've said, borrowed 10p and jogged straight off to the payphone.

HOWARD. I'm not sure I can take this before breakfast.

CRESSIDA. I'm not sure I can take it before coffee.

HOWARD *realises* CRESSIDA *gave him her coffee.*

HOWARD. Hey, let me —

CRESSIDA. No, I . . . (*Pause.*) It's in the cafetière.

HOWARD *makes to go, then turns back.*

HOWARD. Chris. It isn't, honestly. It isn't the affair. It is this.

CRESSIDA. You mean —

HOWARD. I mean, I've noticed how it's changed you. How you dazzle, how you're like a child in a new house, you're running round and flinging open all the doors and windows, letting in the light, and shouting, crikey, look what's here. (*Pause.*) Whereas, for me . . . I've seen the sights before. If not the same, then desperately similar. There is no novel feature, no surprise. (*Pause.*) But I don't want *you* to see it like that, Cressida. I want you to look with wonder. And I worry that

I block your light. That I draw the curtains, close the shutters, shut the door. And that — that isn't fair.

Pause.

CRESSIDA. I was last here when I was ten. In Daniel's position, in reverse. And he was wonderful, my new dad, he was great. He taught me everything. The rocks, the tides, the seaweed, the crustacea. He opened up the wonders of the world. (*Pause.*) Look, all I wanted — 'cos I knew I wouldn't get you touting outside Budgens, but I wanted you to get involved. That's why I said that we could take a kid, or kids. Because I wanted you to get involved. I wanted to see you be right again. I thought that you'd have things to say. That you'd have, wisdom, to pass on. (*Pause.*) He gave me the most dazzling of summers. But however wonderful it is, to be at someone's knee, there comes a point, you have to stand up and confront them face to face.

Pause.

HOWARD. Are you disappointed?

CRESSIDA. What about?

HOWARD. Your news.

A very slight pause.

CRESSIDA. Why should I be?

Pause.

HOWARD. I'll get your coffee, Cressida.

HOWARD *goes out.* CRESSIDA *isn't sure what's happened. Absently, she turns up the TV volume. We hear what is obviously the re-showing of the last lap of the 1500 metres final.* CRESSIDA *turns off the television and goes on to the terrace.* HOWARD *enters, quickly, with* CRESSIDA's *coffee.*

HOWARD. Chris, has the reformation of the working class spread to the girls?

CRESSIDA. What do you mean?

HOWARD. Have they mutated into early risers?

CRESSIDA. Goodness, no.

HOWARD. They've gone.

CRESSIDA. You what?

HOWARD. They've risen. They're not here.

CRESSIDA. Oh, cripes. You're sure?

HOWARD. Of course.

CRESSIDA. Oh gosh, what are we going to say —

    HOWARD, *who's facing towards the beach, suddenly laughs.*
    Howard, this isn't *funny.*

HOWARD. No, it's Frankie. Coming from the beach.

CRESSIDA. The beach?

HOWARD. Hey, you don't suppose they've actually swum?

CRESSIDA. Howard, she is carrying a beach towel.

HOWARD. Stranger things have happened.

CRESSIDA. Kind of, splattered —

HOWARD. Do we — ?

CRESSIDA. We do now.

    They look at each other, and then start to move just as
    FRANKIE *runs on to the terrace, in her bathing suit,*
    carrying a white beach towel splattered with blood.

FRANKIE. Michele.

CRESSIDA. What's happened?

FRANKIE. Uh — Michele. With Terry.

HOWARD. Terry?

FRANKIE. Blood — blood everywhere.

CRESSIDA. Oh, crumbs —

FRANKIE. Huge gash. Blood everywhere.

    Enter TERRY *supporting* MICHELE, *who is indeed bleeding*
    substantially from her foot. They are both in bathing
    costumes. MICHELE *wears a sunhat.*

TERRY. Our early swim. A triumph of logistics, not to say persuasion. Sadly, at the crucial moment, Michele slipped and cut her foot.

CRESSIDA. Are you — is she —

TERRY. We are being very brave. Do we have some TCP?

TERRY is helping MICHELE *on to the recliner.*

CRESSIDA. Sure do.

CRESSIDA goes out through the house. MICHELE *lies back on the recliner, takes off her hat.*

HOWARD. What did she cut it on?

TERRY. Well, we don't think it was broken glass or a tin or anything. But it's better to be sure.

HOWARD. Yes. Right.

TERRY. Now, are you feeling faint at all, Michele?

MICHELE. No. No.

Re-enter CRESSIDA *with* TCP, *a clean towel, bandages, cotton wool and a bowl.*

CRESSIDA. Right. Here we are.

TERRY. Thank goodness for the guides.

CRESSIDA. Now you can stop all that. Is there anything else that you require?

TERRY. Uh — breakfast? If —

CRESSIDA. Dib dib.

She's going out.

HOWARD. I'll help.

HOWARD *follows.* TERRY *sits down to bathe and bandage* MICHELE's *foot.* FRANKIE *stands, agitating.*

FRANKIE. Terry. Will she —

TERRY (*pointedly*). I'm convinced she'll walk again.

MICHELE. Why's Howard back so early?

TERRY. Of that I'm less sure. Why doesn't Frankie go and ask him?

FRANKIE. I'm going sunbathing. Let her get gangrene. See if I care.

FRANKIE *goes out round the side of the house.*

MICHELE. Always a fusser, Frankie.

TERRY. Mm. You should have worn something on your feet.

MICHELE. Well, I would have done. Only Frankie couldn't find her trainers.

TERRY. Sorry?

MICHELE. So I said, okay, I won't wear mine.

TERRY. Um — I'm not sure —

MICHELE. See, if I'd worn mine, and Frankie didn't have hers, she'd have an excuse, like, wouldn't she? So I says, I'll go barefoot, and we're equal, like, and so she don't have no excuse.

TERRY. I see. (*Pause.*) You didn't have to come.

MICHELE. Oh, no, I wanted to. But, see, we wanted to feel easier about the situation here, before consigning our young bodies to the waves. I mean, you know what teenage girls are like.

TERRY *is rather thrown by this.*

TERRY. Well, in a broad —

MICHELE. And particularly, having made such idiots of ourselves the other night.

TERRY. You didn't.

MICHELE. Yes, we did.

TERRY. You wouldn't have thought twice about it, if they'd been your class.

MICHELE. No. But they aren't.

Pause.

TERRY. What did they say? Your mum and dad?

MICHELE. Oh, best behaviour. Emissaries of the strike. Ambassadors for our community.

TERRY. And did you like that? Was that a role you enjoy?

MICHELE *doesn't answer.*

Tell me what you find most strange.

MICHELE. Fellow called Terry.

TERRY. Seriously.

MICHELE. Salad bowls.

TERRY. Beg pardon?

MICHELE. Having food served separate. Salad and vegetables and all that stuff. Like, you've no idea how much you're s'posed to take.

TERRY. And anything annoy you? Or upset you?

Pause.

MICHELE. Not so much 'annoy'.

TERRY. Go on.

MICHELE. It's just . . . It's easy to — be sentimental, if you follow me. The morning mist. The lowering slate-grey sky. The 30s, and the General Strike and stuff like that. You forget, you all know more 'bout that than we do. And of course, it's got its features. Friendliness. Like, everybody caring for each other. Walk along the street, know everybody, say hello. But it can be — restricted. Rather tight. If you don't fit. I mean, there's people who can't wait to go. (*Slight pause.*) I mean, I know I did wrong, making jokes 'bout being queer, and stuff like that. But, a bloke being queer in a mining village, to be honest, he'd not last five minutes. Really.

TERRY. No. I didn't.

Pause.

MICHELE. Pardon?

TERRY. Didn't last five minutes. Really.

MICHELE *can't speak.*

TERRY. When were you born?

MICHELE. The third of April 1969.

TERRY. Well, when you were, God help us, three, some London dockworkers mounted a campaign to save their jobs. And eventually six of them were thrown in jail. And there was a huge campaign to get them out, which culminated in this massive march to Pentonville. The prison, in which they were consigned. And I'd been living in, or rather round, a group of people in West London of an anarchist persuasion, among whom, frankly, being queer was if anything encouraged. But, on this march, surrounded by the best, the brightest, the most militant and self-assured and conscious and aware of all the working class, I had this strange sensation, that I was at home. Back home. But for the first time. Ever. Do you see?

MICHELE nods.

And I had — we used to wear this little triangle, pink triangle, a sort of badge, because that's what the homosexuals had had to wear in the concentration camps in Nazi Germany — you know, like the Jews wore yellow stars. And my badge was in my pocket, for I took it, as indeed I take it, everywhere. And I very nearly put it on. (*Slight pause.*) And last month, we had a march and rally for the miners. Wonderful. So wonderful, in fact, so like that time, I very nearly put it on again.

Pause.

MICHELE. Did they get out? The dockers?

TERRY. Yes, they did.

MICHELE. We thought that you were sweet on Cressida.

TERRY (*with a twinkle*). I am.

MICHELE. No, we meant, like, that — (*She grins, annoyed at missing the twinkle.*) Oh, you.

He pats her foot.

TERRY. Right, then.

MICHELE. I'll walk again.

TERRY. You will.

He stands and helps her up.

MICHELE. You know, you should go home. You should tell 'em. Face 'em up to it. It'd do 'em good. My view.

Pause.

TERRY (*ruefully*). Oh you.

FRANKIE *and* CRESSIDA *come round the side of the house.* TERRY *leaves* MICHELE.

CRESSIDA. So, how's the invalid?

TERRY. We may not have to amputate.

CRESSIDA. I'll post a notice.

TERRY. Howard?

CRESSIDA. Bringing stuff in from the car.

TERRY *a questioning look to* CRESSIDA, *as* HOWARD *enters the living room with a big parcel, his overnight bag, and* FRANKIE's *trainers. He puts the parcel down somewhere inconspicuous and goes on to the terrace.*

He — decided to come back. Now, breakfast, anybody?

HOWARD *appears with the shoes.*

HOWARD. Frankie, I'm sorry. In the boot.

FRANKIE. My trainers.

MICHELE *looks ruefully at her foot.*

TERRY. Did I hear loose talk of breakfast?

CRESSIDA (*pointing round the side*). Thataway.

DANIEL *runs on to the terrace. He bends double and breathes heavily.*

HOWARD. Good morning, Daniel.

TERRY *picks up a note in* HOWARD's *voice.*

TERRY. Right, then. Hobble on.

TERRY *helps* MICHELE *round the side of the house.*

FRANKIE *takes her trainers in through the house.* DANIEL *unbends.*

CRESSIDA. She cut her foot.

DANIEL. Oh dear. How dreadful. Howard, can I use your shower?

HOWARD. Daniel, why did you call Gillian?

DANIEL *looks at* HOWARD, *then* CRESSIDA.

CRESSIDA. She rang last night.

DANIEL. Why shouldn't I?

HOWARD. No reason. But if you're unhappy here, it would be nice if we knew too.

DANIEL *sits.*

DANIEL. Right, then. Family discussion. Minutes of last meeting. Take as read. Matters arising. None. Apologies for absence. Well —

HOWARD. Daniel, this is ridiculous. You're here for a fortnight —

DANIEL. Item four. Holiday. Position on. Characterisation of. A) A time of respite and amusement, often in association with recreation, tourism and travel; or B) guilt trip.

Pause.

HOWARD. All right, then. Go and have your shower.

CRESSIDA. Howard —

DANIEL (*stands*). I mean, do you have any idea how ridiculous you look? You're so keen not to patronise them for being miners' children, you forget they're teenage girls and treat them like they're 40, middle-class and male. And when you're not doing that, it's stuff like accusing them of being pregnant. And that's when you're not giving Frankie the third degree about the fucking Spanish Civil War.

Pause.

Who knows? Who cares? It's something that's embarrassing, or silly, or — just something that she doesn't much want to discuss. It's not like, some great drama. It's like where they live. Sure, for you, it's 'The Rhondda', clenched fists and stirring music and lodge banners fluttering in the wind. But for them, it's dull and grimy and there aren't any decent shops or discos, and it's — just the fucking boring place they live in. And they want to leave it. Just like Terry, eh?

HOWARD. In fact, I've found out about the Civil War. And it's not embarrassing or silly. It's about her grandad. And the International Brigade.

DANIEL. Well, I'm so pleased for you.

MICHELE *has entered.*

MICHELE. Sorry. Me hat. The sun.

MICHELE *limps over, picks up her hat, and goes back out.*

HOWARD (*shortly*). I'm getting bored with this.

DANIEL (*shortly*). Well, so am I, 'cos I have had it up to here.

Slight pause.

HOWARD. Go on.

DANIEL. With everything. From my stupid name, to not having proper toys. To explaining to my friends why my parents dress like freaks and have cats called things like Stalin. Not to mention suffering the delusion they were dangerous revolutionists . . . Until, at least, *she* saw the light.

He turns to go. Then turns back.

You said it. They're just ordinary girls. I'm going to take my shower now.

He goes out, through the house.

CRESSIDA. I s'pose . . . there is a sense . . .

HOWARD. Boy, is there ever.

HOWARD *goes into the living room.*

CRESSIDA (*calls*). Howard, what's this about the International Brigade?

HOWARD. Well. The meeting wasn't quite as long as I'd anticipated. And although I'd got some shopping, I had time to pop into the British Library. There was one person from their village killed in Spain. His name was Owen. First name, Frank.

CRESSIDA. Granddaughter.

HOWARD. Or grandniece. But it would explain the reticence now, wouldn't it?

CRESSIDA. Well, in a way. How was your meeting?

Pause. HOWARD goes back on the terrace.

HOWARD. Well, frankly, not too dazzling. (*Slight pause.*) The problem is, they'd got it in their minds, quite how I don't know, that it was spies. That every 30s lefty ended up as Burgess or Maclean. That's those who didn't see the light, like Orwell in Catalonia. And it was felt, with great regret, that somewhere between Le Carré's latest and the hype for 1984 . . . the thing had, now, how can we put this Howard, just gone off the boil.

CRESSIDA. What, you mean, it's cancelled?

HOWARD. Not their view, of course. They're still as keen as mustard. But they wouldn't put its chances, now, at more than five per cent.

CRESSIDA. Howard, I'm sorry.

HOWARD. Are you?

CRESSIDA. Yes, of course I am.

Enter FRANKIE, having changed.

FRANKIE. Oh, I'm sorry, I —

CRESSIDA. Don't worry. Things had reached a natural break.

She goes out round the side of the house.
FRANKIE goes into the living room. HOWARD follows, picks up the parcel, makes to go. FRANKIE looks at the parcel.

HOWARD (*gnomically*). Beware of freaks, bearing gifts.

He goes out. FRANKIE *is left there.* MICHELE *appears.*

MICHELE. Krrk krrk. Do you read me Delta Foxtrot?

FRANKIE. Krrk krrk. Yes, I read you Delta One Control.

MICHELE. They got the Spain thing.

FRANKIE. Oh, shit.

MICHELE. But they think it's your grand*dad*.

FRANKIE. Grand*dad*?

MICHELE. That's right. They think he was a soldier in the civil war.

FRANKIE. Oh, well.

Slight pause.

Oh, well, *that*'d be all right. I mean, they'd quite like that, wouldn't they?

MICHELE. Krrk krrk. Why need they ever know?

Blackout.

Scene Two

Early evening. A day or two later. Pimms in a jug and glasses in the living room. On the terrace, two parcels wrapped in gift paper are behind a chair. DANIEL sits, to the side, on the recliner, reading the 'I Ching' and sipping a drink. He is dressed smartly. As the scene develops, he'll find three coins in his pocket and start to cast them to form hexagrams. But this, if not surreptitious, is at least a private activity.
HOWARD and TERRY come on to the terrace. They too are both dressed smartly, for an evening out. Both men have drinks. They are arguing.

HOWARD. I'm sorry, I still don't see the problem.

TERRY. Well, can I count the ways. They'll be embarrassed. They'll feel patronised. They'll see it as an act of charity —

TERRY. I'd drop the 'just'.

HOWARD. It is, you know, in fact, a present. From one person to another. Not political, except of course to those who think that everything's political, from toilet roll to Turandot. It is a gift, an act of kindness and affection, given freely by one person, me, to somebody I know. (*Pause.*) Where the hell are they, anyway? Our table's booked for half-past seven.

CRESSIDA. They are getting ready.

MICHELE *and* FRANKIE *enter the living room. They are once again dressed up, but somehow they look more adult than on their first evening.*

They are ready now.

The girls come on the terrace.

You both look lovely.

FRANKIE. Thank you.

HOWARD. Drinks, drinks, drinks.

HOWARD *goes into the living room and pours Pimms into glasses. He puts the full glasses and the jug on to a tray and brings it out.*

MICHELE. We're looking forward to our treat.

FRANKIE. That's right.

MICHELE. Mind, that doesn't mean we haven't liked our dinners here.

FRANKIE. Oh, no. We've liked 'em all.

Pause.

MICHELE. The lobster was particularly toothsome.

HOWARD. It is called Pimms. It's a kind of fruit cup.

TERRY. With a kick.

FRANKIE. Thank you.

They take drinks. He hands a third full glass to CRESSIDA, *puts down the tray, and offers a refill to* TERRY. TERRY

HOWARD. Oh, charity, well I'm *so* sorry —

TERRY. Howard, you know what this strike's all about. T[hey] have been scrupulous. I've seen them sharing out the cornflakes. Virtually counting grains of rice. And it is via rediscovery of those old principles, of equality of sufferin[g] of share and share alike — What do you think?

CRESSIDA *has appeared. She's dressed in a heavily patterned, flowing dress, with dramatic earrings.*

CRESSIDA. What do I think of what?

HOWARD. Ah, Cressida. An Indian restaurant?

CRESSIDA. I'm sorry?

TERRY. Howard. Just think of it, from her point of view. She makes what is by any definition a great sacrifice. Then you turn round and say it wasn't worth it.

HOWARD. That is an utter travesty —

TERRY. She makes that sacrifice first, I imagine, out of a commitment to her family, then to the industry, and finally her community, a community which is itself reasserting its own historical identity, its sense of solidarity, its consciousness . . .

HOWARD. Well, I'm sorry, I'm not hearing that. I'm hearing something rather different.

TERRY. What's that?

HOWARD. I'm hearing a community that Frankie and Michele[?] want to defend, yes, sure, but also want to leave. And I'm hearing — well, we all heard, a cry of something like despa[ir] from a girl who'd found a talent, who'd found something herself that might have *helped* her to —

TERRY. Escape? Get up, get out, get going?

HOWARD. And I'm surprised that you aren't hearing that [?] You of all people.

CRESSIDA. Skating on faces.

HOWARD. That was just a metaphor.

shakes his head. HOWARD *fills his own glass and puts the jug down.* DANIEL *goes and refills his glass from the jug.*

HOWARD. Right then.

Pause. MICHELE *and* FRANKIE *look at each other.*

It is — tonight is our last night together. And instead of yet more boring old lobster, we're going to sample the delights of Blas-Ar-Cymru in Llanwen.

FRANKIE (*correction*). Cymru.

HOWARD. Indeed. But before we — left, I felt I ought to say — well, not to say so much as to, well, mark, our feelings . . . With a little something to remember this, this time we've spent together, here in Wales.

He picks up the two parcels and hands them to the girls. TERRY *refuses to watch.*

Michele, and Frankie. With our love.

MICHELE. Oh, crumbs.

Pause. CRESSIDA *can't bear it.*

CRESSIDA. Are they supposed to —

HOWARD. Yes. Please open them.

MICHELE *looks at* FRANKIE *and then opens her parcel.* FRANKIE *sits opening hers too — which is more complicated, as it contains items in tissue paper — but stops when* MICHELE *finds a pair of leather-bound books. She opens the first and looks up at* HOWARD.

It's a Victorian edition of the works of Tennyson. It includes the 'Morte d'Arthur' and the 'Idylls of the King'. The Arthur legend.

MICHELE (*with a little grin*). 'The Death of Arthur'.

HOWARD (*sharing*): Arthur the King. (*Pause.*) There are some, I think, rather lovely illustrations.

MICHELE *finds a picture in the book.*

MICHELE. Yes. Yes. Thank you, very much.

HOWARD. Whereas, for Frankie, there's some items with which we are sure she'll cut a figure —

FRANKIE *has found a boot and a set of skating blades.*

The boots are WIFA. I'm afraid I had to liberate your trainers for the size. There's a set of figure- and free-skating blades. They're M and K. I'm told —

FRANKIE *pushes the parcel away, bursts into tears, and runs out, back through the living room, to her room. MICHELE runs after. No one else moves.*

DANIEL. Well. That was —

CRESSIDA. Shut up, Daniel.

DANIEL. I'm sorry.

CRESSIDA *looks over to* DANIEL, *a little surprised by his tone. Pause.*

TERRY. Howard. I have to tell you that you've just —

HOWARD. You know, you know what *I* find worst, of all the many things that I find worst about our bleak, mean times, what that bloody woman's done to us, is how we've let her — them — rewrite our history. How in this year of all years, we've allowed them to write off our time.

CRESSIDA. Um, Howard —

HOWARD. And it's — of course it's very easy to write off, all the silliness and grandiosity and triviality, the decade that gave us tower blocks and Chinese heroin and nothing else . . .

TERRY. Well, yur, you can —

HOWARD. But in fact, if you sit down and think about it, if you actually add it up, desegregation, ending of the war, bringing down two presidents, nearly smashing the French state, even dear old here . . . Not to mention all those subtle and yet revolutionary changes in the way we spoke and sang and reached out to each other . . . And of course the rising of the women, and perhaps the rising of the planet, in mute screaming protest against all we'd done to them and her . . . But do you know what it was all about? Why it was so good?

Because it started with four blacks in Carolina who refused to leave a lunch-bar. One young man who was the first to burn his draft card. Students, women, blacks, who laid their, their *own* bodies on a most bewildering array of lines — in order to say, no.

He looks at TERRY, *who shrugs.*

A story. The University of Edinburgh. Where I taught social anthropology, from 1966 to '69. The students' union, divided, men and women. A girl I knew, who had got really pissed off with this situation. So, one Saturday, she dolled herself up in what I think is called a cocktail dress, she went down to the men's union, on her own, and entered the great bar — no doubt among the longest in the western world — and strolled up to the counter bold as brass and inquired if they could furnish her with one small g and t. And the barman said, 'I'm sorry, madam, I can't serve you.' And by now, of course, it being Saturday, not only had her presence been observed, and commented upon, indeed, but by now there was a fearful catcalling, and whistling, and stamping in the gallery; and having asked again, and having been refused again, she began the long walk back, towards the door. And you can imagine both the manner and the matter of the catcalling, and what courage, and indeed what perspicuity, for her to turn back, at the door, to look across that sea of bloated, drunken student faces, smile a withering smile, and drop — one — shoulder strap. And turn, and go. (*Pause.*) In 1967. That time, when young Americans were lying down in front of troop trains. Che Guevara fighting his doomed battles in the hills. Mohammed Ali saying, 'Hell no, I won't go.' That time. That summer.

Silence. HOWARD *looks at* FRANKIE's *parcel. He takes out the other boot and a second set of blades. He looks at them, and sets them down.*

DANIEL. Who was the woman? Was that Cressida?

CRESSIDA. In 1967, dear, I was fifteen. No, I assume that that was Gillian.

HOWARD. That's right. Your mum. In fact, she was actually pregnant at the time. By me. With you.

MICHELE re-enters, alone, through the living room, on to the terrace.

MICHELE. Look.

CRESSIDA. Michele.

MICHELE. Look, Frankie just, just wanted me to tell you, wanted me to say, she's sorry.

HOWARD. Well, she shouldn't be. It was a stupid —

MICHELE. But she was so moved.

Pause.

HOWARD. I'm sorry?

MICHELE. And she just, couldn't speak, you see. She couldn't work out what to say.

Pause.

Because . . . she was so moved. And grateful.

No one can say anything. FRANKIE enters. There is a pause. Then she speaks, slowly and carefully, to the COMPANY.

FRANKIE. I think, if it's okay, I'd like to have my skates now. Take a look at 'em, before we go to dinner. That's, if that's okay.

Pause. MICHELE hands the skates to FRANKIE, and picks up her books.

MICHELE. We'll be ready in five minutes, then. If you don't mind.

She follows FRANKIE out. Pause. DANIEL picks up the 'I Ching' at the hexagram he found earlier in the scene. It is the 54th.

CRESSIDA. I suppose that someone ought to phone —

DANIEL (*reading*). The Hexagram Kuei Mei. The Marriage of the Maiden. Here the great and righteous relationship of heaven and the earth is signified. If heaven and earth were to have no intercourse, they would not grow and flourish as they do. (*Pause.*) Well, that makes sense to me.

He looks at his father.

I didn't know that, about Gillian.

Blackout.

Scene Three

Next day. Around noon. It's hot — when we see them, the residents are dressed in their brightest, summeriest clothes. ALUN stands in the living room, looking around a certain amount of celebratory debris — bottles, glasses, cups, evidence that the party carried on after the restaurant. No people, however.
ALUN goes out on to the terrace, sees the 'I Ching' where DANIEL left it, picks it up and reads. Then he hears voices from the direction of the beach. DANIEL runs on to the terrace.

DANIEL (*turning back, to announce his victory*). I won I won.

ALUN. Congratulations.

DANIEL. Ah. Hullo.

  CRESSIDA *runs in with* FRANKIE.

CRESSIDA. Alun, I'm sorry. We've been saying farewell to the beach.

ALUN. Don't worry. I'm a little early.

  Enter HOWARD, *followed by* MICHELE, *who is being helped over the last few yards by* TERRY.

HOWARD. Alun. Good morning. Afternoon.

MICHELE. Eh, Dad.

ALUN. Michele, what's wrong with you?

TERRY. She cut her foot. It's really not that —

MICHELE. Had a relapse. Trying to do too much, too early.

TERRY. It's really not that serious.

MICHELE. Well, that's all you know!

ALUN. You've had these on the beach?

FRANKIE (*to* ALUN). Oh, they been treating us like something terrible. Making us run about. I nearly rang the NSPCC.

DANIEL. I'm going to have my shower now.

CRESSIDA. Don't be too long!

DANIEL *runs out.*

ALUN. Right, now you girls, I've got to be in Ponty for a meeting —

FRANKIE. But we got to pack.

ALUN. You better get moving, then.

TERRY. Krrk krrk. Wilco.

FRANKIE *and* MICHELE *go to their bedroom,* TERRY *goes out to the hall.*

CRESSIDA. Now, a coffee?

HOWARD. Or indeed a beer?

ALUN. Well, actually, I brought some fizzy wine. It's in the fridge.

CRESSIDA. How — wonderful.

CRESSIDA *goes out to the kitchen.* HOWARD *and* ALUN *are left alone.* ALUN *is still holding the 'I Ching'.* HOWARD *notices.* ALUN *looks at the cover.*

ALUN. The — Itching?

HOWARD. *I Ching.* It's a sort of — sophisticated fortune-telling aid. It's been a feature of the holiday. You know, one year it's frisbees, then its boules, this year it's oriental mysticism.

TERRY *takes the cases from the hall across into the rest of the house.*

What's it say?

ALUN. That 'heaven looks on earthly marriage with great favour, but only where the rightful order is observed. Where the weak become superior to the strong, misfortune will result. The young woman bears an empty basket, there is no advantage.'

HOWARD. Some you win and some you lose.

ALUN *hands the 'I Ching' to* HOWARD, *who looks at the passage* ALUN *has read out as* CRESSIDA *brings in the wine and glasses.*

CRESSIDA. This isn't fizzy wine. This is sparkling Saumur, *méthode champenoise.*

ALUN. Well, I meant, it isn't real champagne.

CRESSIDA. Real schmeal. (*Opening the bottle.*) Right, here we go — here we go —

It pops, as TERRY *joins them.* HOWARD *puts down the oracle.*

HOWARD. Ah, Terry. A little something?

TERRY. Just this once.

They have drinks.

ALUN. So, then:

HOWARD. To the mass defection of the intellectual classes to the cause.

CRESSIDA. To the continued moral vulnerability of the shoppers of North Oxford.

TERRY. To a General Strike.

ALUN. Your health.

They drink.

TERRY. So how was Heysham?

ALUN. Power station?

TERRY. Yuh.

ALUN. Oh, fine.

CRESSIDA. You closed it?

ALUN. Well, no, we didn't — being nuclear, we didn't expect that, but we did, we made our point.

HOWARD. That's good.

ALUN. In fact, to be honest, it was something of an experience.

TERRY. In what way?

ALUN. Well, what happened was —

Suddenly, MICHELE *and* FRANKIE *burst into the living room with their cases. They've changed.* MICHELE *has a carrier-bag.*

TERRY. Be-hold.

TERRY, ALUN, HOWARD *and* CRESSIDA *go into the living room. The girls are breathless.*

MICHELE. The landspeed packing record.

ALUN. Beg your pardon?

MICHELE. Smashed.

CRESSIDA. Well, *that* calls for two more glasses.

HOWARD *gets glasses. As he does so:*

HOWARD. In fact, of course, you'd be most welcome, if you'd care to stay for lunch —

CRESSIDA. Howard, (a) Alun's said he's in a hurry, and (b) we've really only just had breakfast.

HOWARD *pours wine. Enter* DANIEL *from his shower.*

HOWARD. Ah, yes. Frankie's amazing eggs.

CRESSIDA. For which we want the recipe before you go. Now, Daniel, wine?

DANIEL. Yes, please.

HOWARD *pours* DANIEL *wine, as* :

TERRY. Well, one says eggs, but there's onions, bacon, peppers red and green —

ALUN. Ah, now, I know where all that comes from. Frankie's Spanish nan.

Pause.

CRESSIDA. Her Spanish nan?

ALUN. That's right. Why, didn't she —

HOWARD. Her Spanish grandmother?

Pause. ALUN *looks at* MICHELE *and* FRANKIE.

FRANKIE. Well . . . It isn't, like, a terrific mystery. It's just that, in the Spanish war, they sent these kids from the Basque provinces to Britain. You know, like as refugees. And there was three homes in Wales. And almost all of them went back, you know, after the war, but one or two, like if they were orphaned or whatever, they stayed on. Got married. So my nan's name is Francesca Williams. (*Slight pause.*) Lives in Swansea. Near the rink.

CRESSIDA. Why didn't you —

HOWARD. Why did they come, the children.

FRANKIE. 'Cos they lost their homes.

HOWARD. Where did they come from?

FRANKIE. Told you. The Basque provinces.

HOWARD. Which town?

Pause.

FRANKIE. Well, several, as I understand —

HOWARD. Yuh, sure. Your nan. Bilbao? Or the other one?

Long pause.

FRANKIE. She still — she says she still can't hear aeroplanes. Still makes her terrified. To look up, see an aeroplane.

Pause.

HOWARD. Frankie. For heaven's sake. Why didn't you tell us that your nan in Swansea came to Wales from Guernica?

TERRY. *Guernica?*

Slight pause.

CRESSIDA. The bombs? Picasso's screaming horses?

HOWARD. That's the one.

Pause.

ALUN. Good question.

DANIEL. Easy answer.

CRESSIDA (*warning*). Daniel —

DANIEL. Well, it's obvious. You want them all to be like heroes. 'A chapter from your glorious history'. That fits, with a grandad dying in a hail of bullets, head held high. Not so good with a frightened, snivelling little girl, with just the clothes she stands up in, who cries and hides each time she hears a plane. Not so good, with someone thrown on others' mercy. With a refugee.

The adults look at the girls. FRANKIE *shrugs.*

MICHELE. I mean, I didn't know. Ridiculous. I didn't know why Frankie's nan was called Francesca. And had a kind of funny accent. Before it came up on this holiday, I never thought to ask.

Pause.

ALUN. Ah, well. There's been a lot of digging. Lot of stuff we'd let get buried. High time it got dug up. (*Slight pause. He drains his glass.*) Well, now, perhaps the time has come —

MICHELE. Well, no, not quite.

ALUN. Beg pardon?

MICHELE *picks up the carrier. To* ALUN:

MICHELE. See, we had a little present session yesterday, but it all got out of hand. So we didn't give out ours.

HOWARD. Oh, for heaven's sake —

CRESSIDA. Well, goodness.

FRANKIE. It's not much, only strike stuff really. There's a cassette of mining songs, for Terry . . .

The girls hand out the presents.

MICHELE. And a pit lamp key-ring, that's for Howard.

FRANKIE. And a Women Against Pit Closures teatowel, that's for Cressida . . .

MICHELE. . . . or you could swap 'em round —

FRANKIE. And there's a Rhondda mug for Daniel.

MICHELE. So he'll remember how to say it, like.

FRANKIE. And everybody gets a badge.

MICHELE. That is, except for Terry.

Pause.

TERRY. Sorry?

MICHELE. Terry doesn't get a badge.

TERRY. And why not, pray?

MICHELE. 'Less we get a badge from him.

Pause.

FRANKIE. That is a definite decision.

MICHELE. For we know he takes it everywhere. (*Pause.*) 'Cos if you show 'em ours, it's only fair, it's only right we show 'em yours.

After a moment, TERRY feels in his pocket, and takes out a pink triangle badge. He gives it to MICHELE, who looks at it in her hand. Then she speaks to the COMPANY. But she can't yet look at her FATHER.

MICHELE. You see, the way we look at it, is it's not as if you knew us. Not as if we're family or somebody you know. You asked us here as strangers. You accepted us, because our families are suffering. 'Course, you know us *now*. But when you said you'd help us, we were strangers.

Pause.

And it's not just — hospitality. You taught us things about our lives. What's wrong with, you know, with our attitudes. The way we've been brought up, like. Like, the way we are.

CRESSIDA. Oh, no.

HOWARD. No, really not.

MICHELE. Oh, yes. Oh, yes.

Pause.

Oh, yes, there's lots of things, that you passed on to us.

She pins the badge on to herself.

Yes, there's no doubt about it, in my view.

Pause. At last, she looks at ALUN.

ALUN. Um, that's — the gay thing, isn't it?

MICHELE. That's right.

ALUN *turns to* TERRY.

TERRY (*pause*). Oh, yes. (*Pause.*) 'Fraid so.

FRANKIE (*brightly*). Okay. We're ready.

HOWARD. Hey, you didn't tell us about Heysham.

MICHELE. And that recipe —

FRANKIE. Oh, Christ —

CRESSIDA. No. No, I think you should just go.

HOWARD *looks to* CRESSIDA.

And of course we'll see you again soon, and yes, we'll write, and phone, and indeed we want the recipe for Frankie's Spanish eggs, but at this, at this moment, I do think it's best — if you just go. Out through that door.

They all look at her.

Because I think that when we came here, Howard, Daniel and I — and Terry, too, p'raps — we were in a room. And it was quite a pleasant room, we could have stayed for years, quite happily. And that was good, because the door, the only door, in fact, had clicked shut, quietly, behind us . . . But you see, what I think we may have found, the four of us, is that there might be — might just be another door, a different door from the one we came in by, the sort of door we'd never think of, even masquerading as a window or a curtain or a picture on the wall . . . And I think we might have found the strength, and perspicuity, to find that door, that secret door, and open it, and go beyond our cosy room, to something new. (*Pause.*) And of course it may be that it all goes wrong, and even if it doesn't, memories will fade, and it may look as if things have gone back to the way they were before . . . But I think that once we've found the new door, once the old paint's cracked, the locks turned and the hinges loosened, then we'll always know it's there. And even if *we* never open it again, we'll pass it on.

CRESSIDA *is face to face with* HOWARD. *The phone starts to ring.*

Good. Go.

After a moment, HOWARD *shrugs and goes out.* CRESSIDA, DANIEL *and* TERRY *are still. The phone stops.* ALUN *picks up one suitcase,* FRANKIE *the other. But he can't go. He puts down the suitcase.*

ALUN. You know, at Heysham, we didn't get much change, from the power workers, if the truth be told. Bit disappointing really. But where we did get help was from this kind of group who turned up, from the anti-nuclear. Bit freaky actually. Not sure we liked the look of 'em, when they first showed. Not quite sure, to be honest, they was that hygenic. But I have to tell you, that up against our 'brothers' from the power station, going into work, and catcalling, and throwing pennies, all that stuff — well, up against all that, they came up trumps. They stood their ground. And in a day or two, the powermen stopped catcalling, and started looking pretty sheepish, if I'm honest. As they hurried past. And I mean, I can't agree with all they said, but they did all right. Our gypsies. (*Pause.*) 'And it shall come to pass, that all they that look upon thee shall flee from thee, and say, Nineveh is laid waste: who will bemoan her? Whence shall I seek comforters for thee?'

A moment. Then ALUN *goes to* TERRY.

So long, our Terry.

Very gently, he presses his fist against TERRY's *shoulder.* TERRY *responds. Then* ALUN *turns, picks up the suitcase and goes out, followed by* FRANKIE, MICHELE *and* DANIEL.

TERRY. Love it and want to leave it? That's so strange? Is that unprecedented?

CRESSIDA *shakes her head. Enter* HOWARD. TERRY *goes out to the kitchen.*

CRESSIDA. Who was that?

HOWARD. It was for you. He'll ring you back.

CRESSIDA *looks questioning.*

He wouldn't give his name.

CRESSIDA. That's odd.

HOWARD. But I think, in fact, he might be — or he might describe himself — as the bearer of the five-per-cent solution.

CRESSIDA. What.

HOWARD. Or put another way, I have an inkling that, in the hexagram Kuei Mei, where in the sixth place there's an Old Yin line, once again the oracle is wrong.

He walks towards the terrace. As he reaches the windows, he looks around them.

Good heavens. Funny door.

He mimes opening an imaginary door, walks through it to the terrace, and away. CRESSIDA *is looking mystified. Then, suddenly, she rushes round, searching for the 'I Ching'.* DANIEL *re-enters.*

CRESSIDA. Where is it? Where's the *'I Ching'*?

DANIEL. Left it on the terrace.

CRESSIDA. Terrace.

CRESSIDA *goes on to the terrace.* DANIEL *goes out. She finds the book. She reads the section* HOWARD *quoted. She is mystified.*

(*Calls:*) Terry! I think . . . I think in fact, I might be . . . That in fact, you see . . .

She goes out after HOWARD. *The lights change. It's darker, colder.* TERRY *enters with breakfast things. He wears a sweater. He puts down the tray and goes and looks at the weather.*

TERRY. I see.

HOWARD (*calls, from off*). So what's it like?

TERRY (*calls back*). What's what like?

Enter HOWARD *with more breakfast things to put on the table. Like* TERRY, *he is dressed for cooler weather.*

HOWARD. Well, the outlook, comrade.

TERY. Pretty dire.

HOWARD. 'The slightest puff of cloud . . .'

TERRY. Ah me.

They sit at the table for breakfast.

HOWARD. So, do you hear from them?

TERRY. Yes, sure. Don't you?

HOWARD. Well, yes. I mean, from time to time.

TERRY. It's been a year. It's bound —

HOWARD. It's sometimes hard to know, what's best to say.

TERRY. They were betrayed. They were let down.

HOWARD. You think, it's that —

TERRY. Oh, yes. Oh, yes.

Slight pause.

And can *any* of us say, we did enough?

CRESSIDA *enters. She wears the kimono she wore at the beginning of the play. She has a plate of Spanish eggs.*

CRESSIDA. I have made eggs.

She brings the eggs to the table and puts them down.

Yes, I, who could not organise a piss-up on a whelkstall; I, who have misunderstood the situation once again and turned up as a teepee; I, the Married Maiden, whose basket was so unexpectedly not empty after all, I have made eggs. Today. This time. This summer.

A baby has begun to cry. HOWARD *looks up to* CRESSIDA.

HOWARD. Shall I go?

CRESSIDA. Yes. Yes. Why not. You go.

Fade to blackout.